CONTEMPORARY ISSUES
IN BUSINESS ETHICS

CONTEMPORARY ISSUES IN BUSINESS ETHICS

MARY W. VILCOX
AND
THOMAS O. MOHAN
EDITORS

Nova Science Publishers, Inc.
New York

NOTICE TO THE READER

The Publisher has taken reasonable care in the preparation of this book, but makes no expressed or implied warranty of any kind and assumes no responsibility for any errors or omissions. No liability is assumed for incidental or consequential damages in connection with or arising out of information contained in this book. The Publisher shall not be liable for any special, consequential, or exemplary damages resulting, in whole or in part, from the readers' use of, or reliance upon, this material.

Independent verification should be sought for any data, advice or recommendations contained in this book. In addition, no responsibility is assumed by the publisher for any injury and/or damage to persons or property arising from any methods, products, instructions, ideas or otherwise contained in this publication.

This publication is designed to provide accurate and authoritative information with regard to the subject matter covered herein. It is sold with the clear understanding that the Publisher is not engaged in rendering legal or any other professional services. If legal or any other expert assistance is required, the services of a competent person should be sought. FROM A DECLARATION OF PARTICIPANTS JOINTLY ADOPTED BY A COMMITTEE OF THE AMERICAN BAR ASSOCIATION AND A COMMITTEE OF PUBLISHERS.

LIBRARY OF CONGRESS CATALOGING-IN-PUBLICATION DATA
Contemporary issues in business ethics / Mary W. Vilcox and Thomas O. Mohan (editors).
    p. cm.
  Includes index.
  ISBN-13: 978-1-60021-773-9 (hardcover)
  ISBN-10: 1-60021-773-7 (hardcover)
  1. Business ethics. 2. Social responsibility of business. I. Vilcox, Mary W. II. Mohan, Thomas O.
HF5387.C6628 2007
174'.4--dc22
                        2007019180

Published by Nova Science Publishers, Inc. ✦ New York

CONTENTS

PREFACE

Business ethics is a form of the art of applied ethics that examines ethical rules and principles within a commercial context, the various moral or ethical problems that can arise in a business setting, and any special duties or obligations that apply to persons who are engaged in commerce. Business ethics can be both a normative and a descriptive discipline. As a corporate practice and a career specialisation, the field is primarily normative. In academia descriptive approaches are also taken. The range and quantity of business ethical issues reflects the degree to which business is perceived to be at odds with non-economic social values. Historically, interest in business ethics accelerated dramatically during the 1980s and 1990s, both within major corporations and within academia. For example, today most major corporate websites lay emphasis on commitment to promoting non-economic social values under a variety of headings (e.g. ethics codes, social responsibility charters). In some cases, corporations have redefined their core values in the light of business ethical considerations.

Catching business ethics in action, however, remains a seldom-spotted nugget for in reality it depends on the characters of the characters.

Chapter 1 - This chapter reviews and updates much of the literature on social responsibility including the author's own [2001] "Social Responsibility Within and Without Self-Interest." The chapter relates the debate's history from its development in the 1960's to its current global emphasis. It reviews "social responsibility" as "window-dressing," as well as "the market for virtue" in several key companies including Dow, Merck, Malden Mills and others. It presents the arguments from altruism and utilitarianism found in the work of Peter Singer, John Rawls and R.E. Freeman (stakeholder theory) and then addresses and defends the "free market" side of Milton Friedman against his critics. The author argues that we should widen the idea of self-interest and reject altruistically motivated ethics. Getting rid of altruism and utilitarianism will leave plenty of egoistic social responsibilities that are also responsible to business needs and demands.

Chapter 2 - In this paper, the authors discuss ethical foundations of well being marketing. Specially, the authors argue that well-being marketing is a business philosophy based on duties of beneficence and non-maleficence, deontological ethics, normative ethics, and moral idealism.

Chapter 3 - Newly emerging evidence suggests that global warming could endanger human existence itself, unless there is quick, effective, and worldwide collective action. In particular, runaway global warming mechanisms have been identified that in past eons apparently replaced much of atmospheric oxygen with hydrogen sulphide, causing the

Permian (and perhaps other) mass extinctions of most of the world's land and water species. Accepted climate models suggest that anthropogenic global warming is capable of triggering those mechanisms [Ward, 2006]. Even assuming less catastrophic scenarios, human institutions have ethical responsibilities to support, or at least not impede, solutions to global warming. Yet many major corporations contribute adversely to global warming through two channels: first, by actively producing products and services that emit a major part of all greenhouse gas emissions; and second, by exerting political power via lobbying and other means that impede governments from appropriately regulating those emissions. With respect to the second channel, Burress [2005] contrasts two major ethical frameworks, showing that the stakeholder approach recommends that corporations should support corrective government action, while the neoclassical profit-maximizing approach sometimes recommends opposition to corrective action. In practice, major corporations have lobbied heavily against environmental regulation. A straightforward interpretation is that these corporations are in fact motivated by systematic incentives to maximize profits, even when this entails considerable damage to the common world we inhabit. These corporate choices are inconsistent with ordinary ethical facts accepted by most individuals. Therefore both internal incentive structures and external controls on corporate political action are matters of considerable ethical importance. This paper raises the following question: should incentive structures regulating corporate business be reformed to reduce ethically dubious lobbying on climate change? The stakeholder and neoclassical frameworks suggest rather specific, and contrasting, ethical criteria for incentive structures. This Chapter considers how these criteria are, or might be, operationalized. It suggests for example that representation for non-shareholder interests on a Board of Directors are forbidden by neoclassical ethics, but obligatory under stakeholder ethics. Perhaps surprisingly, the neoclassical approach provides considerably more support than the stakeholder approach for limitations on the lobbying and political activities of major corporations.

Chapter 4 - Business ethics, especially among top managers, has become a topic of concern to the public and business community. As a result, much attention has focused on the development of moral reasoning in corporate individuals. Past research examining individual and business decision behavior, indicates that several variables such the level of moral reasoning, perceived ethical climate, education, age, management level, work tenure, industry types and gender have a significant impact on individual decisions. This chapter outlines the major findings by researchers investigating these variables.

Chapter 5 - The passage of the Federal Election Campaign Act of 1971 and its subsequent amendments had a significant impact on the relationship between business and politics. With this piece of legislation, the U.S. Congress made available to corporate executives an ideal avenue to express themselves in the political arena through a newly legalized political tool, the corporate political-action committee (Shipper and Jennings, 1984). Since their allowed existence, these committees (hereafter, PACs) flourished as they increased in number from 89 in 1974 to over 1,600 in 2004 (Federal Election Commission, 2007). In addition, during the 2003-2004 election cycle, corporate PACs donated over $211 million to congressional candidates (Center for Responsive Politics, 2007).

In this chapter, the author gives an overview of the history behind corporate PACs; determine when, how and why such entities were created; examine their organizational and disclosure requirements; and analyze their operations. Second, the author examines PACs related to specific industries subject to tighter regulation, thus greater public policy pressure, and study their spending behavior during recent election cycles. The author selects a cluster of business industries which activities are harmful to the natural environment, classified as the Energy and Natural Resources sector by the Center for Responsive Politics (CRP), and analyze their PAC contributions over the period 1998-2004. This research provides evidence that corporations from these industries generally hold a defined political agenda illustrated by the amount and allocation of their political contributions to legislators who are supportive (or not) of their business activities.

Chapter 6 - This chapter examines how improving daily management practices can increase the level of civil aviation safety. Various internal and external factors have an impact on an airline's flight safety performance. Historically, accident investigations have focused on primary factors related to operational failure and human error. In addition to the training and maintenance programs required by regulatory agencies, airlines have created safety management systems in order to prevent, control, or mitigate primary causes of safety breaches. In recent years accident investigators have begun seeking the latent factors behind primary causes, shedding light on management factors that impact flight safety. Industry efforts are turning to identifying opportunities to proactively address management factors as a way of further improving flight safety.

This research identifies key management factors that are considered to have a significant impact on flight safety, through extensive literature review and in-depth interviews with safety experts. Then, the relative importance of these key management factors are measured by a questionnaire survey with airline employees and civil aviation experts. Thirty-eight individuals from five continents have responded to the questionnaire. The research analysis has indicated that safety culture has the most significant impact on aviation safety improvement. Therefore, management needs to give a priority to enhance organization's safety culture in daily business operations in order to improve safety performance.

Chapter 7 - This study addresses the way to develop a new corporate responsibility audit system, which is speedy, simple and easy to conduct. Many organizations today show great interest in assessing their daily operational performance in order to be a good corporate citizen. However, various currently existing corporate responsibility audit systems are often complex and make organizations, especially small & medium size enterprises, hesitate to engage in the corporate responsibility initiative despite their willingness. An audit system without much time, resource or budget constraint is highly likely to encourage more organizations to take part in the corporate responsibility initiative.

This research shows that there is no single broadly accepted definition, despite the widespread debate on corporate responsibility, which makes corporate responsibility audit development truly challenging. This study highlights key issues to be focused on during the development process of corporate responsibility audits, which were identified through extensive literature review and in-depth interviews with key representatives from various sectors in the United Kingdom. The research suggests that the proposed audit system needs to assess the key corporate responsibility performance of organizations comprehensively by their stakeholder groups. The study also discusses what is required for such audit systems to be effectively implemented in order to improve corporate responsibility performance of organizations.

Chapter 8 - Despite extensive corporate responsibility research into both *what* products firm produce and *how* they produce them, research is lacking in one product category in which the *what* and *how* linkage create questionable corporate practice – luxury products.

Luxury is in some cases created by companies controlling the so-called user imagery of their customers, i.e., by companies encouraging 'desirable' individuals to consume their products and obstructing 'undesirable' individuals from consumption. This chapter critically analyses the implications of this corporate practice based on a study of Sweden's most luxurious nightclub. The study's results show that the nightclub has organised its activities to allow categorisations of individuals into 'desirable' and 'undesirable' customers. Furthermore, the study shows that a creation of 'misery' for the vast majority of individuals (the 'undesirable') is essential for creating 'enjoyment' for the selected few (the 'desirable'). The chapter concludes by discussing implications for practitioners interesting in altering this situation.

Chapter 9 - The focus of this paper will be to analyse the relationship between corporate social responsibility and corporate governance adopting a stakeholder perspective. Moreover, the authors also try to go in depth about how internal governance mechanism can contribute both to reinforce company's values and to take into account the stakeholders' interests. So, the authors explain that the internalisation of stakeholder preferences implies a three- stage process: allocation of ownership rights, board composition, and the influence of important stakeholders. All the above lead us to propose that the future research would aim to clarify the roles and the importance of the diverse participants of the corporate governance systems (owners, directors, managers) in achieving a social responsible behavior of the firm, in order to secure its sustainability and legitimacy.

In: Contemporary Issues in Business Ethics
Editors: M. W. Volcox, Th. O. Mohan, pp. 1-3

ISBN: 978-1-60021-773-9
© 2007 Nova Science Publishers, Inc.

Expert Commentary A

BUSINESS ETHICS AND MANAGEMENT RISKS

Nikolay A. Dentchev[1] and Derrick P. Gosselin[1,2]*
[1]Ghent University, Ghent, Belgium
[2]University of Oxford (James Martin Institute), United Kingdom

Contemporary theorizing on business ethics is been predominantly approached through a normative approach. The meaning of this approach is well explained in the work of Donaldson & Preston (1995), who argue that "The normative approach [...] is [...] categorical; it says, in effect, 'Do (Don't do) this because it is the right (wrong) thing to do." Being developed as a branch of general ethics, business ethics focuses on the moral adequacy of corporate activities (Goodpaster, 1997). In this context, it is often argued that managers are obliged to pay more attention to the moral implications of their actions. The concern about the moral (in)adequacy of decisions taken by business leaders is argued when using examples of corporate scandals (e.g Enron), industrial accidents (e.g. Chernobyl) and environmental disasters (e.g. Bophal). Indeed, these examples, as well as many others, indicate the reckless behavior of some managers, which influences negatively the life of large groups of people. However, business ethics requires more than the mere use of rhetoric arguments in favor of morality in business. In fact, we should be able to tell practitioners how to adopt higher norms of ethics in their daily businesses. Therefore, we will argue in the remainder of this commentary that our field of research needs to comprehensively approach the management risks that executives may encounter in their practice of business ethics.

Our arguments are based on the premises that business ethics has not only moral, but also strategic implications for business organizations. Therefore, we need to study into more detail the empirics of business ethics (e.g. Treviño & Weaver, 2003), or in the words of Donaldson & Preston (1995), to adopt more descriptive approaches in our research. As scholars, we cannot provide advise to managers when only preaching morality and avoiding the challenges that executives face in their practice of business ethics. We propose to go even beyond the discussion on the difference between the normative and descriptive approach to business ethics (cf. Donaldson, 1994; Frederick, 1994; Treviño & Weaver, 1994; Victor & Stephens, 1994; Weaver & Treviño, 1994; Werhane, 1994). According to us, more attention should be

---

* Coordinates of corresponding author: Nikolay Dentchev, Ghent University, Tentoonstellingslaan 27, 9000 Ghent, Belgium; Tel: +32.477.91.71.21; e-mail: nikolay.dentchev@gmail.com

devoted to addressing the managerial risks of business ethics. Although these risks have been identified and discussed in recent publications (cf. Dentchev, 2004; Heugens & Dentchev, forthcoming; Kotler & Lee, 2005), the discussion on the management risks of business ethics still remains a *taboo* in our field of research. The reason to avoid such a discussion is arguably the possible reaction of executives. Knowing that business ethics is associated also with management risks, some scholars are concerned with a potential conclusion of managers: they may think that they are better of when adopting lower norms of morality in the corporate conduct of their companies. Such a concern is, however, rather hypothetical and does not reflect the principle of scientific rigour. Avoiding the discussion of managerial risks does not contribute to our knowledge of how executives should best approach the practice of business ethics, but on the contrary.

This commentary is concerned with those managers who truly believe in business ethics and who are determined to integrate higher norms of morality in their corporate identity. What can we advise them? How should they proceed in their endeavour to embrace higher norms of morality? In addition, this commentary is also concerned with managers who have adopted higher norms of morality, but, unfortunately, have encountered problems as a result. How should they approach these problems? We can answer these questions and provide intelligent advise to managers only when having a comprehensive knowledge on the management risks of business ethics. Hence, it is opportune to address concrete research questions in studying these management risks, some of which may be the following: *What are the different types of management risks? Are they related to a specific activity, sector, firm size, operational strategy or past performance? What is the context in which these risks materialize? Do they materialize under any condition, or are these risks a subject to specific contingencies? How do executives manage or proactively prevent management risks of business ethics? Can executives adopt already known generic strategies to the management of business ethics? Could we identify new management strategies that are applicable only to the management of business ethics?*

In conclusion, we would like to emphasize that the knowledge on how to manage business ethics is as important to the development of this field of research as the normative advocacy in favour of adopting higher moral norms in corporate performance. A rigorous knowledge of management is build when focusing on the problems that executives have to solve. Hence, we have argued in this commentary for research attention to the management risks of business ethics. We are convinced that comprehensive knowledge of the management risks associated with the adoption of higher moral norms will not only strengthen the theory of business ethics, but also its practice.

REFERECES

Dentchev, N. A. (2004). Corporate social performance as a business strategy. *Journal of Business Ethics, 55*(4), 395-410.

Donaldson, T. (1994). When integration fails: The logic of prescription and description in business ethics. *Business Ethics Quarterly, 4*(2), 157-170.

Donaldson, T., & Preston, L. E. (1995). The stakeholder theory of the corporation: Concepts, evidence, and implication. *Academy of Management Review, 20*(65-91).

Frederick, W. C. (1994). General introduction: The elusive boundary between fact and value. *Business Ethics Quarterly, 4*(2), 111-112.

Goodpaster, K. E. (1997). business ethics. In P. H. Werhane & R. E. Freeman (Eds.), *The Blackwell ecyclopedic dictionary of business ethics*. Oxford: Blackwell.

Heugens, P. P. M. A. R. & Dentchev, N. A. (forthcoming). Taming the trojan horse: Mitigating the potentially negative effects of corporate social performance. *Journal of Business Ethics*.

Kotler, P., & Lee, N. (2005). *Corporate social responsibility: Doing the most good for your company and your cause*. Hoboken: John Wiley & Sons.

Treviño, L. K., & Weaver, G. R. (1994). Business ETHICS/BUSINESS ethics: One field or two? *Business Ethics Quarterly, 4*(2), 113-128.

Treviño, L. K., & Weaver, G. R. (2003). *Managing ethics in business organizations: Social scientific perspectives*. Standford, California: Standford University Press.

Victor, B., & Stephens, C. U. (1994). Business ethics: A synthesis of normative philosophy and empirical social science. *Business Ethics Quarterly, 4*(2), 145-156.

Weaver, G. R., & Treviño, L. K. (1994). Normative and empirical business ethics: Separation, marriage of convenience, or marriage of necessity? *Business Ethics Quarterly, 4*(2), 129-143.

Werhane, P. H. (1994). The normative/descriptive distinction in methodologies of business ethics. *Business Ethics Quarterly, 4*(2), 175-180.

In: Contemporary Issues in Business Ethics   ISBN: 978-1-60021-773-9
Editors: M. W. Volcox, Th. O. Mohan, pp. 5-48   © 2007 Nova Science Publishers, Inc.

Chapter 1

SOCIAL RESPONSIBILITY REVISITED

James Stieb
Drexel University, Philadelphia, PA, USA

ABSTRACT

This chapter reviews and updates much of the literature on social responsibility including the author's own [2001] "Social Responsibility Within and Without Self-Interest." The chapter relates the debate's history from its development in the 1960's to its current global emphasis. It reviews "social responsibility" as "window-dressing," as well as "the market for virtue" in several key companies including Dow, Merck, Malden Mills and others. It presents the arguments from altruism and utilitarianism found in the work of Peter Singer, John Rawls and R.E. Freeman (stakeholder theory) and then addresses and defends the "free market" side of Milton Friedman against his critics. I argue that we should widen the idea of self-interest and reject altruistically motivated ethics. Getting rid of altruism and utilitarianism will leave plenty of egoistic social responsibilities that are also responsible to business needs and demands.

INTRODUCTION: THEORY MEETS PRACTICE

Business professionals quarrel more intensely over corporate social responsibility (CSR) than perhaps anything else. Social Responsibility is the doctrine that businesses, governments, individuals or other such entities have a moral obligation to 1) promote the positive welfare or 2) not infringe upon the rights or property of others, or 3) both. 1) indicates a positive obligation to help or assist; the second is "negative" indicating a responsibility to refrain from harming.

The idea that corporations should be responsible for their actions developed in earnest in the 1960s when public protests and boycotts against Dow Chemical prefigured those against Shell in the 1990's [Vogel 2006, 6]. According to David Vogel, many new "contemporary strategies of civil regulation" developed during this period "including voluntary codes of conduct, social audits, ... social investment funds" and a plethora of ways to assess and rank [2006, 6]. The heightened state of corporate awareness reflected increasingly global politics. According to James Rowe:

> The first wave took place in the 1960s and 1970s, when revelations about corporate corruption, tax evasion, and involvement in clandestine political activities, including the U.S.-backed coup that ousted Chilean president Salvador Allende, fueled populist attempts to rein in corporate power and increase accountability. In 1976, the United Nations began negotiating a binding international code of conduct for corporations. [Rowe, quoted by McNulty 2005]

As in the '60s, the public currently demands more social responsibility. However, corporations now respond differently. With "globalization" corporations are more likely to form "compacts" among international members [Rowe, 130]. According to BSR (Business for Social Responsibility) a global corporate nonprofit and the self-proclaimed "world leader in corporate social responsibility (CSR) research and consulting":

> Today's business landscape requires that companies navigate a complex and evolving set of economic, environmental and social challenges and address stakeholder demands for greater transparency, accountability and responsibility. These factors affect all aspects of business operations -- from supply chain to marketplace and from employee productivity to investor return. [BSR website]

"Stakeholders," according to R. E. Freeman who coined the term, comprise people affecting or affected by a corporation or more narrowly customers, suppliers, employees, and the local community [2002, 41]. Freeman says that he can "revitalize the concept of managerial capitalism by replacing the notion that managers have a duty to stockholders with the concept that managers bear a fiduciary relationship to stakeholders" [2002, 49].

In short, activists and others demand transparency and accountability. "Transparency" is "obviousness—the ability to be "easily seen through, recognized, or detected" [www.dictionary.com]. An "accountable" person can give a (presumably satisfactory) "account" of their actions. Critics want businesses to improve the environment, the economy, and society itself. A considerable wealth of philosophical and business argument backs their demands. And yet the arguments may mislead. Is transparency really possible? How might we make everyone "accountable" and what exactly does that mean?

After a brief "history of social responsibility," this chapter first addresses the philosophical and political arguments that try to define social responsibility and our desperate need for it. Debates are confused, so one must distinguish the primary philosophical question, which is not so much the definition of social responsibility as it is altruism's split from egoistically minded ethics. Do businesses have duties to help others at a cost to themselves, or only when it is in their enlightened interest?

After equating altruism with its near cousin utilitarianism, I review and attempt to refute Luis Pascal's and Peter Singer's "shaming" arguments. Pascal's and Singer's arguments try to make one feel bad for not doing enough to help worldwide suffering. Actually, I find such arguments either religiously motivated (and therefore rationally arbitrary) or hopelessly oblivious of economic realities.

Economics and political structures are just as important as philosophy and ethics. Duties to "distributive" or social justice are instantiated in and *in turn depend on* certain forms of government and economics. Yet, economics also needs philosophy and ethics. Economics should never be reduced to the attempt to rank preferences scientifically without suggesting them. Economics without ethics is sort of like tabulating the weights of prisoners in concentration camps without any regard for their condition. Business needs an ethical economics of the sort that Plato meant. In short, it needs an adequate social and political philosophy. Therefore, this chapter reviews the main options given in John Rawls' *Theory of Justice* as well as the numerous critics condemning Milton Friedman's doctrine. Exploring America's capitalist foundations a bit and the so-called "purpose" of the corporation, I argue for an amendment to Milton Friedman but not a wholesale dismissal.

A BRIEF HISTORY OF SOCIAL RESPONSIBILITY

In 1966, no one had ever heard of public protest against a major United States corporation. But, those days against Dow Chemical have since transformed traditional civil disobedience and activism. "In 1966, there was no pre-packaged corporate apologia upon which Dow could model its own defensive campaign. There were, for instance, no widespread environmental or consumer protection movements, ... " [Huxman & Bruce, 1995]. Newly declassified "rhetorical artifacts," shed light on nationwide student protests and the public condemnation of the use (or abuse) of technology in a hugely unpopular war.

The scenario resembles our own times (esp. the Persian Gulf war). Dow manufactured "Agent Orange," (or napalm) a chemical defoliant also designed to debilitate the enemy by burning their bodies chemically. Dow neither invented napalm nor was the first to use it. Nor did napalm ever make much money, "accounting for merely one half of one percent of total sales (which in 1967 totalled [*sic*] $1.3 billion)" [Huxman & Bruce, 1995]. Nevertheless, charges of war profiteering proliferated, as did the student protests. Dow's official response, as could be expected, was "understated and reactive."

What were the students seeking? A complete change in corporate practice? An overhaul of capitalism itself? Vogel relates an argument he used to hear in graduate school: "that as a new generation of more socially committed managers moves into positions of responsibility, we can expect corporations to become increasingly responsible" [2006, xxi]. Unfortunately, the scandals since have rendered such zeal shortsighted or even misleading. Business needs something more than social commitment, and that something includes an understanding of how business has developed and what it has become:

> Important social and political forces encourage firms to behave more responsibly, and they
> have accomplished much more than almost anyone could have predicted a decade ago. But,
> there are also important restraints on more responsible business behavior. [Vogel 2005, xxi]

Early corporations were hardly "corporations" in the modern sense that endows them with all the attendant rights and responsibilities of persons. Before 1886[1] the state granted "corporate charters" to churches, charities, and even cities" [Lipshitz and Rowe 133 quoting Hans 2000, 80]. The government, of course, carefully directed the power of such corporations to what it saw as the public good. After 1886, social responsibility became voluntary and a

---

[1] See Santa Clara County v. Southern Pacific Railroad.

period of huge commercial growth, scandal and apologetic philanthropy (say Andrew Carnegie's) followed. Meanwhile, a new player emerged, replacing the "robber baron" or the lone entrepreneur. She was the investor, or stockholder. When asked whether higher worker salaries or lower consumer prices should take "priority over stockholder interests" [Bowie and Beauchamp 2001, 46], *Dodge v. Ford Motor Company* [1919] resounded, no:

> A business corporation is organized and carried on primarily for the profit of the stockholders ... , It is not within the lawful powers of a board of directors to shape and conduct the affairs of a corporation for the merely incidental benefit of shareholders and for the primary purpose of benefiting others, ... [quoted in Bowie and Beauchamp 2001, 87]

No doubt, World War II and its aftermath woke the United States from its industrial slumber. The government encouraged corporations to train their newly found domestic might on helping Europe recover economically. This "abetted the outflow of foreign direct investment" and the transnational corporation was born; a "symbol of American economic power" [Lipschitz and Rowe, 135]. But, few were happy.

Domestically, Americans came to view corporations as huge autonomous Goliath's "'He' [the corporation] was power without personality, without proximity, 'he' was cold and distant" [Lipschitz and Rowe, 134]. Meanwhile, the public searched for civil rights and domestic equality, all the while mistrusting the huge corporations they saw buttressing the old system. In response, they created a regulation-friendly environment and enacted many familiar laws including those governing occupations, consumer products, clean air and water and others [Lipschitz and Rowe, 136].

Edwin Epstein claims that the 1960's saw governments "no longer reluctant to enact laws that transformed general public expectations about business responsibilities into specific legal requirements" [Epstein 1998, 6 quoted by Lipschitz and Rowe 2005, 134]. However, a distinction arose between laws that protect the rights of so-called economic "externalities" (those affected by business) and laws that confer positive benefits upon them. In this respect, post WWII governments have possibly been a little "benefit happy" at least with its own citizens.

Internationally, relationships changed. Colonialism gradually released its grip, though the colonialist powers still found time to carve out Israel over local resentment. The League of Nations and the United Nations promised self-determination. With their new-found freedom, "Salvador Allende's Chile and some 20 other developing nations" sought to control the transnational corporations (TNCs) they could not nationalize [Lipschitz and Rowe 2005, 136].

Moreover, these "developing nations" attempted unsuccessfully to control TNCs internationally. Lipschitz and Rowe write of the G-77 (Group of 77) nations who, partly emboldened by the "OPEC-orchestrated oil crises of 1973" sought to pass what they called a New Economic Order (NIEO). Complete with binding corporate codes of ethics, the NIEO would erase the "international division of labor" that resulted from unrestrained market capitalism [136-138].

However, the G-77 misunderstood both market capitalism and the possible responses of the dominant powers in a way that now seems hopelessly naïve. The "global North" simply conceded everything the G-77 wanted *on paper* seeing that often the best way to deal with an incredibly ambiguous proposal is to embrace it. Lipschitz and Rowe explain that the worldwide recession of 1980-82 helped the "global North" quash international regulation more than politics and more than the misguided and counterproductive help of International Telegraph and Telephone in Chile's coup leading to Allende's death. I believe that they are right: corporate responsibility (CSR) emerged in this period as "business strategy" and it has mostly remained there ever since. As they say

> The primary reason for business's trenchant interest in corporate codes is that they are an effective means of quelling popular discontent with corporate power and the political change that discontent might impel. Our research has convinced us to approach corporate codes of conduct less as exemplars of business ethics and more as effective business strategy. [Lipschitz and Rowe 2005, 132]

It may be that something can be done to further corporate responsibility not only domestically but also internationally. Indeed, global warming and the approaching environmental crisis may thrust responsibilities upon us. Nevertheless, simple demands for transparency or the dissolution of capitalism will not work. Perhaps a new way of thinking will. Therefore, let us look at the theory and philosophy behind social responsibility to see if we can find one.

THE PRIMARY PHILOSOPHICAL QUESTION

The Need for Ethics: What is Social Responsibility?

Philosophical questions may be divided from scientific questions by assessing how much and what kind of argument they need. In science, the lay community expects explanations, not arguments. In such a way scientists use observation and experiment to "settle" (at least in principle) questions about the boiling point of mercury or the origin of sunspots. Not so in philosophy. Observation and experiment rarely settle philosophical questions (hence business ethics questions). Philosophers do not disdain these any more than science disdains argument. Indeed, science without argument is dogmatic, and philosophy without observation and experiment is silly. However, philosophers use *conceptual analysis* and *arguments* to "settle" philosophical questions, if at all. If we do not settle them, we at least try to clarify them.

One might think that the most pressing philosophical question about social responsibility is its definition: "what is it?" However, I think the etymology has always explained its meaning. Something is "social" if it involves other people: one either owes something *to* others (the dative sense) or cannot have something *without* others (the generative sense).

The generative sense is interesting. In this sense, one has to derive the form and function of a language from society before she can speak it. "The social" includes language and other "socially constructed" entities.[2] But we can set the generative sense aside for the moment. This meaning of social responsibility bears on some *arguments* for social responsibility (say that corporations owe their position and conditions to society, so they *owe* society X, Y, Z in return). However, including arguments in definitions is usually a case of "begging the

---

[2] See Berger and Luckman 1966, Searle 1997. See my reply to John Searle in Stieb 2004b.

question" or "rhetorical definition" and these should be avoided. If a responsibility is an obligation, i.e. something we have to do or face the consequences, then the non question begging definition of social responsibility is: one's social responsibilities *are what one owes to society or what one is obligated to do for society.*

But, what about the consequences? What consequences confront the irresponsible? Obviously, the law condemns certain forms of irresponsibility (failing to do what one "must" for others). And some, even some who call themselves business ethicists, seek to reduce all responsibility to legal responsibility as if the law or the political system could capture what one ought to do for or to others, or in general, how we ought to live. A businessperson should find legal responsibility very important, but hardly the only thing that is. Yet another field seeks to go beyond that law or even critique the law when *it* is irresponsible, this field is Ethics.

So, when one speaks of consequences for social irresponsibility, we mean primarily if not exclusively *moral* consequences. We say: not only is embezzlement illegal, it is *wrong*. As I use the idiom, Ethics covers theories of what is good or bad right or wrong in human conduct, while each person/society has his or her individual morality or moral view. Business Ethics, then, studies how different moral theories apply in business, and then recommends how they *should* be applied.

In short, our social responsibilities are what we are ethically or morally required to do for or to society. Our legal or contractual responsibilities are important but separate. They may derive from given moralities or they may simply regulate (like "drive on the right-hand side of the road" when in the U.S). It is not like driving on the left-hand side of the road is unethical; it just probably means you are British.

Which Ethics Applies to Social Responsibility?

So, what kind of things do ethical theories or moralities oblige? This question has two different senses: it has an actual sense and a prescriptive sense.

The 'actual' sense indicates what businesses *actually* oblige of those who work in them. For example, Enron and Google ask for (or asked for) very different things. Enron officials touted "integrity" and "honesty" on huge banners in their parking lots but flouted these in their private offices. Or so it is alleged, cases are still pending. Google, it seems, goes above and beyond the "standard of the industry" devoting "20 percent of employees' schedules for their own intellectual pursuits" [Coughlin 2005]. Computer scientist Rob Pike left Nobel winning Bell Labs for a pay cut at Google and an "exciting place to work" [Coughlin 2005].

However, Business Ethics does not primarily concern what corporations actually do, it concerns what they *should* do. Business ethicists are concerned with the "prescriptive" sense of obligation.[3] What moral obligations does a businessperson have, regardless of who keeps them? Are any of these "social"? What must a moral businessperson do for others even when everyone else is acting differently?

First, an exhaustive list of responsibilities cannot be provided, however numerous ethical theories, codes and faith traditions seem right: these moral responsibilities include honesty,

---

[3] I tell my students: if you are not making arguments you are not doing philosophy; and if you are not talking about how things should or should not be, you are not doing ethics.

integrity, determination, passion, and many others. Not one of these is always a "virtue" for any time or place except perhaps integrity (remaining true to one's chosen values). Here the reader is referred to Robert Solomon's work [Solomon 1999]. Solomon gives a whole list of virtues and admirably explains how they are situational.

Instead, consider one specific list of "social responsibilities," that which Milton Friedman proposes and rejects in his important essay "The Social Responsibility of Business is to Make a Profit." He writes:

> The businessmen believe that they are defending free enterprise when they declaim that business is not concerned "merely" with profit but also with promoting desirable "social" ends; that business has a "social conscience" and takes seriously its responsibilities for providing employment, eliminating discrimination, avoiding pollution and whatever else may be the catchwords of the contemporary crop of reformers. [Friedman 1991, 78]

In addition to "providing employment" and the rest, one can include eliminating poverty or inflation as "catchwords of the contemporary crop of reformers."

I am not going to argue for or against this list right now, but it is worth presenting because it highlights a crucial distinction: that between egoism and altruism. This distinction is essential. According to egoism, I should seek my overall, enlightened, "best" interest; according to altruism I should *always* put others ahead of myself.

Egoism

Fundamentally, people misunderstand the egoist, accusing her of crass selfishness [Rand 1964, 33]. However, an egoist sacrifices much along the way. She may work to go to school, pay taxes, take classes she finds boring, and even care for a sick relative she values. Still, an egoist always pursues (to the extent she acts voluntarily) what she at least *thinks* to be in her best interest or most conducive to her overall happiness.[4] This theory has its appeal, though others think it hardly amounts to an ethical theory at all as they level arguments against it. I will oppose some of these objections to egoism later, but for right now the egoist theory is clear.

Altruism

For an altruist, consider Auguste Comte who said "[Man must serve] Humanity, whose we are entirely" [Comte 1973, quoted by Machan 2006]. Like L. Ron Hubbard (*Dianetics*), Comte attempts to craft a "secular" religion from the ashes of supernaturalism. Unlike Hubbard, Comte's "positive religion" (Comte began the "positivist" philosophical school) reproduces much Christian sentiment. For example:

> We are born loaded with obligations of every kind, to our predecessors, to our successors and to our contemporaries. ... Whatever our efforts, the longest life well employed will never enable us to pay back but an imperceptible part of what we have received [Comte 1973, quoted by Machan 2006]

---

[4] Psychological egoism motivates me psychologically to do whatever I think is in my best interest (when I act voluntarily). Ethical egoism says I should do what is really in my best interest. The first explains psychological motivation; the second is an ethical theory (a theory about what I should or should not do). My true best-interest only relates tangentially to what I may think it is.

This reflects the debt that supernaturalism says one owes to a creator. Comte substitutes other people for God. On his view, rights are nonsense. No one could possibly have a right: "All human rights then are as absurd as they are immoral."

Economics and Law

Others object that such an "extreme view of altruism" does not capture anyone's actual view. Yet, Tibor Machan, a classical liberal (libertarian), writes extensively on the altruism (or "welfare"/positive rights view) he finds in economist Amartya Sen and co-author Martha Nussbaum [*Rationality and freedom* [2002]], as well as in legal theorist Ronald Dworkin [*Sovereign virtue, the theory and practice of equality* [2000]]. These are important arguments, but there are philosophers who shed more light on social responsibility and the foundation of business ethics.

Religious Ethics

For this reason, religion should not be discussed much as well. I also want to base my arguments on reason and not faith. Religion *is* perhaps the most powerful source of altruism. Currently theologians such as Philip Hefner, Denis Edwards, Gerd Theissen, and Sallie McFague are debating several fundamentals of the Christian faith in numerous books and articles. McFague, in particular, finds the universe "directed toward inclusive love for all, particularly the oppressed" [CTNS-Vatican]. Of course, this "inclusive love" is altruistic: "The religious traditions carry altruistic values, particularly trans-kin altruism, and the biblical commandments ground altruism ultimately in God" [CTNS-Vatican]. Hefner goes so far as to say "Altruistic love holds the status of a cosmological and ontological principle" [quoted in Edwards 1999, 15].

The arguments complicate quickly, but the basic story relates God's totally uninterested sacrifice of his beloved son. Jesus heroically saves unworthy human beings including us. He "turns the other cheek" and allows himself to be killed. Instead, of remaining mired in sin, one should follow Jesus' example and sacrifice her self to save others.

Two thirds of our nation wants to be "like Jesus" and much of the rest of the world follows similar prophets. Far from obscurity, this "extreme version of altruism" has won the greatest "market-share" by far! Many theologians seek non-altruistic, and perhaps more plausible, ways to interpret the Christian story. Even so, the altruistic account carries the day.

Business Ethics

Altruism's prescribed sacrifices may seem tangential to social responsibility, but they are not. These sacrifices form the lynchpin of the social responsibility theorist's argument. It is not enough to argue that one should live up to his social responsibilities only when they conduce to his best-interest or convenience. Business people do not object to that view since in business most everyone wants to contribute to the bottom line without violating law and ethical custom. If one can do so by helping others in the process, then why not? No, the social responsibility theorist must argue that one should live up to her social responsibilities even when these contradict her best-interest or when they are very inconvenient or expensive. Put schematically (with 'a' for altrust; 'e' for egoist):

Social responsibility (a): one must help others even if doing so harms one's self.

Social responsibility (e): one must help others if doing so helps one's self.

Now, on the other side, Friedman and other "free-market" theorists do not object to "Social responsibility (e)." In fact, Friedman writes in a famous passage:

> In practice the doctrine of social responsibility is frequently a cloak for actions that are justified on other grounds rather than a reason for those actions.
>
> To illustrate, it may well be in the long run interest of a corporation that is a major employer in a small community to devote resources to providing amenities to that community or to improving its government. That may make it easier to attract desirable employees, it may reduce the wage bill or lessen losses from pilferage and sabotage or have other worthwhile effects. Or it may be that, given the laws about the deductibility of corporate charitable contributions, the stockholders can contribute more to charities they favor by having the corporation make the gift than by doing it themselves, since they can in that way contribute an amount that would otherwise have been paid as corporate taxes. [Friedman 1991, 78]

So, on the egoist or "free-market" view, businesses can contribute time, energy, and money to community resources when that will contribute most to business interests. An executive who spends her time making money rather than taking advantage of other socially responsible opportunities should not be condemned. She should rather be praised. She is not harming anyone. (The law and ethical custom make sure she is not). And, in fact, she is helping others by providing jobs, goods and services, and paying taxes.

The Plan of this Chapter

This chapter largely takes altruism as equivalent to utilitarianism as found (for example) in the work of that theory's present day champion Peter Singer, although it then explores the variant "responsibility sensitive egalitarianism" [Matravers 2007, 71] of John Rawls' *difference principle*. Altruism clearly resembles utilitarianism. An altruist puts the good of others ahead of his own in most if not every case, while a utilitarian seeks the "greatest good of the greatest number." "The greatest number" almost always means others, but it may also include the self, so utilitarianism is a *little* more benign in seeking one's own good. Yet, since it is not difficult to find at least two people worse off than oneself, utilitarianism, like altruism, often demands too much or is inconsistent. Or, so I shall argue. If you find one person worse off than you are, then you do not have to do anything. If you find two, they comprise a "greater number" and that "greater number" obliges you to give them everything until you are as worse off as they [Singer 1997, 42].[5] Consistency in altruism, and utilitarianism, seems to require a *sacrifice* of individual good.

Actually, no consistent theory of altruism seems available, though I do not pretend to refute them all at this point. A paradox, however, should be pointed out. When the altruist is asked why one should always (or even often) seek the interests of others before her own, she may only respond in two ways. She may answer, "because it is good for you" thus defeating her own argument, or she may answer "just because" thus giving an article of faith, not reason.

---

[5] Singer writes: "One possibility, ... , is that we ought to give until we reach the level of marginal utility—that is, the level which, by giving more, I would cause as much suffering to myself or my dependents as I would relieve

Of course, many supposedly 'altruistic' acts may be good for the individual, but those acts still sum into egoism and not altruism if they really are "good for the individual."

The Primary Philosophical Question(s)

The primary philosophical question is, therefore, not what social responsibility is, it is: *what grounds are there for the principle that one should sacrifice her good for another's?* There are very little or no grounds when *enlightened* interest frames the question and all social responsibilities become egoistic (a matter of convincing people that x or y policy is really in their best interest).

Of course, if all of our interests where those of brutes—if one only wanted to eat, propagate and rule—then inevitably some must sacrifice their "good" for another's. Having taken care of eating, propagating, and "ruling," at least to a large extent in the so-called "developed" nations; we turn our attention to other values like loving, wisdom, and making money. In his influential book *The Market for Virtue* (2006), David Vogel describes the contemporary development of CSR thought:

> Friedman had no quarrel with corporate social policies or programs that benefited shareholders—a category in which he included contributions to the community where the firm's employees resided. What he objected to were expenditures that benefited "society." And in the late 1960's there was no shortage of business initiatives that appeared to violate his criteria. [19]

The 1960's were both more volatile and more optimistic. Vogel explains that times have changed:

> Were Friedman now to revisit the subject, he would find much less to concern him. Virtually all contemporary writing on CSR emphasizes its links to corporate profitability. The typical book on CSR consists either of examples of companies that have behaved more responsibly and thus have also been financially successful, or advises managers how to make their firms both responsible and profitable. [19]

Vogel is probably right about today's "typical book." Authors can publish a thousand explanations about how to make money through pacifying the public, and no doubt they will. None of these will touch the core of Business Ethics: which is about what businesses should or should not do. Arguments about *whether* one has any social responsibilities to sacrifice his interests for the good of others are very different from arguments about *how* to help one's self by helping others. These latter are, no doubt, important. But, they are not the issue.

As should be clear, I agree with the modern trend. The best and perhaps only way to truly help others *is* by helping ourselves. As Adam Smith author of the *Wealth of Nations* famously put it, a person who does this

by my gift. This would mean, of course, that one would reduce oneself to very near the material circumstance of Bengali refuge." [1997, 404].

generally, indeed, neither intends to promote the public interest, nor knows how much he is promoting it. By preferring the support of domestic to that of foreign industry, he intends only his own security; and by directing that industry in such a manner as its produce may be of the greatest value, he intends only his own gain, and he is in this, as in many other cases, led by an invisible hand to promote an end which was no part of his intention. [2002, 159]

However, a focus on arguments about social responsibility (e)--that is, ways that corporations *can* be successful and responsible--runs two risks. First, such a focus runs the risk of marginalizing dissenting voices within American capitalist culture and begging the question for that system. Secondly, one runs the risk of marginalizing dissenting voices and alternative systems from *other* cultures thereby spreading intellectual colonialism.

The point is about pedagogy and fairness. Suppose that one agrees that the best way to get businesses to shoulder "responsibility" is to convince them that it is in their best interest. We still need to hear and refute arguments for social responsibility (a) that corporations should be responsible regardless of those interests. Let us turn to those.

AM I MY BROTHER'S KEEPER?

At the University of Pennsylvania in Philadelphia, mere blocks from my office at Drexel University, sits the Roy and Diana Vagelos Laboratories for Advanced Science and Technology. Roy Vagelos headed Merck research labs in 1978, when a senior researcher in parasitology, Dr. William Campbell, suggested that a drug they were currently studying for animal use might also help humans.[6] As late as 1978 a severely debilitating disease struck millions living along fast-moving rivers in the so-called "Third World." The World Health Organization considered "some 85 million people in thousands of tiny settlements throughout Africa and parts of the Middle East ... at risk" [Donaldson et al 2002, 238].

Tiny black flies would bite their victims and thereby deposit parasitic worms. These in turn grew to more than two feet, thereby creating ugly but harmless skin nodules. The real problem came when the worms reproduced, spawning hordes of microfilariae that swarmed the body's tissues, making the victim itch like mad. The microfilariae attacked the skin causing lesions and de-pigmentation and soon attacked the eyes causing blindness. Doctors used diethylcarbamazine (DEC) and Suramin to combat the parasite, but these had bad and sometimes lethal side-effects.

Merck, of course, is a major pharmaceutical company headquarted in Rahway New Jersey. Like most pharmaceuticals, it realized that "its success ten and twenty years in the future depended upon present investments" into research and development [Donaldson et al, 2002, 239]. At the same time, Merck also thought itself socially responsible. According to George W. Merck, former chairman and the founder's son: "We try never to forget that medicine is for the people, ... It is not for the profits. The profits follow, and if we have remembered that, they have never failed to appear" [quoted in Donaldson et al, 240].

Scientists discovered Ivermectin in a soil sample from a Japanese golf course. Ivermictin promised to eradicate *onchocerca cervalis* a relatively unimportant horse parasite [Donaldson et al, 242]. "Could a safe, effective, drug, for community-wide treatment of river blindness

---

[6] Details of this case study derive from Donaldson et al 2002.

[caused by the related *onchocerca volvulus*] be developed?" [Donaldson et al, 242]. Should it be developed? After all, the people who needed it would never be able to afford it. "Some diseases were so rare that treatments developed could never be priced enough to recoup the investment in research, while other diseases afflicted only the poor in rural and remote areas of the Third World" [Donaldson et al, 241].

It is difficult to find much in the way of *argument* for the principle that one should sometimes or always sacrifice one's good for another's. This is the principle of altruism (or here utilitarianism) which says that we should put the good of other people ahead of our own, or what amounts to the same thing, certainly never put our own good ahead of that of others. I have described it as social responsibility (a).

The principle can get pretty complicated when it is applied. Suppose I want to become a doctor, and I even have some skills and aptitude for it. Would altruism move me to helping the poor in the streets of Calcutta where Mother Theresa pursued her calling? Could I spend ten or more years becoming a doctor? Probably, I could go to school if I could show that my becoming a doctor would help more people or help them better. The idea that "inequalities" or self-interested actions are *allowable* if they tend to contribute to the good of the whole or of the disadvantaged (a version of John Rawls' "difference principle") will be important in what follows. But, for right now, let me just keep to the basics.

The "arguments" from religious sources that I am my brother's keeper, that I have a moral obligation to at all times seek their good (Jesus' commandment to love our neighbor as ourselves) are already too well understood and obvious to need review. In fact, I do not consider these to be arguments. Arguments consist of premises that are importantly different from the conclusion but that lead to the conclusion by reason rather than divine fiat. An understanding of theology should be left up to the theologians.

Turning to the philosophical literature (which supposedly depends on rational arguments), one finds little in the way of *arguments* for altruism. Numerous *examples* are present. There arguments *about* whether it is our duty to cure world hunger [Govier 1975; Singer 1972; Hardin 1974]; to provide jobs or employment [Miller 1998; Orlando 1999; Stieb 2004a] or to stem overpopulation [Pascal 1980, 1986]. However, arguments about a duty to cure world hunger may *turn on* whether one has a duty to put other people's interest ahead of his own *without being an argument* that one has a duty to put other people's interests ahead of his own. In other words, proponents of the principle simply assume it in their *further* arguments.

I agree more with Nicholas Rescher. In his book on welfare, Rescher writes of the "superogative" (above and beyond) duties of a society to its own members. Many think that welfare is a moral imperative. However, Rescher thinks the story is more complicated:

> In what respects and to what extent is society, working through the instrumentality of the state, responsible for the welfare of its members? What demands for the promotion of his welfare can an individual reasonably make upon his society? These are questions to which no answer can be given in terms of some *a priori* approach with reference to universal ultimates. Whatever answer can appropriately be given will depend, on the final analysis, on what the society decides it should be. [Rescher 1972, 114 quoted by Govier 1997, 378]

Rescher says that a non-question begging arguments for the desert of welfare or of social responsibility (a) cannot be found. There can, however, be many reasons that providing welfare is in society's best interest. For example, it may help quell civil unrest.

The different motives must be separated. Society's pursuit of *its best interests* differs entirely and importantly from categorical duties to help others regardless. Again, altruism or utilitarianism does not say, "do what is best for society." They say do what is best *for the afflicted* regardless of any self interest, whatever "self" one means: whether that is the individual self or society as a self. Sometimes society itself is "the afflicted." But, when society acts as an *agent* to help the victim, it is not itself the victim and is not supposed to act for itself. It is supposed to act for the good of others. Altruism by definition requires a sacrifice of the agent's good (utilitarianism almost always does).

At least a couple of papers explain the altruist or utilitarian "arguments" such as they are. Louis Pascal writes one. He is not a philosopher, and his arguments are less guarded and easier to refute. His paper does put a lot of issues on the table, though. Peter Singer writes the second, and a discussion of that paper will follow.

An Uncomfortable "Utilitarian" Question

Utilitarians are fond of asking "train track" or lifeboat type questions. "Imagine that your spouse is tied to one track of a train track and five world leaders are tied to the other and you control the track on which a speeding train descends," they say. In his paper, "Judgment Day" [Pascal 1986], Louis Pascal applies an interesting test of "how morally committed the students of a good school are." He creates a fictitious lecturer giving a speech to 300 students at Columbia University. The lecturer, Walter Bradford Ellis, asks the students to raise their hands if they say "yes" to a host of "train track" type ethical questions. He then lectures on overpopulation, trying by that means to have the student's responses elicit ethical action.

Pascal (or Ellis) recognizes that 300 students do not make a scientific sample. The group is "neither large enough or diverse enough to give an especially accurate picture" [105]. Still, he says, the test should indicate roughly how "morally committed" the students are. Pascal has good reasons for his questions:

> In today's world of racial prejudice, Vietnam, and above all, the miseries of overpopulation, it will take an uncommonly dedicated and selfless generation to grapple with these issues successfully. [105]

One can agree that Vietnam, racial prejudice and overpopulation continue to be big problems. However, notice how Pascal has snuck in the idea that only "selflessness" will grapple with these issues successfully. Philosophers call that "sneaking in' "begging the question" or "insinuation" and it has been found in so-called arguments at least since Socrates.[7] Pascal has so far given no evidence that these problems demand selflessness. He has stacked the deck.

---

[7] Most famously, see the dialogue called "Meno." Arguably, Socrates "coaches" the slave boy through the necessary steps to find the diagonal of a given square. Socrates (or Plato) argues, perhaps facetiously, that he has awakened dormant knowledge that everyone possesses prior to their birth. For me, the dialogue suggests

No wonder, then, that scenarios meant to test "moral commitment" make students uncomfortable. These do not test "moral commitment" to *whatever* code of values, they test whether the students agree with Pascal's altruism and are willing to stand up for it. At any rate, here is his first scenario:

> Imagine yourself to be in an ancient country which is ruled over by an evil king who has absolute power of life or death over all his subjects—including yourself. Now this king is very bored, and so for his amusement he picks 10 of his subjects, men, women, and children, at random as well as an eleventh man who is separate from the rest. Now the king gives the eleventh man a choice: he will either hang the 10 people picked at random and let the eleventh go free, or he will hang the eleventh man and let the other 10 go free. And the eleventh man must decide which it is to be.

Pascal distinguishes two questions: 1) Should the eleventh man give up his life for the other ten? 2) If you were the eleventh man, would you give up your life for the other ten? The distinction between these two questions is interesting, because in Ethics one often believes in "universalizability" which roughly says that whatever moral standards apply to everyone should apply to the individual and vice versa.[8] One should not make a moral exception of herself or of any one else.

Pascal wants one to give up her life to save ten others. There are two ways to go about disagreeing. First, if the answer to 2) differs from 1)--that is, if *our* being the eleventh man means ten others could die in one's stead--then one denies the principle of universalizability: we say it is ok to make an exception of ourselves. It is ok to "kill" ten others so that we may live. Or rather, it is morally permissible to let someone else kill ten people when the only way to prevent it is our certain death. The fire fighters in 9/11 were sort of this way. They raced in to save people's lives but *not* when it meant certain death for them. Pascal presumably has a problem with denying universalizability, however he need not. For example, it is morally ok to send your kid to college and not everyone else's.[9] It is ok, to make an exception for your kid. One can make himself a moral exceptions in a lot of ways. One feeds himself first, houses himself, and so on.

Once again, Pascal is trying to convince the reader to allow the king to kill her so that ten others may live. I think universalizability can be dismissed. However, anyone wishing to preserve it may disagree with Pascal in another way. Libertarians argue that the situation *itself* is fundamentally unjust. A king or a "gunman" forcing a person to do something immoral (such as killing 10 people with her inaction or other means), bears the full brunt of responsibility. Responsibility lies with the person initiating the force (or fraud) and not on the person used as an instrument.

This goes back to Aristotle's distinction between voluntary and involuntary. An action cannot be moral or immoral unless it is voluntary—one is not responsible for what she could not do otherwise. Our own law preserves this distinction when it distinguishes between murder and manslaughter. Manslaughter is "accidental," i.e., the agent did not intend to kill

---

that there may be forms of knowledge that are "logical" but no items of knowledge embedded in our collective unconscious.

[8] The Theory derives from Immanuel Kant in the liberal tradition. See Kant 1993.

[9] The example derives from Marcia Baron, a contemporary deontologist (duty-based ethicist in the Kantian tradition). See Baron 1991.

and did not do so voluntarily. In some cases, "ignorance of the law is no excuse" but these cases can be set aside.

After these initial inroads, Pascal shifts the burden of his question. He asks how many students would save ten people if the king only required twenty years in prison. Pascal's fictitious pole has many more people give up twenty years of freedom to save ten people. I think this case resembles the first. Twenty years of life is still a lot of life to give up, and twenty years of prison will almost certainly sour one's subsequent life.

Pascal then has the king say he will release the ten "if you will agree to give him all the money you have and all the money you will make in the future, except of course enough for you to feed yourself and house yourself and take care of all the absolute necessities" [107]. Readers who think their taxes too high already may find this situation upon them. All the same, a huge number of people starve to death each year.

Pascal argues that failing to give up one's money is murder.

> If you are poor and kill 10 people in order to steal their money, that is surely murder. But morally speaking that situation is exactly the same as this one. In both situations if the people die, you will be rich; if they live, you will be poor, and it is within your power to decide which it is to be. In either situation if you decide that they should die in order that you can be rich, you have put your happiness, or not exactly even that, you have put material riches for yourself above 10 people's lives. That is the moral error you have made and it is exactly the same for both cases. [108]

Pascal says, "Morally speaking the situation is exactly the same." However, he does not seem to be right. *Killing* 10 people to take their money is very different from *failing to save* 10 people by refusing to give up *all* of one's money. Even if one uses utilitarianism the situations do not come out the same "morally speaking." Here are the situations:

1. Keep my money and have 10 people die who I could have helped.
2. Murder 10 people for their money.

Utilitarianism looks at consequences, or the greatest good for the greatest number. In case one, ten people are dead, but the murderer is still as happy or miserable as he ever was. In case two, ten people are dead and the murderer is much happier because now he has their money. Case two thus shows a net increase in happiness. Of the two cases, utilitarianism actually seems to prefer the second. This is reason for dispensing with utilitarianism.

If Pascal is not using utilitarianism, what theory he *is* using is not clear. Virtue ethics, Aristotle's theory, would morally prefer case 1 because, although 10 people are dead in either case, one is not a murderer. In case 1, murder does not stain one's character, give her bad habits, or set the law at her heels. Virtue ethics posits a big difference between killing 10 people and keeping one's money when the alternative is giving up *all* (or most all) of one's money.

Obviously, Pascal should change the alternative, although he does not. He should ask, "what if the king asked you to give up say 10 or 20 percent of your money so that 10 people may live?" This is commonly known as "tithing." What if the king asked one to tithe in order to save the lives of 10 people? (We may also dispense with the idea that he will actually kill them if one does not agree; he will just be unable to prevent their deaths.) That *I should help others when the cost to myself is little* convinces more than that I should help others at great cost to myself. This first idea might be enough for "social responsibility," so it is discussed in the next section.

Should we Give Something?

Peter Singer argues that one should at least give something to the needy in his paper "Famine, Affluence, and Morality" [1997]. Singer writes more carefully and skillfully than Pascal. He puts it this way:

> If it is in our power to prevent something bad from happening, without thereby sacrificing anything of comparable moral importance, we ought, morally to do it. By "without sacrificing anything of comparable moral importance" I mean without causing anything else comparably bad to happen, or doing something that is wrong in itself, or failing to promote some moral good, comparable in significance to the bad thing that we can prevent. [1997, 400]

Singer says:

> An application of this principle would be as follows: if I am walking past a shallow pond and see a child drowning in it, I ought to wade in and pull the child out. This will mean getting my clothes muddy, but this is insignificant, while the death of the child would presumably be a very bad thing. [400]

Fair enough. But, a drowning child represents only *one* application of Singer's principle, and probably the least contentious. Singer mainly discusses the famine in East Bengal in 1971 where "constant poverty, a cyclone, and a civil war have turned at least nine million people into destitute refugees" [399]. Singer laments that individuals "have not responded to the situation in any significant way." Governments, on the other hand, are more interested in "supersonic transports" and Opera houses. Singer implies "that the British government values a supersonic transport more than thirty times as highly as it values the lives of the nine million refugees"; Australia values its Opera House twelve times as much.

Singer's strategy, like Pascal's, seeks to analogize and shame. If a drowning child compels our aid, a starving refugee should do the same. One stuffs his face, while people starve.

First, Singer says that his principle "requires us only to prevent what is bad, and not to promote what is good" [400]. This seems incorrect. The two cannot be divided so neatly. If I feed a starving man, am I promoting his good or just preventing something bad? After all, he receives a service.

More importantly, Singer writes: "It is not beyond the capacity of the richer nations to give enough assistance to reduce any further suffering to very small proportions" [399]. Singer also wants each individual to give until it hurts, he writes:

> One possibility, ... , is that we ought to give until we reach the level of marginal utility—that is, the level which, by giving more, I would cause as much suffering to myself or my dependents as I would relieve by my gift. This would mean, of course, that one would reduce oneself to very near the material circumstance of Bengali refuge.

Singer approves of reducing one's material circumstances to those of a Bengali refugee:

> It will be recalled that earlier I put forward both a strong and a moderate version of the principle of preventing bad occurrences. The strong version, which required us to prevent bad things from happening unless in doing so we would be sacrificing something of a comparable moral significance, does seem to require reducing ourselves to the level of marginal utility. I should also say that the strong version seems to me to be the correct one. ... I can see no good reason for holding the moderate version of the principle rather than the strong one. [404]

He concludes that, "It does follow from my argument that we ought, morally, to be working full time to relieve great suffering of the sort that occurs as the result of famine or other disasters" [403]. However, what is missing from Singer's "argument" is any sociological or economic input about how viable societies actually run. He seems oblivious of how "rich nations" got that way in the first place. Marx's famous slogan (actually Thomas More's) "From each according to his means, to each according to his need" illustrates this problem as well. Someone has to have means before anything goes to the needy.

Singer should ask, "How did these rich nations become rich in the first place?" Undoubtedly, a certain amount of force, fraud, and deceit underlies any nation's history. America itself rests on slavery and near genocide. Our country exports wastes to countries where the laws are more lenient and wars against sovereign nations without clear evidence of destructive intent or capability (such as weapons of mass destruction). Things have not necessarily changed much since 1971. However, reducing America's material circumstance to that of the Bengali refugees simply makes us prey to less altruistically minded nations.

Singer's principle cannot be universalized. One cannot give everything to others because that would leave nothing left to give. If it cannot be universalized in general (that is for everyone everywhere), then it cannot be universalized in particular (that is for you or me now). I mean that a principle of production must precede a principle of distribution. Or, as Plato put it "If our servant goes empty-handed to another city, without any of the things needed by those from whom he is trying to get what his own people need, he will come away empty-handed, won't he" [370a10]? If, in general, a city must produce, then one cannot fault those who concentrate solely on production. If people must produce in general, then some must produce in particular. Production must be a virtue or value preceding distribution. If some focus on creation and others on distribution, who can fault either?

Now, whether a city must give as well as produce, and therefore, whether some individuals in the city must give in particular and how is still an open question. Apparently, Plato did not think that a city owed anything to any other in virtue of need (though something was owed in virtue of contracts or alliances or in times of disaster). Moreover, he is very murky about what citizens owe each other. Plato was an aristocrat who never argued against the institution of slavery. Both Plato and Aristotle thought slavery quite natural.[10] On the other hand, Plato's hero Socrates, spent his life relying on the good graces of his friends whom he sought to educate philosophically. There is an aura of caring about city politics (i.e., the good of the city and the individual) in Plato and Aristotle, but the altruistic impulse is absent. Apparently, it had to wait for Christianity.

---

[10] I may have missed something in The *Laws* or another dialogue, however Aristotle's defense of slavery is notorious.

My critics might think this historical review an easy way to dispense with the issue: should one tithe? Should we individually or collectively give up only 10 or 20 percent of our wealth in order to help starving nations? They say, surely we can without making ourselves "prey to less altruistically minded nations."

Perhaps we can. But let us not lose sight of whether we should and why. So far, we have not seen very good moral arguments for social responsibility (a), that one should help others regardless of his own interests. Internationally, there are of course, very good reasons for *caring* about starving refugees (or economically depressed countries). There are very good reasons for social responsibility (e), the kind that is also in our best interest.

For example, few Americans seemed to care or know that the Taliban (the former government of Afghanistan) destroyed two thousand plus year old monuments to the Buddha. They shot them out of the rock face with artillery. These are cultural icons of the age and status of the pyramids. However, most every American knows that many of the 9/11 terrorists trained in formerly Afghani camps. This was the *casus belli* (cause of war) against that country (that and the wish to hunt out the mastermind Bin Ladin). The rather horrible point is that sometimes it takes planes crashing into New York City skyscrapers to remind Americans of the bedraggled plight of much of the rest of the world. Such acts remind us not only to protect our security, they remind us of the self-interest involved in making sure that "most of the world" lives "nearly as well as its most privileged part" (Margolis 2004, 407; Stieb 2005).

Still, as Rescher implied, whether one should tithe depends on the governmental structure and economics in question and not on some supposed *apriori* moral duties. Of course there can be better or worse governmental structures. Let us look next at the arguments from economics and social and political philosophy that suggest alternative structures fostering social responsibility (a).

TWO THEORIES OF POLITICS

The City of Pigs

> If you were founding a city of pigs, Socrates, isn't that just what you would provide to fatten them?
>
> Plato [2004, 372d5] attributed to Glaucon

According to Plato, a city is a man "writ large" and justice fundamentally orders both. Of course, justice is not easy to define and Socrates seeks a definition through most of the *Republic*. Traditionally, Plato has his mouthpiece Socrates refute the troubling and half-baked ideas of foils like Thrasymachus who thinks that justice is the advantage of the stronger. However, the *Republic* also offers a theory of city construction from the ground up.

One by one Socrates ticks off the city's needs. The city (my translator calls it "Kallipolis"—literally beautiful city) needs farmers, builders, and weavers to take care of the fundamentals; cobblers and toolmakers to take care of secondary needs. Notice, however, that Socrates makes the "real creator" of the city "our need," not the needs of *others*. He bases the city in rational self-interest assuming that each role will work productively and collectively for the good of all. Altruism is foreign to Socrates.

Socrates adds that the settlement will not be very large "even if we added cowherds, shepherds and other herdsmen, so that the farmers will have cows to do their plowing, the builders oxen ... [and so on]" [370a10]. And, naturally it will trade: "Our citizens, then, must produce not only enough for themselves at home, but also goods of the right quality and quantity to satisfy the needs of others" [371a5]. Sharing *is* very important to Socrates: "It was in order to share, after all, that we associated with one another and founded a city." Citizens will build a marketplace and establish a common currency. Some become retailers and accountants.

Socrates says that citizens of the "healthy" city

> will mostly work naked and barefoot, but in the winter will wear adequate clothing and shoes. For nourishment, they will provide themselves with barley meal and wheat flour, which they will knead and bake into noble cakes and loaves and serve up on a reed or on clean leaves. They will recline on couches strewn with yew and myrtles and feast with their children, drink their wine, and, crowned with wreaths hymn the gods. They will enjoy having sex with one another, but they will produce no more children then their resources allow, lest they fall into either poverty or war. [372a5-372c]

At this point, Glaucon interrupts: "If you were founding a city of pigs, Socrates, isn't that just what you would provide to fatten them" [2004, 372d5]? Glaucon means that barley meal and wheat flour feasts will not please everyone. The "feverish" city must have painting, gold and ivory, actors, jewelry and even prostitutes. The healthy city is fit for pigs, not for people. A city fit for people must exceed one's basic needs. And when, one oversteps her basic needs, war is sure to follow. One will

> have to seize some of our neighbor's land, then if we are to have enough for pasture and plowing[.] And won't our neighbors want to seize ours in turn, if they too have abandoned themselves to the endless acquisition of money and overstepped the limit of their necessary desires. [373d5-10]

Of course, the idea that pursuing luxury beyond the bare minimum inevitably causes war [373e5] is a *non sequitor*. There is no reason to believe that citizens in the *healthy* city will not have to fight for their parcel of land. However, Socrates is right that exceeding our natural due is importantly related to injustice.

Altruists or utilitarians tend to equate going beyond the bare minimum with selfishness (or egoism) and argue that one should live at the bare minimum so as to leave as much as possible for others. Some Christians even blame acquisitiveness on "original sin" and a fallen nature. However, these arguments appear too fast. Socrates tries to define what is in one's best interest; he does not argue that one should sacrifice it in order to avoid war. In fact, Socrates implies that one should avoid excess and luxury *because* he thereby avoids strife and war. We gain our true self-interest by sacrificing our illusory wants.

Postmodern Economics: The Ethics of Impartiality

Times have changed since Plato. Today theorists discuss "distributive justice." Distributive justice "uses some principle or criterion to give out a supply of things. Into this process of distributing shares, some error may have crept. So, it is an open question whether redistribution should take place; ... " [Nozick 2002, 203]. In Plato's time, economics meant "house things"—i.e., taking care of the house, and men left the job to women. Today economics is the province of elite forecasters (mostly men).

According to Mark Fleurbay, economics explains distributive justice through theories of inequality and poverty measurement, social choice, bargaining and cooperative games, fair allocation and welfare economics [Fleurbay]. Since economic naivety riddles the philosopher's analysis (Pascal's and Singer's) then one might want to embrace modern economic theory. However, that is not the solution either. Embracing modern economics is a mistake because it really does not have much say about "distributive justice" at all. In fact, it is purposely irrelevant to the question of altruism—hence of social responsibility (a). Rather, one should go back to a pre 20th century understanding of economics to find a relevant economics. Turning to philosophers other than Pascal and Singer might also help.

The supposed difference between the "normative" (the ethical) and the "positive" (non-ethical, scientific) illustrates economics' obliviousness to moral questions. In the first half of the 20th century, noted economists involved themselves with helping the less fortunate [Fleurbay]. But, something happened. Today, the economist is more "positivistic," more uninvolved and scientific. "Normative economics itself may be partly guilty for this state of affairs, in view of its repeated failure to provide conclusive results and its long-lasting focus on impossibility theorems" [Fleurbay].

The whole "postmodern" effort to replace narrative, patriarchy, and colonialism with behaviorism (cf. B.F. Skinner) and science can be blamed. Postmodernism has transformed questions of "house things" (*oeconomicos*) into questions of subjective value-preferences. It has eroded the metaphysical question of *the* good. There is not any independent thing to be preferred, there is what one happens to prefer and questions about how she may get it most efficiently.

Actually the supposed value objectivity of economics is just a story. Ethically, it defaults to utilitarianism. For example consider "poverty measurement." Obviously, the only reason to measure poverty is in order to do something about it. (I certainly hope that economists do not measure poverty simply as an academic exercise).

Second, consider welfare economics. Fleurbay notes the strategy:

> The proponents of a "new" welfare economics (Hicks, Kaldor, Scitovsky) have distanced themselves from their predecessors (Marshall, Pigou, Lerner) by abandoning the idea of making social welfare judgments on the basis of interpersonal comparisons of utility. Their problem was then that in absence of any kind of interpersonal comparisons, the only principle on which to ground their judgments was the Pareto principle, according to which a situation is a global improvement if it is an improvement for every member of the concerned population (there are variants of this principle depending on how individual improvement is defined, in terms of preferences or some notion of well-being, and depending on whether it is a strict improvement for all members or some of them stay put). Since most changes due to public policy hurt some subgroups for the benefit of others, the Pareto principle remains generally silent. [Fleurbay]

This requires a bit of unpacking. Basically, it says that Hicks, Kaldor and Scitovksy (or others like them) have tried to avoid "interpersonal comparisons of utility"--i.e., they want to avoid saying what is good for one person vs. what is good for another. The motive is clear. One does not want to judge someone's life or choices as good or bad; rather one seeks a neutral measurement such as what they prefer or what the market will allow. The neutral measurement will prevent hypocrisy or condescension. Some economists think the "Pareto principle" provides that neutral measurement. According to the "Pareto principle" "a situation is a global improvement if it is an improvement for every member of the concerned population." Moreover, the "Pareto Principle" tries to remain "silent" because "most changes due to public policy hurt some subgroups for the benefit of others."

However, the Pareto Principle does not provide a neutral measurement: *there is no neutral measurement*. Second, the alternative to utilitarianism (hurting some subgroup for the benefit of others) is not silence (or as I prefer to call it postmodern catatonia). It is a better ethics. First, how could a measure that measures a "global improvement" on the basis of "an improvement for every member of the concerned population" not make significant value judgments about what is good or bad for the members of the "concerned population"? Obviously, one exports and transports his values—one should rather try to have good values than to remain 'neutral.' This leads to a second point. The alternative to utilitarianism (sacrificing some for the greater good of the greater number) is not silence; it is redefining social responsibility so that it does not require sacrifices. Social responsibility (e) can be defined so as to avoid unnecessary sacrifices if one reads the economist Milton Friedman the right way.

The "Theory of Social Choice" and the "Theory of Cooperative Games" fail even worse in these respects. "Social choice ... deal[s] with the problem of synthesizing heterogeneous individual preferences into a consistent ranking." Arrow argued that such a ranking could not be set up. Nash argued that it could. He, Nash, refocused on game theory: "Nash (1950) published a possibility theorem for the bargaining problem, which is the problem of finding an option acceptable to two parties, among a subset of alternatives" [Fleurbay].

The history of economics is all well and good. But whether all "heterogeneous individual preferences" can be ranked consistently or not has little to do with how to rank certain important individual preferences (such as whether to go to school, take a job, etc). Nash and others realized this and hence refocused economics on bargaining and games. But, that did not help much, for game theory has spun wildly and irrelevantly out of control. It has lost most of its relevance (and even intelligibility) to the phenomenon it was supposed to explain. One such example of game theory is the much cited "prisoner's dilemma," (PD) which authors argue refutes egoism [Lucas 2003, 16; Boatright 2007, 50-51].

Persons A and B are arrested; the charges will be dropped against whoever confesses, unless both confess. "Whatever the other does, each is better off confessing than remaining silent. But the outcome obtained when both confess is worse for each than the outcome they would have obtained had both remained silent" [Kuhn, 2003]. If both remain silent then both A and B are better off (no charges stick). The egoist is likened to the prisoner who "rats out" her partner with the result that egoism does not appear to be the best policy for individual betterment.

However, the PD argument assumes too much. Ethical egoism is the view that we should do what is *really* in our best interest. First, the PD assumes that *not* doing time for one's crime is in one's true best-interest. However, paying for one's mistakes might actually be best. Second, the PD depends on raising an *unjust* situation and on not adequately distinguishing between psychological and ethical egoism. In the first case, it is not just to let someone go free just because she confesses. One could easily say that there is no moral way out of an unjust situation [Gillespie 2002], and leave the PD at that.

In the second case, the PD claims that the prisoners *think* that confessing (while the other remains silent) is in their best interest, while both prisoners remaining silent is really to each's best-interest. If this is true, then ethical egoism councils doing what is really in their best interest (not what they think is), so there is no contradiction: on this supposition, they should both remain silent. I see no way that the PD gains any purchase without assuming that there is something that is really to the best interest of the participants that differs from what they think is. Ethical egoism says, once again, that an agent should do *what is really in her best interest* whether or not there are situations in which she does not or cannot know that.

The "purely economic view," or the view that "ethics and economics can be neatly and sharply separated" [Freeman 2004, 364] is unlikely to settle any question of Business Ethics. As Freeman says, "In this context, the challenge of doing business becomes a Sisyphean task because business ethics is, by definition, an oxymoron" [2004, 364]. Economics is not a pristine oasis for retreat.

The problem is that economic naivety limits Pascal's and Singer's ethical theories. Pretensions to value objectivity limit economics. What is left? The answer is now called "social and political philosophy" though it was once called "economics." Altruism (or social responsibility (a)) will not come out of the ethical theories. Nor will it come out of purposely oblivious economic theory. Unfortunately the best example of social and political philosophy rather smuggles altruism (a) instead of deriving it. Hence, the need for an alternative social and political philosophy recalling Plato.

Justice as Fairness

According to Fleurbay, "Rawls' difference principle (Rawls 1971) has been instrumental in making economic analysis of redistributive policies pay some attention to the maximin criterion, which puts absolute priority on the worst-off, and not only to sum-utilitarianism" [Fleurbay]. Rawl's distributive justice theory favors altruism to the "worst off" while avoiding the sacrifices of "sum-utilitarianism." Actually, Fleurbay is wrong. Rawls does not avoid utilitarianism. The idea that inequalities are justified by improving everyone's lot *is* a kind of utilitarianism. As for altruism or social responsibility (a), Rawls assumes these for his theory; he does not derive them. But let us look at the theory.

John Rawls' theory of justice (justice as fairness) is important because it shows what not to do in social and political philosophy. It is famous and widely read. It proceeds systematically spanning a number of volumes often in outline form and with ample response to objections. Finally, Rawls intends it to be very altruistic. Rawl's second ("difference") principle justifies inequalities only when they favor the disadvantaged. It is the job or the social responsibility (a) of the economic system (or perhaps of business) to stamp them out otherwise.

Here are Rawls' two principles as he first states them:

1. The "Liberty Principle": Each person is to have an equal right to the most extensive basic liberty compatible with a similar liberty for others. [1971, 60]

2. The "Difference Principle": Social and economic inequalities are to be arranged so that they are both (a) reasonably expected to be to everyone's

advantage, and (b) attached to positions and offices open to all. [1971, 60]

Libertarians and "negative" minded social responsibility (e) theorists such as Robert Nozick [2002] agree with the first principle, but not with the second. I am not sure that anyone would disagree with the first principle, so I set it aside. The second, occasions a lot of difficulty, not least of all because Rawls' 1971 formulation is really just an obscure piece of writing. The 1971 formulation in *A Theory of Justice* makes the difference principle sound like the liberty principle. However, a 1967 chapter reprinted in at least one important Business Ethics textbook [Donaldson et al, 2002] gradually clarifies what Rawls means:

> Now the second principle holds that an inequality is allowed only if there is reason to believe that the institution with the inequality, or permitting it, will work out for the advantage of every person engaged in it. In the case of the basic structure [,] this means that all inequalities which affect life prospects, say the inequalities of income and wealth which exist between social classes, must be to the advantage of everyone. Since the principle applies to institutions, we interpret this to mean that inequalities must be to the advantage of the representative man for each position; .... [2002, 196]

Now, this formula does not obviously improve over the previous. It does introduce a central government stamping out all sorts of inequalities "affecting life prospects." They stamp them out unless leaving them alone helps the "representative man." But, who is the representative man? Rawls says, "The one obvious candidate is the representative man of those least favored by the system of institutional inequalities" [197]. Hence,

> We interpret the second principle to hold that these differences are just if and only if the greater expectations of the more advantaged, when playing a part in the working of the whole social system improve the expectations of the least advantaged. The basic structure is just throughout when the advantages of the more fortunate promote the well-being of the least fortunate, that is, when a decrease in their advantages would make the least fortunate even worse off than they are.

So, Rawls says that the centralized government should stamp out inequalities such as wealth, talent, health, looks, and so on, if preserving these inequalities does not help those worse off. Otherwise these inequalities are unjust. Second, it should stamp out inequalities unless doing so harms those already disadvantaged. For example, Bill Gates. It is better that Gates has more computers than others, because he will provide jobs with them while I would only play more video games. Gates' having more computers improves everyone's status, while my having more computers does not.

At any rate, Rawls attempts to put much social responsibility (a) into his system; indeed, he seems to be a leading advocate of such responsibility. However the arguments for his "difference principle" are lacking. These arguments are well known although they are hard to get exactly right. One begins by thinking of a social contract situation, i.e., in Rawls' idiom "an agreement among free and independent persons in an original position of equality ... [that] reflect[s] the integrity and equal sovereignty of the rational persons who are the contractors" [2002, 195]. Our "representatives" (curiously it is not us) in such a thought-experiment choose "in one joint act, what is to count among them as just and unjust" [195].

Of course this "suitably defined initial situation" is supposed to be "Kantian."[11] To be "Kantian" is to be independent of wants and desires--that is, to be based solely on the *apriori* (oblivious of experience) resources of reason. Of course this comprehension "prior to experience" baffles. However, the *apriori* rather means "oblivious" to experience rather than temporal priority. This is purposeful obliviousness of the sort present in modern economic theory.

Descartes *cogito* (his saying "I think; therefore, I am") also provides a good example. In his *Meditations*, Descartes says that he wants to assess each of his former opinions for soundness and validity, to find out whether they are indeed right or wrong. He resolves to doubt anything that can possibly be doubted, which he finds to be the case with anything that comes through his senses. He could be dreaming that he is seeing a fire before him, or his senses could be deceiving him. When train tracks recede in the distance, supposedly parallel lines appear to meet. But, they do not. Our senses deceive us.

Descartes then moves on to mathematical propositions. Is not 2+2=4? Not so, says Descartes because an evil deceiver (a sort of anti-god) could make one only think 2+2=4 when really it equals 5. At any rate, even if an evil deceiver grips me icily and deceives me mightily he/she can never make me doubt one thing: I am a deceived being. And as long as I think I am a deceived being, then I know I exist. *Cogito; ergo sum*. I think; therefore, I am.

I cannot doubt that I exist, because in my doubting I am existing. Scholars often find it difficult to get any other "indubitable" *apriori* knowledge (although they fought for a while over what they called "synthetic" vs. "analytic" propositions). Certain axioms, postulates or common notions might count as *apriori* knowledge. For example, Euclid's famous 5th postulate says that parallel lines do not meet. One cannot prove that parallel lines do or do not meet without assuming that they do. Strangely, all of mathematics (from the Greek *mathemata*—"true knowledge"), hence all science, depends on certain improvable postulates, axioms and common notions. Moreover, one can have perfectly sensible Euclidian geometries based on the premise that parallel lines *do not* meet, and Lobachevskian geometries based on the premise that they *do*.

At any rate, Rawls wants his original position to be Kantian in this respect: independent of experience and also necessary (if he can get it). For this purpose, he introduces a "veil of ignorance." In Rawls' system, the veil actually shields the wearer from knowledge of others and themselves.

> This decision is thought of as being made in a suitably defined initial situation one of the significant features of which is that no one knows his position in society, nor even his place in the distribution of natural talents and abilities. ... A veil of ignorance prevents anyone from being advantaged or disadvantaged by the contingencies of social class and fortune; and hence the bargaining problems which arise in everyday life from the possession of this knowledge do not affect the choice of principles. [2002, 195]

Rawls' account of the veil of ignorance has much going for it. Consider the intense fighting between the Palestinians and the Israelis and the many attempts at negotiation. The parties cannot forget their differences. If they could, they would hammer out a peace.

---

[11] For an account of Kantian constructivism vs. Rawls' political constructivism see Stieb 2006a.

Moreover, justice is supposed to be blind. Judging on character and not on skin color or gender would eradicate many modern problems such as racial profiling or sexism.

Few authors if any (I have not seen any) describe exactly how the two principles of justice are supposed derive from the original position. I do not think it is even possible for one to really imagine that she does not know her gender, race, monetary and societal position, history, natural talents, abilities and so on. The best one can do is to pretend that these do not matter. She then asks, "If I could be anyone, then what principles of justice would I endorse." Rawls thinks that I would endorse the maximal liberty compatible with like liberty for all and that I would only allow some persons to have more than others if doing so left everyone better off.

If I could be anyone, then it is in my best interest that everyone has maximal liberty compatible with like liberty for all. *Whoever* I actually turn out to be when the veil is lifted, then, I too will have maximal liberty. Similarly, if I could be anyone, then I could be one of the disadvantaged, so it is in my best interest to make the disadvantaged as best off as possible. Though Rawls thinks social responsibility (a), i.e., egalitarianism, motivates his system; social responsibility (e), egoism, or self-interest, actually motivates it. We may think of Rawls' (and Kant's) systems as ways of "taming egoism" for the ultimate good of the individual. However, if they are ways of "taming egoism" *for the ultimate good of the individual*, then they are not ways of "taming egoism" at all.

Moreover, scholars seem to exaggerate the system's importance, but there seems to be little reason for preferring "Kantianism" to other hypotheses:

> I guess there may be something special about putting our representatives behind a veil of ignorance (as Rawls proposes). But, I can't see the general difference between that and any scientist that proffers a hypothesis while ignoring what she thinks is irrelevant. The question, of course, is how much can we safely ignore?
>
> ...
>
> The "ideal gas law" (PV=nRT) assumes that there are no intermolecular forces and collisions are perfectly elastic.[12] Both Rawls' theory of justice and the ideal gas law are "idealized" constructions. The difference between Rawls and the scientist is that the latter realizes that her scientific law doesn't work in every situation, while Rawls thinks that his theory of justice might work for *any* democratic society. [Stieb 2006a, 381-382 refering to Rawls 1993, xvi]

Hence, I cannot really see any argument for social responsibility (a) coming out of Rawls' theory of distributive justice. One favors the disadvantaged in his system (the difference principle) because that is best for one given the knowledge restrictions of the original position. If an action helps others and helps us then that is social responsibility (e), not social responsibility (a). We are trying, and apparently failing, to find arguments for social responsibility (a) that business people have a responsibility to put others before any interest they may have however enlightened. It does not appear that we have a duty to give to others at an *overall* cost or inconvenience to ourselves.

---

[12] PV=nRT (Pressure x Volume = Number of moles x Universal gas constant x Temperature). See ("Ideal Gas Law." Georgia State U. 8 Mar. 2005 <http://hyperphysics.phy-astr.gsu.edu/hbase/kinetic/idegas.html>).

THE CLASSICAL MODEL OF CORPORATE SOCIAL RESPONSIBILITY

The Social Responsibility of Business is to Increase its Profits

Having no luck with positive arguments for social responsibility (a), perhaps we should start from the negative side, with the conclusion that business has no extra social responsibilities other than those that are in its best interest. Maybe we can compose the critics' objections into a single coherent argument for social responsibility (a).

Milton Friedman, a "Chicago school," nobel winning economist is best known for his defense of the free market. "Social responsibilities" or the lack of them are key to Friedman's defense. In the by now notorious paper "The Social Responsibility of Business is to Increase its Profits" Friedman concludes that the only social responsibility of business it to make a profit provided it follows law and ethical custom.

> That responsibility is to conduct the business in accordance with their desires, which generally will be to make as much money as possible while conforming to the basic rules of the society, both those embodied in law and those embodied in ethical custom. [1991, 79]

Friedman, of course, puts the point in an unfortunate way. He makes it seem like business must take advantage of every opportunity ("make as much money as possible"). Industrialists should, therefore, set up lemonade stands because they could thereby make "more" money, legally and ethically. No, "opportunity costs," the fact that one cannot do X if she does Y, make this reading of Friedman preposterous. Yet, most of Friedman's critics (at least in Business Ethics) either miss the subtlety of Friedman's arguments or obviate them "on principle." Let us first look at the arguments before we look at the critics.

Friedman's argument may be divided into four particulars. First, the CEO is an employee of the stockholders and should do what they want. They want a return on their investment, since they could have put their money into charity otherwise.

> In either case, the key point is that, in his capacity as a corporate executive, the manager is an agent of the individuals who own the corporation or establish the eleemosynary institution, and his primary responsibility is to them. [79]

If one hires an engineer to build a bridge and the engineer gives the funds to charity, one should perhaps applaud his philanthropy before suing him. But, one should sue him nonetheless.

Second, there are other experts such as social workers and economists. Friedman lists "providing employment, eliminating discrimination, avoiding pollution and whatever else may be the catchwords of the contemporary crop of reformers" [78]. Surely, social workers, economists, and governmental officials are better trained to deal with these problems than are corporate executives:

> On the grounds of consequences, can the corporate executive in fact discharge his alleged "social responsibilities? ... How is he to know how to spend it? He is told that he must contribute to fighting inflation. How is he to know what action of his will contribute to that

end? He is presumably an expert in running his company—in producing a product or selling it or financing it. But nothing about his selection makes him an expert on inflation. [80]

Third, the government is charged with taking care of "social responsibilities." This may sound like an appeal to "other experts," but it is a bit different because of Friedman's list of proposed social responsibilities. For better of worse, since the depression, American government has assumed the goal of putting of "a chicken in every pot." There are complex reasons why the process of improving living conditions is slow and sometimes not possible. Nevertheless, Friedman argues that arguments that affect everyone should be made by everyone otherwise one is "seeking to attain by undemocratic means what they cannot attain by democratic procedures" [81]. This is why Friedman accuses advocates of social responsibility (a) of "preaching pure and unadulterated socialism" and "undermining the basis of a free society these past decades" [78].

Lastly, the executive is what one might call "a small fish in a big pond"; she does not have that much *ability* to effect change even were trained to do so. I tell my students that Bill Gates could cure poverty in the United States—for about an hour and then there would be one more poor person. Society must look at and ameliorate the complex reasons why people are poor, not simply throw more money at the problem. Critics counter that small CEOs can pool their resources. However, in keeping with Friedman's arguments, such "collusion" may form the sort of monopoly Friedman detests. The government is slow but separate from the public sphere for a reason.

To me, these form a powerful bulwark of argument against social responsibility (a). As noted before, Friedman does not reject social responsibility (e) and at times even embraces it:

> In practice the doctrine of social responsibility is frequently a cloak for actions that are justified on other grounds rather than a reason for those actions.
>
> To illustrate, it may well be in the long run interest of a corporation that is a major employer in a small community to devote resources to providing amenities to that community or to improving its government. That may make it easier to attract desirable employees, it may reduce the wage bill or lessen losses from pilferage and sabotage or have other worthwhile effects. Or it may be that, given the laws about the deductibility of corporate charitable contributions, the stockholders can contribute more to charities they favor by having the corporation make the gift than by doing it themselves, since they can in that way contribute an amount that would otherwise have been paid as corporate taxes. [Friedman 1991, 78]

Friedman even revisits the issue in a recent [2005] debate with Whole Foods CEO John Mackey. Mackey posits, among other things, that "The most successful businesses put the customer first, instead of the investors" and that "There can be little doubt that a certain amount of corporate philanthropy is simply good business and works for the long-term benefit of the investors." Friedman disputes Mackey in two ways. First he says, "Had it [Whole Foods] devoted any significant fraction of its resources to exercising a social responsibility unrelated to the bottom line, it would be out of business by now or would have been taken over" [Friedman et al, 2005]. Second, Friedman disputes "Mackey's flat statement that 'corporate philanthropy is a good thing'" by noting no reason to believe that a "stream of profit" directed to corporate philanthropy "would do more good for society than investing that stream of profit in the enterprise itself or paying it out as dividends and letting the stockholders dispose of it."

Whole Foods donates 5 percent of net profit to charity. Contrary to what his critics expect, Friedman agrees that this practice makes sense: "They were clearly in their rights in doing so." However

> it makes sense only because of our obscene tax laws, whereby a stockholder can make a larger gift for a given after-tax cost if the corporation makes the gift on his behalf than if he makes the gift directly. That is a good reason for eliminating the corporate tax or for eliminating the deductibility of corporate charity, but it is not a justification for corporate charity. [Friedman et al, 2005]

In other words, the government has set up a system that makes corporate philanthropy make sense. It is a fluke. For, corporations will actually better achieve real end-goals such as jobs, improved working conditions, and a cleaner environment, by reinvesting the money than by giving it away for a tax break.

Stakeholder Theory

Many see R. E. Freeman's "stakeholder theory of the corporation" as a welcome and leading alternative to Milton Friedman's "stockholder" theory. Stockholder theory prioritizes stockholders or investors. They are the beneficiaries of corporate effort and dividends. Freeman argues that others have a "stake" in the success or failure of the firm and that corporations should be "responsible" to these "stakeholders."

> Until recently [there] ... was no constraint at all. In this century, however, the law has evolved to effectively constrain the pursuit of stockholder interests at the expense of other claimants on the firm. It has, in effect, required that the claims of customers, suppliers, local communities, and employees be taken into consideration, though in general they should be subordinated to the claims of stockholders. [2002, 39-40]

Certainly, one can doubt that there was "no constraint at all" on the pursuit of stockholder interests. However, Freeman's point is well taken. He seems to agree with John Orlando that "the business ethics literature has yet to identify a morally relevant distinction between the situation of the shareholder and that of the worker in relation to the corporation" [Orlando 2003, 32-33]. If there is no morally relevant distinction between the stakeholder and stockholder, then fairness and respect for persons demand that we treat both alike.

Freeman says "My thesis is that I can revitalize the concept of managerial capitalism by replacing the notion that managers have a duty to stockholders with the concept that managers bear a fiduciary relationship to stakeholders" [2002, 39]. "The crux of my argument," he writes, "is that we can reconceptualize the firm around the following question. For whose benefit and at whose expense should the firm be managed" [39]? Freeman thinks that firms should be managed to benefit and exact costs from stakeholders equally. There seems to be no way to assess whether one stakeholder has made a greater contribution than another. So, all should be treated equally and all should have equal decision making power: "That is, each of these stakeholder groups has a right not to be treated as a means to some end, and therefore must participate in determining the future direction of the firm in which they have a stake" [39]. They must have real and not simply illusory or token decision making power.

First, in a previous paper, I addressed the idea that "the business ethics literature has yet to identify a morally relevant distinction between the situation of the shareholder and that of the worker in relation to the corporation" [Orlando 2003, 32-33]. In fact I think the morally relevant distinction is between presently owned money and the prospect of future work:

> indeed a significant difference in the *kind* of risk that each shareholder or worker assumes. Shareholders already *have* their money, earned (we may assume rightfully) from their own work. ... Workers, on the other hand, *don't have* the money in question yet. Money from the *future* employment that Orlando feels workers ordinarily deserve is money that can be legally and morally obtained by the worker only on the condition of *future* performance adequately agreed to (i.e., under a contract). Shareholders risk present money; workers risk future earnings. Shareholder money (to use Kant's terminology) is "categorical"; worker money is "hypothetical." Should we not assume, then, that the nature of the moral imperative involved follows the nature of the money in question? A manager's duty to a shareholder is categorical, while to a worker it is hypothetical. [Stieb 2004, 65]

Second, Freeman does not seem to give valid arguments for his conclusions. Stakeholder theory is the theory proposed by Freeman that we should a) change the beneficiaries, and b) give them serious decision making power. He argues for this on the basis of a legal argument and an economic argument.

According to Freeman's legal argument,

> The law has evolved to effectively constrain the pursuit of stockholder interests at the expense of other claimants on the firm. It has, in effect, required that the claims of customers, suppliers, local communities, and employees be taken into consideration. [Freeman 2002, 39-40]

Instances of such requirements are "privity of contract" in Winterbottom vs. Wright, "strict liability" in Greenman vs. Yuba Power. Freeman also includes the National Labor Relations Act, Title VII of the Civil Rights Act of 1964, and the Age Discrimination act of 1967. In a nutshell the argument goes like this.

> There are all these new laws constraining corporations.
> ...
> We should change the beneficiaries and give them serious decision power.

One can see that the conclusion does not follow. We may justly approve of these laws some of which protect consumers, others of which clear gender gaps and the like without concluding that any stakeholder is now *benefited*. Those who respect our dignity regardless of race or age do not benefit us. They merely give us what we rightly deserve as human beings.

Moreover, stockholder theory can accept new constraints on businesses without changing their primary message. One should not tar stockholder theory with racial or age prejudice; it is simply the theory that investors should be and are the primary beneficiary of what businesses do with stockholder money. Even if the new laws "benefit" the public in some sense, it does not follow that they ever could replace the investor as the primary beneficiary. Yes, new laws constrain corporations. But they only protect some third party, against pollution, for example. If A and B are doing business and C gets polluted, the law then allows greater protection of the "economic externality" C. The law makes C whole again. However, it does not give C anything she did not have before. She does not seem to have any new decision power either.

I cannot see in what sense the new laws would give its new "beneficiaries" greater decision-making power. Title VII may give a worker more options, but that is not the same thing. Greater decision-making power is the ability to have one's decisions listened to and acted upon. Improved working conditions such as a minimum wage do not confer such power on workers. The minimum wage may frustrate the decisions of some managers, yet workers do not decide anything about the minimum wage (except as voters): the government decides for them.

Freeman's economic argument is similar. According to Freeman

> In its pure ideological form managerial capitalism [stakeholder theory] seeks to maximize the interests of stockholders. In its perennial criticism of government regulation, management espouses the "invisible hand" doctrine. ... However, we know that externalities, moral hazards, and monopoly power exist in fact, whether or not they exist in theory.
>
> The problem of the "tragedy of the commons" or the free-rider problem pervades the concept of the public goods such as water and air. ...
>
> Similarly, moral hazards arise when the purchaser of a good or service can pass along the cost of that good ...
>
> Finally, we see the avoidance of competitive behavior on the part of firms, each seeking to monopolize a small portion of the market and not compete with one another. [2002, 41]

In other words,

Capitalism has numerous problems

...

We should change the beneficiaries and give them serious decision power.

Once again, we can agree with the premises without the conclusion being true.

Yes capitalism, as they like to say, is the worst system there is *except for all the others*. But, again, that does not make any alternative such as stakeholder theory better for that reason. Freeman does not show that the tragedy of the commons, the free-rider problem, moral hazards or "the avoidance of competitive behavior" result from *stockholder theory*. There is nothing in stockholder theory that councils morally questionable behavior that may in fact diminish the return to stockholders. Stockholder theory may be a cornerstone of capitalism, but it is not, thereby, heir to capitalism's problems (which, by the way, are problems for any economic system).

Moreover, I cannot see that laws that prevent the abuse of the commons, that make everyone pay his share, or that disallow monopolies, challenge the investor's primacy at all. Surely, the investor has fewer options. Law constrains the potentially lucrative behavior of harming others. But, the investor is still Queen. The law rather provides the conditions for free trade; it does not direct that trade to altruistic ends. (The exception of course is government produce, but even that is strategically directed.)

Freeman writes about how stakeholder theory is supposed to affect each stakeholder. Here are two. First the supplier: "When the firm treats the supplier as a valued member of the stakeholder network, rather than simply as a source of materials, the supplier will respond when the firm is in need" (43). However, I do not know what it means to treat anyone "simply as a source of materials," and there is no guarantee that any supplier will "respond" to any "need" no matter how well treated. Nor is there any reason to believe that the supplier has a responsibility to act altruistically.

Second,

> The local community grants the firm the right to build facilities ... The firm cannot expose the community to unreasonable hazards in the form of pollution, toxic waste, and so on. If for some reason the firm must leave a community it is expected to work with local leaders to make the transition as smooth as possible. Of course, the firm does not have perfect knowledge, but when it discovers some danger or runs afoul of new competition, it is expected to inform the local community and to work with the community to overcome any problem. When the firm mismanages its relationship with the local community, it is in the same position as a citizen who commits a crime. It has violated the implicit social contract with the community and should expect to be distrusted and ostracized. It should not be surprised when punitive measures are invoked. [2002, 43]

It is a play on words to say the local community grants anything: *representatives* of that community sit on zoning boards. Government bodies are instituted (as the Declaration of Independence says) to "secure the rights of the governed" not to grant them. At any rate, I am not sure what the local community may validly "expect" but a firm that fails to inform the community of a new source of competition or fails to "work with the community to overcome any problem" is hardly criminal. The law decides what is criminal, not the community. *Members* of the community certainly have the right to "distrust" and "ostracize" any firm they want (within the prescribed limits of civil disobedience and occasionally beyond), but they may invoke "punitive measures" only when laws are broken. Stockholder theory specifically says, "Follow law and ethical custom." There is no extra-legal, punitive community sanction that the community can level against firms.

Freeman's recent (coauthored) articles merely repeat these arguments, if they offer any arguments at all for changing the beneficiaries and giving them serious decision-making power. More often than not the recent articles simply offer business strategy. For example:

> We would argue that stakeholder theory gives managers more resources and a greater capability to deal with this challenge [of getting stakeholders to sign on and give their best for the firm], because they can offer not only financial reward, but language and action to show that they value relationships with other groups and work to advance their interests over time. [2004, 365]

Managers have more resources and greater capabilities because they can offer more language and action. No doubt some companies value "language and action to show that they value relationships with other groups." Such language and action will encourage employees to "sign on and give their best for the firm." Yet, other "stakeholders" do not value these things in the companies they associate with. They believe that too much "language and action," emphasis on "value relationships with other groups," and "group advancement" all divert them from the already daunting task of creating a quality product and competing in the market place. These individuals do not lack values because they lack "collective" or "altruistic" values. They value competence and precision more and prefer not to waste their time with corporate handholding (or whatever it is that Freeman means that one should do for other stakeholders that they are not already doing. Freeman is not exactly clear).

One more quote should adequately seal Freeman's view of business under stakeholder theory:

> Finally stakeholder theory does a better job of explaining and directing managerial behavior in markets. Stakeholder theory claims that whatever the ultimate aim of the corporation or other form of business activity, managers and entrepreneurs must take into account the legitimate interests of those groups and individuals who can affect (or be affected by) their activities (Donaldson and Prestion 1995, Freeman 1994). It is quite natural to suggest that the very idea of value creation and trade is intimately connected to the idea of creating value for stakeholders. Business is about putting together a deal so that suppliers, customers, employees, communities, managers, and shareholders all win continuously over time. [2004, 365]

Freeman thinks that business is about making all stakeholders win. However, Business is not about "putting together a deal so that suppliers, customers, employees, communities, managers, and shareholders" (the stakeholders) will "all win continuously over time." Business, the free market, is about trade. One person or a group of people put mental and/or physical labor into materials in order to create a product. They then attempt to advertise and sell their product. There are no "winners" and "losers." There are those who buy and those who sell. The government sets minimal conditions of trade in order to verify quality and insure delivery (for example). All other associations, assistance giving, or team sports analogies are up to the traders involved. There is no "right" or "wrong" beyond following law and ethical custom. There is the stupid and the intelligent (course of action). Of course everyone should best look out for his interests, social responsibility (e)). As of yet, I still see no reason (beyond law and ethical custom) that one needs to put the interests of others first. Even following law and ethical custom is not putting the needs of others first, because one certainly has a self-interest in *their being* law and ethical custom that they and others follow.

Some Other Objections to Milton Friedman:

J.R. Lucas

According to J.R. Lucas

> Many thinkers deny the possibility of businessmen having responsibilities or ethical obligations. ... Admittedly, there is a framework of law within which he has to operate, but that is all, and so long as he keeps the law he is free to maximize profits without being constrained by any moral or social considerations, or any further sense of responsibility for what he does. [2003, 16]

Lucas thinks that a businessman who maximizes profits is "unconstrained by any moral or social considerations, or any further sense of responsibility." Lucas believes this view is mistaken because

It is a mistake to construe rationality in terms of maximizing. Even though some economists, influenced by the Theory of Games, offer it as a definition, it is, as the prisoner's dilemma shows, an incoherent one. For individuals each seeking to maximize their own payoff can lead to sub-optimal outcomes assessed in maximizing terms. [16]

Instead, rationality also requires us "to widen our range of concern. We accept that it would be foolish to be guided only by immediate payoffs without considering future ones; ... ." Like Freeman, Lucas believes that

cooperation, not competition, is the most fundamental aspect of business. ... The obligations of a businessman arise from the cooperative nature of business and the shared values and mutual understanding of the cooperative associations within which business transactions take place.

I can entice someone into wanting to do business with me only by attempting to figure out and serve her needs. Lucas best explains his point with the inconsistency he calls "scepticism." He thinks that many in business are "sceptical":

It would still be possible for a businessman to remain sceptical. ... The tough-minded can dismiss all concern for the environment as unrealistic woolly-mindedness, and may defer payment to his suppliers until the last possible moment: but when the Mafia call and suggest that he might like to purchase protection from arson attacks, he is likely to be indignant. He believes vehemently in the rule of law, and that violence has no place in a civilized society; his skepticism, in short, is selective. ... Morality and self-interest remain opposed, but each version of self-interest is seen ultimately to belacking in enlightenment. Scepticism is always possible, but never in the long run reasonable. [2003, 18]

In sum, those who cleave to the law to determine business' social responsibilities, "deny the possibility of businessmen having responsibilities or ethical obligations." This view is inconsistent even on egoist terms, both because of the prisoner's dilemma and because of the businessperson's insistence on the rule of law in his own case "when the Mafia call."

Unfortunately, Lucas' arguments are unsound. One cannot follow the law and simultaneously deny all responsibilities or ethical obligations. This is why Friedman called following the law (and much else) plausible "social responsibilities" (e), though they are not social responsibilities (a).

Of course, the corporate executive is also a person in his own right. As a person, he may have many other responsibilities that he recognizes or assumes voluntarily–to his family, his conscience, his feelings of charity, his church, his clubs, his city, his country. He may feel impelled by these responsibilities to devote part of his income to causes he regards as worthy, to refuse to work for particular corporations, even to leave his job, for example, to join his country's armed forces. If we wish, we may refer to some of these responsibilities as "social responsibilities." But in these respects he is acting as a principal, not an agent; ...

As far as this view being inconsistent, I fail to see the inconsistency. First, I tried to show (above) that the prisoner's dilemma does not show that construing rationality in terms of maximizing is incoherent. Understanding the prisoner's dilemma depends on what one is maximizing. The prisoner's dilemma may show that maximizing short term or immediate profit seeking goals contradicts maximizing long term goals. But, ethical egoism is the view that we should do what is *really* in our best interest, whatever that is, not what we *think* is. The PD claims that the prisoners *think* that confessing (while the other remains silent) is in their best interest, while *we know* that both prisoners remaining silent is really to each's best-interest. If this is true, then ethical egoism councils doing what is really in their best interest (not what they think is), so there is no contradiction: on this supposition, both are better off when both remain silent.

The PD represents an unjust situation anyway. If the world where truly just there would be no crime in the first place. Even if there were, each prisoner would confess honestly so that each could better receive the correction he deserved. Any contradictions stem not from maximizing one's best interest but from the injustice of the situation.

Similarly, Lucas supposes that it is contradictory for me to call the police (or be indignant) when the Mafia come calling offering their protection. However, I do not see the inconsistency since it is supposed that I fully believe in following the law. I would then expect others to follow the law, and be indignant when they do not.

Robert Hannaford

Like Lucas, some authors such as Hannaford object that stockholders want a lot of things besides money: "it is not clear whether our interest is to be given a purely financial interpretation" [1991, 86]. Of course, Hannaford is right: stockholders might want an improved environment and a cure to poverty. However one probably better cures these ills by giving her money to Greenpeace than by investing in IBM.

Hannaford accuses Friedman of just such an equivocation: that a "theoretical twist" allows Friedman to advocate *greed* while defending *self-interest*. Yet, it is Hannaford who equivocates. As separate *people*, each of us seeks "to better his or her condition" [85]. He claims "To say that all persons will seek what they regard as useful does not tell us anything about what in particular they so regard, nor what they will seek" [86]. Of course he is right. And, it does not follow that because we seek our own self-interest continuously that "we have a right to say each of us seeks his or her own financial interest continuously" [86]. We have other interests besides financial ones. Yet, as stockholders, our interests are more specific and limited. The stockholder's interest *can* be given a "purely financial interpretation" because that is why one invests money—to make money.

Friedman wrote:

> In a free-enterprise, private property system, a corporate executive is an employee of the owners of the business. He has direct responsibility to his employers. That responsibility is to conduct the business in accord with their desires which generally will be to make as much money as possible while conforming to the basic rules of the society, both those embodied in law and those embodied in ethical custom. [Friedman 1991, 79]

But, he never denies that CEO's represent only one interest among a stockholder's many plausible interests. "Instead, he argues that they or their duly elected government represent their other interests better than would a CEO hired to represent one's financial interest (within the rules of law and ethical custom)" [Stieb 2001, 242]. As noted before, Friedman explicitly recognizes other *personal* responsibilities:

Of course, the corporate executive is also a person in his own right. As a person he may have other responsibilities that he recognizes or assumes voluntarily—to his family, his conscience, his feelings of charity, his church, his clubs, his city, his country. [79]

Friedman's point is crucial: public outcry against companies and their CEO's merely fixates on the closest source of power. In this way the public forgets "its proper democratic role in the generation and check of that power. It is 'seeking to attain by undemocratic procedures what [it]…cannot attain by democratic procedures' (81)" [Stieb, 2001, 242].

The whole justification for permitting the corporate executive to be selected by the stockholders is that the executive is an agent serving the interests of his principal. This justification disappears when the corporate executive imposes taxes and spends the proceeds for "social" purposes. He becomes in effect a public employee, a civil servant…If they are to be civil servants, then they must be elected through a political process. If they are to impose taxes and make expenditures to foster "social" objectives, then political machinery must be set up to make the assessment of taxes and to determine through a political process the objectives to be served. [Friedman 1991, 80]

For better or worse, democracy is rule by the people for the people. "Friedman doesn't defend greed by defending self-interest; he defends "greed," or the pursuit of profit, by paying attention to job descriptions and the real source of political power" [Stieb 2001, 243].

Robert H. Frank

First of all, Frank mischaracterizes Friedman:

In Friedman's view managers who pursue broader social goals—say by adopting more stringent emissions standards than required by law, or by donating corporate funds to charitable organizations—are simply spending other people's money. Firms run by these managers will have higher costs than those run by managers whose goal is to maximize shareholder wealth. According to the standard theory of competitive markets, the latter firms will attract more capital and eventually drive the former firms out of business. [2002, 252]

Frank thinks that Friedman will disallow any investment of stockholder funds to anything else than "the bottom line." However, Friedman recognizes that the bottom line is not precise and well-defined. Contributing to "broader social goals" may also contribute to the bottom line (social responsibility (e)).

It is true that managers who pursue *any* corporate goals are spending someone else's money unless they, themselves are investors. Friedman also thinks that we can do anything we like with our own money: "the individual proprieter … is spending his own money, not someone else's. If he wishes to spend his money on such purposes, that is his right, and I cannot see that there is any objection to his doing so" [36]. However, Friedman clearly recognizes that corporate management or philanthropy is far from an easy matter of "simply spending other people's money."

To illustrate, it may well be in the long-run interest of a corporation that is a major employer in a small community to devote resources to providing amenities to that community or to improving its government. That may make it easier to attract desirable employees, it may reduce the wage bill or lessen losses from pilferage and sabatoge or have other worthwile effects. Or, it may be that given the laws about the deductibility of corporate charitable contributions, the stockholders can contribute more to charaties they favor by having the corporation make the gift than by doing it themselves, since they can in that way contribute an amount that would otherwise have been paid as corporate taxes. [1991, 82]

So Friedman does not think that *necessarily* "firms run by these managers will have higher [overall] costs than those run by managers whose goal is to maximize shareholder wealth." He recognizes that "higher costs" in one area may be offset by greater returns in other areas.

Frank continues:

In the years since Friedman wrote this article, the development of the theory of repeated games has given us ever more sophisticated accounts of the forces that often align self-interest with the interests of others. For example, Robert Axelrod (1984) suggests that firms pay their suppliers not because they feel a moral obligation to do so but because they require future shipments from them. [2002, 252]

Frank makes two claims 1) game theory helps explain better how self-interest aligns with others' interests (than Friedman does, presumably). 2) paying suppliers because one requires future shipments is not part of a "moral obligation" while paying them for some other reason is. Let me start with 2). Moral obligations are at least in part those duties we owe to others in virtue of being part of the same shared, human enterprise. We all strive (or should strive) to be happy, to please God (perhaps), to do our duty. One theory could be called, after the literature, "consequentialist," another "divine," a third "deontological." Paying suppliers (doing on to others) so that we may then have a reasonable expectation of them continuing to supply to us (do onto us), seems the very call of morality whether Aristotelian, Christian, or Kantian.

As for 1), it has often been asserted that game theory improves and perhaps falsifies the famous "invisible hand" of Adam Smith. I have already dealt with this assertion previously.

Thomas Donaldson, et al.

Donaldson, Werhane and Cording seem to think that Friedman's arguments have something to do with the "purpose" of business. They ask: "As a businessperson, is it sufficient to manage one's firm such that it operates within the confines of law?" (Friedman's point). They follow with the suggestive question "In its most basic sense, what is the purpose of a large business organization?

Next, they also imply that Friedman's position is nonethical (or perhaps unethical). They write:

Some argue that ethics has nothing to do with business, nor business with ethics. For example the obligation of a firm that generates pollution as a byproduct to its manufacturing processes is to comply with pollution-control laws; it is up to the government to set these standards such that the public welfare is protected [again, very close to Friedman's point]. Others claim that because business involves people, by definition it involves ethical considerations. In determining the amount of corporate funds to spend on abatement, they argue firms must consider the damage their actions may have on innocent people. Both sides of this argument are presented throughout the text. (12)

All of these assertions miss the point. Friedman was not describing the purpose of a business; he was describing what its social responsibility is *not*. Second, we need not accept the false dichotomy that one is ethical *or* profit-minded. One can be ethical *and* profit-minded. Indeed, running a successful business would seem impossible otherwise. In "determing the amount of corporate funds to spend on abatement" (which all corporations do), one must do more than "consider the damage their actions may have on innocent people." One must offer specific recommendations and numbers and follow through. For example, the National Pollution Discharge Elimination system (NPDES) specifies the total amount of chromium that municipalities may discharge into the waterways [Gunn & Vesilind 2003, 10]. We may conclude from these specific recommendations that a municipality that failed to meet the law's requirement is immoral; while one that failed to *exceed* it is decidely not immoral.

We must go beyond the vague language of "giving greater consideration" to stakeholders. Male chauvinists "consider" women all the time; they "consider" them to be greatly inferior. In business, this is basically Kenneth Goodpaster's point:

> We can imagine decision-makers doing "stakeholder analysis" for different underlying reasons, not always having to do with ethics. A management team, for example, might be careful to take positive and (especially) negative stakeholder effects into account for no other reason than that the offended stakeholders might resist or retaliate ... . [2002, 51]

Goodpaster argues that we must do more than talk about and analyze who the stakeholders are. I think that we are already doing that "more" the best way we can: by attempting to pass legislation.

Robert Solomon

Solomon seems to argue against Friedman, although it is not exactly clear why given his emphasis on Aristotelian virtue ethics. He writes: "The Aristotelian approach to business ethics begins with two concepts, the individual embedded in the community and the ultimate importance of happiness as the sole criterion of success" [1999, xxii]. This seems clearly egoistic: we should pursue our true self interest. The crux of the argument lies in *what* is to our true self-interest. Aristotle, Solomon and Friedman all seem to *agree* that our true self-interest lies partly in community:

> The underlying assumption was that a person is who he or she is by virtue of his or her place and role in the community, and the virtues of the community in turn, nurture and encourage each of its members to be a good person. ... On the Aristototelian approach to business, a good corporation is one that is not only profitable but that provides a morally rewarding enviroment in which good people can develop not only their skills but also their virtues. [1999, xxiv]

However, later Solomon calls Friedman's view "a more sophisticated version of the myth of the profit motive." This myth, Solomon suggests "causes more damage than any amount of sleaziness or dishonest dealings on the part of the business community. It is the narrow-minded language of the profit motive that gives rise to public suspicion" [1999, 30]. One should note that so far the argument such as it is seems entirely *ad hominem*: Friedman should not talk about the profit motive (or a social responsibility to make a profit) because the public suspects it. We may refuse to use certain words or phrases because of public distaste (supposing that a good reason). However, retiring a word does not change the idea(s) the word stands for. We would simply invent another word for "profit."

Solomon adds: "Milton Friedman adds to the confusion with his famous charge that charitable giving (on the part of corporations, not individuals) is nothing less than theft (from stockholders) an insidious form of socialism" [1999, 33]. As noted before, Friedman did not argue that charitable giving is theft. Friedman agrees that the practice of corporate charitable giving makes sense: "They were clearly in their rights in doing so." However

> it makes sense only because of our obscene tax laws, whereby a stockholder can make a larger gift for a given after-tax cost if the corporation makes the gift on his behalf than if he makes the gift directly. That is a good reason for eliminating the corporate tax or for eliminating the deductibility of corporate charity, but it is not a justification for corporate charity. [Friedman et al, 2005]

It may be true that Friedman "adds to the confusion." But, that is not the point. The point is whether he is correct or not. And a statement may be correct no matter how much confusion it adds.

Friedman's point was that business has no other social responsibility but to use investor money to make more money without violating the "rules of the game." In the end, Solomon seems to concede the point: "But does it have to be proven to the myopic stockholder who can see only his share price and dividends that such community-minded activities do indeed improve profitibility? (Could one ever conclusively prove this?)" (33). I think the answer (Vogel's answer) is that we have to try to prove whether social responsibility is profitable or not, even if we could never do it conclusively. It does have to be proven to the "myopic" stockholder that community-minded activities are worthwhile and not just ways of throwing away money.

SOCIAL RESPONSIBILITY REVISITED

In a paper aptly titled "You Don't have the Right to do it Wrong" [2001] Robert Gotterbarn declares "The world will no longer accept the view that BUGS arise in programs by Spontaneous Generation. The BUGS (errors) were put there by people who should know better." Gotterbarn has vastly improved the computing profession and to the professional responsibility movement. However, enough is enough. Programmers do not *purposely* put bugs in their programs. They try to avoid them, which is difficult in millions of lines of code.

I advocate that business has no other social responsibility (a) but to make a profit provided it follows law and ethical custom. Of course Friedman's picture has its problems. [Stieb 2001]. Certain responsibilities devolve to government, while Friedman limits the power of that "laissez-faire" government. Of course there might be inconsistencies in Friedman's overall picture. "It is possible to keep passing the buck until there is no one left to take responsibility" [Stieb 2001, 243].

In my 2001 paper, I talked about responsibilities that arise for "non-exhortative" issues occuring when emergency (or emergent) situations, or other technological or secretive issues prevent appeal to law and ethical custom. I concluded that these special cases force genuine responsibilities on CEOs regardless of self-interest. For, sometimes there is no one else. However each of these cases represents either a case of social responsibility (e), the kind that helps the actor *and* the beneficiary, or a case of that does not have to do with self-interest at all (it is "without self interest"). This chapter has tried to show that there really are no good arguments for social responsibility (a), that business must sacrifice its true self-interest for the good of stakeholders.

It has looked at the "history of social responsibility," and addressed the philosophical and political arguments that try to define social responsibility and our desperate need for it. We distinguished the primary philosophical question, which is not so much the definition of social responsibility as it is the question of altruism. Do businesses have duties to help others at a cost to themselves, or only when it is in their enlightened interest?

After equating altruism with utilitarianism (the view that moral behavior seeks the greatest good of the greatest number) I attempted to refute Luis Pascal's and Peter Singer's "shaming" arguments. They try to make one feel bad for not doing enough to help worldwide suffering. Such arguments either seem religiously motivated (and therefore rationally arbitrary) or hopelessly oblivious of economic realities.

Then, of course we turned to "economic realities." Economics and political structures are very essential to an account of social responsibility. Still, they will not determine those responsibilities. Economics should never be reduced to the attempt to rank preferences scientifically without suggesting them. Business needs an ethical economics of the sort that Plato meant, although we should avoid Plato's excesses as much as Friedman's. Business needs an adequate social and political philosophy. After reviewing John Rawls' *Theory of Justice* as well as the numerous critics condemning Milton Friedman's doctrine, I have argued for an amendment to Milton Friedman but not a wholesale dismissal.

According to David Vogel, a leading expert in the field of Corporate Social Responsibility (CSR), all current CSR projects are or should be based on the self-interest of business anyway. Partly this is because of the incredible complexity of measurement:

> It is hard to draw broad conclusions about the relationship between CSR and profits because the studies often measure different things. In the ninety-five studies summarized by Margolis and Walsh, *financial* performance is measured in seventy different ways: these studies employ forty-nine different accounting measures that mix accounting and market indicators and four other measures ... .
>
> ... Measurements of *social* performance also vary widely. In the ninety-five studies, twenty-seven different data sources were used. These range from multidimensional screening criteria, surveys, conduct in South Africa (which has since become irrelevant), organizational programs and practices, disclosure, money spent, environmental performance and reputation. [2005, 30]

We may also come to the same conclusion by looking at case studies. Here are two:

Beech Nut

These days chemists can make Styrofoam taste like a turkey dinner. Executives at Beech Nut saw nothing wrong with making corn syrup taste like apples.[13] Back in the 80's Beech Nut got their "apple" concentrate from a Bronx supplier called the "Universal Juice Company." Beech Nut, a competitor with huge company Gerber in the baby food industry, was doing everything it could to improve its fifteen percent market share including selling corn syrup as "apple juice" to infants. There was no evidence that the juice was harmful [Boatright 2007, 30], although it depends on what one means by "harmful."

When the Swiss giant Nestle bought Beech Nut in 1981, and made Lars Hoyvald company President, Hoyvald promised Nestle that he would return a $7 million dollar profit that year. Switching suppliers and a juice recall would not make that profit. Indeed, Hoyvald complains: "I could have called up Switzerland and told them I had just closed the company down. Because that would have been the result of it." In the famous Ford Pinto case (the reckless endangerment or wrongful death suits against Ford), Ford executives expected an imminent recall and "attempted to squeeze as many Pinto's out "before the gun" as it were" [Stieb 2001, 246]. Beech Nut acted similarly. Hoyvald unloaded thousands of cases to its distributors in Puerto Rico and the Dominican Republic.

Malden Mills

Solomon writes of Malden Mills:

> Here is a contemporary role model for executives. He is not historical but very contemporary. ... He is Aaron Feuerstein, who was and is CEO of Malden Mills, a textile company in Massachusetts.
> Just before Christmas 1995, a fire destroyed the manufacturing plant in Lawrence, Massachusetts, and three thousand employees were put out of work. Feuerstein announced that he would keep all of them on the payroll while the business was being rebuilt, and in January, and again in February, he continued to pay them and assure them of jobs. The plant was back in full operation by March, and needless to say, Malden Mills now has the most loyal, hardworking, workers around.
> Feuerstein is not the usual candidate for business hero. He has no pretensions of being a "master of the universe." He is just a very successful businessman and human being. ... True, Feuerstein paid out several million dollars that others might have seen as "unnecessary," but in the "long run" (about six months!), Malden Mills came out just fine. [Solomon 1999, 10]

Unfortunately, the real case is not as rosy as Solomon (or Desjardins 2003) would have us believe. A 2003 CBS "60 Minutes" report (Safer, 2003) holds the 1995 fire and resulting debt (Feuerstein's good intentions) at least partly responsible for driving Malden Mills into bankruptcy. Other factors include the long decline of the U.S. textile industry and warm winters that have cut into the sales of Polartec, the Mill's main product. "Feuerstein [also] decided to rebuild right there in Lawrence - not to move down South or overseas as much of the industry had done in search of cheap labor."

---

[13] I get most of the details of this case from Boatright 2007 who in turn gets it from Traub 1988.

The "60 Minutes" report emphasizes the countrywide acclaim greeting Feuerstein's exercise of social responsibility: "The press loved him, and so did politicians. President Clinton invited him to the State of the Union Address as an honored guest. He also received 12 honorary degrees, including one from Boston University" [Safer, 2003]. Indeed, Feuerstein credits the Hebrew Bible:

> You are not permitted to oppress the working man, because he's poor and he's needy, amongst your brethren and amongst the non-Jew in your community," says Feuerstein, who spent $300 million of the insurance money and then borrowed $100 million more to build a new plant that is both environmentally friendly and worker friendly.

That is hard to argue with. Nonetheless the Harvard Business School details the struggle on behalf of Feuerstein's " creditors "to decide whether to lend Feuerstein additional funds to enable him to regain control of the company after emerging from bankruptcy" [Nohria et al, 2006].

Meanwhile, a recent New York Times article (Oct 27, 2004) reported Feuerstein's unsuccessful bid to regain control of the company that had been in his family for three generations. Instead, "the reorganization put lenders, including the GE Capital Corporation, in control." [Malden Mills Rejects Purchase Bid]. The board wasted no time. On July 26, 2004 the board named Michael Spillane, the former President for Children's Apparel & Men's Underwear and Loungewear at Tommy Hilfiger, the new CEO at Malden Mills.

***

Business is rarely easy. Let us not make it more difficult by politicizing it more than we have to.

REFERENCES

Axelrod, R. (1984). *The evolution of the corporation.* New York: Basic Books.

Boatright, J. (2007). *Ethics and the conduct of business 5th edition.* New Jersey: Prentice Hall.

Berger, P. & Luckmann T. (1966). *The social construction of reality.* New York: Anchor Books.

Bowie, N. & Beauchamp T. (Eds.) (2001). *Ethical theory and business 6th edition.* New Jersey: Prentice Hall.

BSR. (2006). Business for social responsibility [On-line website]. <http://www.bsr.org/>.

Comte, A. (1973 [1852]). *The catechism of positivist religion.* Clifton, NJ: Augustus M. Kelley.

Coughlin, K. (2005). Google recruits mature minds to join brainiac kids. Newhouse News Service [On-line serial]. <http://www.newhouse.com/>.

CTNS-Vatican Observatory. (2006). Edwards, Denis. Original sin and saving grace in evolutionary context. The CTNS-Vatican Observatory book series. [On-line serial]. <www.metalibrary.net/other/ctns-body.html>.

Debtor Inc. (2001). Malden mills files for bankruptcy. The Trumbull group. [On-line]. <http://www.mmreorg.com/>.

Denis, E. (1999). *The god of evolution: a trinitarian theology*. New York: Paulist Press.

Desjardin, J. (2003). *An introduction to business ethics*. New York: McGraw Hill.

Desjardins, J. (2006). *An introduction to business ethics 2nd edition*. New York: McGraw Hill.

Donaldson, T. & Werhane, P. & Cording, M. (Eds.) (2002). *Ethical issues in business; a philosophical approach 7th edition*. New Jersey: Prentice Hall.

Fleurbay, M. (2006). Economics and economic justice. Stanford encyclopedia of Philosophy. [On-line Encyclopedia]. <http://plato.stanford.edu/entries/economic-justice/>.

Frank, R. (2002). "Can socially responsible firms survive in a competitive environment?" In T. Donaldson, & P. Werhane, & M. Cording (Eds.), *Ethical issues in business; a philosophical approach 7th edition* (pp. 252-262). New Jersey: Prentice Hall.

Freeman, R. E. (2004). Stakeholder theory and "The corporate objective revisited." *Organization science 15*, 364-369.

Freeman, R. E. (2002). A stakeholder theory of the corporation. In T. Donaldson, & P. Werhane, & M. Cording (Eds.), *Ethical issues in business; a philosophical approach 7th edition* (pp. 38-48). New Jersey: Prentice Hall.

Friedman, M. (1991). The social responsibility of business is to increase its profits. In Johnson D. (Ed.), *Ethical issues in engineering* (pp. 78-83). New Jersey: Prentice Hall.

Friedman, M. & Mackey, J. & Rogers, T. J. (2005). Rethinking the social responsibility of business. *Reason magazine* [On-line magazine]. <http://www.reason.com/news/show/32239.html>.

Goodpaster, K. (2002). Business ethics and stakeholder analysis. In T. Donaldson, & P. Werhane, & M. Cording (Eds.), *Ethical issues in business; a philosophical approach 7th edition* (pp. 49-60). New Jersey: Prentice Hall.

Gillespie, N. (2002). The business of ethics. In T. Donaldson, & P. Werhane, & M. Cording (Eds.), *Ethical issues in business; a philosophical approach 7th edition* (pp. 112-118). New Jersey: Prentice Hall.

Gotterbarn, D. (2000) You don't have the right to do wrong!" [author's On-line website] <http://csciwww.etsu.edu/gotterbarn/>.

Govier, T. (1997). The right to eat and the duty to work. In T. Mappes & J. Zembaty (Eds.), *Social ethics; morality and social policy* (pp. 377-389). New York: McGraw Hill.

Gunn, A. & Vesilind, P. A. (2003). *Hold paramount; the engineers responsibility to safety*. New York: Thompson Engineering.

Hardin, G. (1997). Living in a lifeboat. In T. Mappes & J. Zembaty (Eds.), *social ethics; morality and social policy* (pp. 406-412). New York: McGraw Hill.

Hannaford, R. (1991). The theoretical twist to irresponsibility in business. In D. Johnson (Ed.), *Ethical issues in engineering* (pp. 84-92). New Jersey: Prentice Hall.

Hoffman, A. (2000). Integrating environmental and social issues into corporate practice. *Environment 42*, 22-33.

Huxman, S. & Bruce, D. (1995). Toward a dynamic generic framework of apologia: a case study of Dow Chemical, Vietnam, and the napalm controversy. *Communication studies 46*, 57-73.

Kant, I. (1993). Grounding for the metaphysics of morals. J. Ellington (Trans.). Indianapolis, IN.: Hackett.

Kuhn, S. (2003). Prisoner's dilemma. *Stanford enclyclopedia of philosophy* [online encyclopedia]. <http://plato.stanford.edu/entries/prisoner-dilemma/>.

Lipschutz, R. and Rowe, J. (2005). *Globalization, governmentality and global politics: regulation for the rest of us?* New York: Routledge.

Lucas, J. R. (2003). The responsibilities of a businessman. In W. Shaw (Ed.), *Ethics at work; basic readings in business ethics* (pp. 15-29). New York: Oxford U. Press.

Margolis, J. (2004). *Life without principles; reconciling theory and practice.* New York: Blackwell.

Machan, T (2006) Two philosophers skeptical of negative liberty. [On-line serial]. <http://www.mises.org/journals/scholar/Machan8.pdf>.

Malden mills rejects purchase bid. Company news; malden mills rejects purchase bid from former owner. *The new york times.* 27, October 2004. [On-line serial] <http://query.nytimes.com/gst/fullpage.html?res=9401E4D9153DF934A1 5753C1A9629C8B63>.

Matravers, M. (2007). *Responsibility and justice.* Malden, M.A.: Polity Press.

McNulty, J. (2005). Corporate self-regulation falls short, says author. [Interview with James Rowe]. *Uc santa cruz currents* [On-line serial]. <http://currents.ucsc.edu/05-06/11-07/rowe.asp>.

Mitchell, P. & Larsen, T. (2006). U.S. socially responsible investment assets grew faster than rest of investment world over the last decade. *Social investment forum.* [On-line serial]. <http://www.socialinvest.org/areas/news/2005Trends.htm >

Miller, R. (1998). Lifesizing in an era of downsizing: an ethical quandary. *Journal of business ethics 17*, 1693-1700.

Milchin, J. (2000). Inherent rules of corporate behavior. Reclaimdemocracy.org. [On-line site] http://reclaimdemocracy.org/corporate_accountability/corporations_cannot_be_responsible.html

Mulligan, T. (1986). A critique of Milton Friedman's essay. *Journal of business ethics 5*, 265-269.

Nohria, N. & Piper, T. & Gurtler, B. (2006). Malden mills. [On-line serial]. <http://harvardbusinessonline.hbsp.harvard.edu/b02/en/common/item_detail.jhtml?id=404072>.

Nozick, R. (2002). The entitlement theory. In T. Donaldson, & P. Werhane, & M. Cording (Eds.) *Ethical issues in business; a philosophical approach 7th edition* (pp. 203-209). New Jersey: Prentice Hall.

Orlando, J. (2003). The ethics of corporate downsizing. In W. Shaw (Ed.), *Ethics at work; basic readings in business ethics* (pp. 21-48). Oxford: Oxford University Press. Orginally in (1999). *Business ethics quarterly 9.*

Pascal, L. (1986). Judgment day. In P. Singer (Ed.), *Applied ethics* (pp. 105-123). New York: Oxford U. Press.

Plato. (2004). *Plato's republic.* Reeve, C. D. C. (Trans.). Indianapolis: Hackett.

Rand, A. (1964). *The virtue of selfishness.* New York: Penguin.

Rawls, J. (2002). Distributive justice. In T. Donaldson, & P. Werhane, & M. Cording (Eds.) *Ethical issues in business; a philosophical approach 7th edition* (pp. 193-203). New Jersey: Prentice Hall.

Rawls, J. (1993). *Political liberalism.* New York: Columbia U. Press.

Rawls, J. (1971). *A theory of Justice.* Cambridge: Harvard U. Press.

Rescher, N. (1972). *Welfare: the social issues in philosophical perspective.* Pittsburgh: U. of Pittsburgh Press.

Safer, M. (2003). The mensch of malden mills. CBS news "60 Minutes." [On-line serial]. <http://www.cbsnews.com/stories/2003/07/03/60minutes/main561656.shtml>.

Searle, J. (1997). *The construction of social reality.* New York: Free Press.

Singer, P. (1997). Famine, affluence and morality. In T. Mappes & J. Zembaty (Eds.), *Social ethics; morality and social policy* (398-405). New York: McGraw Hill.

Smith, A. (2002). Benefits of the profit motive. In T. Donaldson, & P. Werhane, & M. Cording (Eds.), *Ethical issues in business; a philosophical approach 7th edition* (pp. 155-159). New Jersey: Prentice Hall.

Smith, K. & Smith, M. (2003). Business and accounting ethics. [On-line paper.] <http://acct.tamu.edu/smith/ethics/ethics.htm>.

Solomon, R. (1999). *A better way to think about business; how personal integrity leads to corporate success.* New York: Oxford U. Press.

Stieb, J. (2006a). Moral realism and kantian constructivism. *Ratio juris 19,* 402-420.

Stieb, J. (2006b). Clearing up the egoist difficulty with loyalty. *Journal of business ethics 63,* 75-87.

Stieb, J. (2005). Three philosophical difficulties with 'preemptive wars.' [On-line conference proceedings]. <http://www.usafa.af.mil/jscope/JSCOPE05/Stieb05.html>.

Stieb, J. (2004a). The morality of corporate downsizing. *Business and professional ethics journal 23,* 61-76.

Stieb, J. (2004b). *Toward a constructivist theory of realism.* [unpublished dissertation.]

Stieb, J. (2001). Social responsibility within and without self interest: emergent technologies and situations. *Business and society review 106,* 241-253.

Traub, J. (1988). Into the mouths of babes. *New york times magazine,* 24 July.

Wagner-Tsukamoto, Sigmund. (2006). Moral agency, profits and the firm: economic revisions to the Friedman theorem. Listed as forthcoming in the *Journal of business ethics.* [Online article]. <http://www.le.ac.uk/ulmc/academics/wsigmund.html>.

Vogel. D. (2005). *The market for virtue; the potential and limits of corporate social responsibility.* Washington D.C.: Brookings Institution Press.

In: Contemporary Issues in Business Ethics
Editors: M. W. Volcox, Th. O. Mohan, pp. 49-66

ISBN: 978-1-60021-773-9
© 2007 Nova Science Publishers, Inc.

Chapter 2

ETHICAL FOUNDATIONS OF WELL-BEING MARKETING

*M. Joseph Sirgy**
Virginia Politechnic Institute and State University, USA
Dong-Jin Lee
Yonsei University, Korea

ABSTRACT

In this paper, we discuss ethical foundations of well being marketing. Specially, we argue that well-being marketing is a business philosophy based on duties of beneficence and non-maleficence, deontological ethics, normative ethics, and moral idealism.

Keywords: well-being marketing, marketing and quality of life, consumer well-being, customer well-being, consumer welfare, marketing ethics, and corporate social responsibility

INTRODUCTION

Generally speaking, ethics is the study of what constitute good and bad conduct including the values that influence conduct (Barry 1979). Recently, we have seen much emphasis placed on corporate social responsibility and marketing ethics (e.g., Kotler and Lee 2005; Samli 1992). There are many ethical issues in marketing. Examples of ethical issues in marketing practices include issues in purchasing (receiving gifts and entertainment), product development (planned obsolescence, arbitrary product elimination, altering size and quality of products, price discrimination), retailing (unresponsiveness of retailers to customer

---

* Contact person and address: *M. Joseph Sirgy*, Department of Marketing, Virginia Tech, Blacksburg, Virginia 24061-0236, USA, tel.: 540-231-5110, fax: 540-231-3076, e-mail: sirgy@vt.edu.

complaints, coercion), salesperson (bribes, conflicts of interests, entertaining), advertising (puffery, exaggerated claims), international marketing (foreign corrupt act, social values, and de-marketing), and marketing education (ethics training for enhanced sensitivity and changes of value) (Tsalikis and Fritzsche 1989).

The practice of ethical marketing has the ability not only to deal with the aforementioned problems (i.e., reducing the negative impact of marketing) but also the ability to enhance consumer well-being (i.e., fostering the positive impact of marketing). Thus, ethical marketing can increase its positive impact by providing consumers with goods and services that can enhance their overall quality of life. Ethical marketing can reduce its negative impact by providing consumers with goods and services that are safe—to the consumers themselves, to other publics, and the environment. Reflecting this need, Kotler et al (2002) has emphasized marketing's impact on the quality of life by stating that marketers should determine the needs, wants, and interests of target consumers and deliver satisfaction more effectively and efficiently than competitors in a way that preserves or enhances consumer well-being. The firm should deliver superior value to customers in a way that maintains or improves the customer's and the society's well-being. The traditional marketing concept overlooks possible conflicts between consumer short-run wants and consumer long-run welfare (Armstrong and Kotler 2002). In this paper, we discuss the concept of *well-being marketing* as an ethical concept grounded in societal marketing as first introduced by Kotler (1979, 1986, 1987), and we focus on ethical foundations of well-being marketing.

Well-being marketing is a business philosophy that guides managers to develop and implement marketing strategies that focuses on enhancing consumer well-being through the consumer/product life cycle (acquisition, preparation, consumption, possession, maintenance, and disposal of consumer goods) and to do so safely in relation to consumers, other publics, and the environment. We define *consumer well-being* (CWB) as a desired state of objective and subjective well being involved in the various stages of the consumer/product life cycle in relation to consumer goods. By providing need satisfaction over the entire consumer/product life cycle, well-being marketing guides the firm to establish long-term relationships with target consumers. Thus, the long-term objective of well-being marketing is the enhancement of CWB. In addition to enhancing CWB, well-being marketing prescribes that enhancement of CWB should not come at the expense of adverse conditions experienced by other organizational stakeholders (e.g., employees, the local community, the general public, and the environment).

Although much has been discussed about well-being marketing and its implications to CWB (e.g., Lee and Sirgy 1999a, 2004, 2005; Lee, Sirgy, and Su 1998; Sirgy 1986, 1991a, 1991b, 1996, 2001; Sirgy and Lee 1994, 1996, 2006; Sirgy, Lee, and Reilly 2006; Sirgy and Mangleburg 1988; Sirgy, Meadow, and Samli 1995; Sirgy and Morris 1986; Sirgy, Morris, and Samli 1985; Sirgy, Samli, and Meadow 1982;), we still have a limited understanding regarding its ethical basis. We will an attempt to establish the ethical foundations of well-being marketing by contrasting the ethics of transactional and relationships marketing with the ethics of well-being marketing. We will argue that well-being marketing is grounded in duty ethics of beneficence and nonmaleficence, deontological ethics, normative ethics, and moral idealism.

OUR CONCEPTUAL DEFINITION OF WELL-BEING MARKETING

Kotler et al (2002) emphasized marketing's impact on the quality of life by stating that marketers should determine the needs, wants, and interests of target consumers and deliver satisfaction more effectively and efficiently than competitors in a way that preserves or enhances CWB. Based on Kotler's notion of marketing and quality of life, we define well-being marketing as *marketing practice that serves to enhance CWB while preserving the well being of other stakeholders.*

In turn, we define CWB as a state of objective and subjective well-being involved in the various stages of the consumer/product life cycle in relation to a particular consumer good. The consumer/product life cycle deals with various types of marketplace experiences a consumer has with a product from purchasing the product to its disposal. Specifically, the stages of the consumer/product life cycle are: product acquisition (purchase), preparation (assembly), consumption (use), ownership (possession), maintenance (repair), and disposal (selling, trade-in, or junking of the product). See Table 1.

The distinction between objective and subjective CWB is important. *Subjective* CWB refers to feelings of satisfaction/dissatisfaction the consumer experiences in a manner that contributes to his or her quality of life. What we are talking about here is consumer-life satisfaction or the link between consumer satisfaction and life satisfaction (overall happiness in life, overall sense of subjective well-being, or the perception of life quality). In contrast, *objective* CWB refers to an assessment by experts (e.g., engineers, scientists, consumer economists, safety experts) regarding consumers' costs and benefits as well as safety assessments (safety to consumers, others that come in contact with the product, and the environment). Specifically, in relation to *product acquisition*, subjective CWB translates into consumer satisfaction with the shopping for and the purchase of the product in a manner contributing to the consumer's life satisfaction. In contrast, objective CWB in relation to product acquisition means experts' assessment that the product is high quality and the price is fair and affordable; also that the purchase experience is safe to the purchasers, the sales people and facilities, the general public, and the environment.

With respect to *product preparation*, subjective CWB reflects consumer satisfaction with the preparation or assembly of the product in a manner contributing to the consumer's quality of life (life satisfaction). Objective CWB in relation to product preparation means that the preparation or assembly of the product is assessed by experts to be easy (or convenient) and safe to the people who elect to prepare or assemble the product, the assembly facility, the general public, and the environment.

The *product consumption* dimension captures consumer satisfaction with the use of the product in a manner contributing to consumer's quality of life. In comparison, the objective CWB dimension captures experts' assessment that the consumption of the product is significantly beneficial to those who use the product, and that the product is safe to consumers, the general public, and the environment.

The *product ownership* dimension of subjective CWB refers to consumer satisfaction with the ownership of the product in a manner contributing to the consumer's quality of life. In contrast, the objective CWB dimension captures experts' assessment that the ownership of the product has appreciable value and is safe to the owners, the general public, and the environment.

Table 1. Our Conceptualization of Consumer Well-Being

	Subjective well-being (consumer satisfaction)	Objective well-being (experts assessment of consumers' and societal costs and benefits)
Product acquisition	Consumer satisfaction with the shopping for and the purchase of the product in a manner contributing to the consumer's quality of life	Experts' assessment that • the product is high quality and the price is fair and affordable, and • the purchase experience is safe to the purchasers, the sales person/facility, the general public, and the environment
Product preparation	Consumer satisfaction with the preparation or assembly of the product for use in a manner contributing to the consumer's quality of life	Experts' assessment that the product is • easy (or convenient) and • safe to prepare or assemble to the preparer, the general public, and the environment
Product consumption	Consumer satisfaction with the use of the product in a manner contributing to the consumer's quality of life	Experts' assessment that the consumption of the product is • significantly beneficial to consumers and • safe to consumers, the general public, and the environment
Product ownership	Consumer satisfaction with the ownership of the product in a manner contributing to the consumer's quality of life	Experts' assessment that the ownership of the product • has appreciable value and • is safe to the owners, the general public, and the environment
Product maintenance	Consumer satisfaction with product maintenance and repair in a manner contributing to the consumer's quality of life	Experts' assessment that the maintenance of the product is • easy (or convenient), • not costly (affordable), and • safe to the repair person/facility, the general public, and the environment
Product disposal	Consumer satisfaction with product disposal (or trade-in or re-selling) in a manner contributing to the consumer's quality of life	Experts' assessment that the disposal of the product is • easy (or convenient), • not costly (affordable), and • safe to the disposal person/facility, the general public, and the environment

The *product maintenance* dimension of subjective CWB reflects consumer satisfaction with product maintenance and repair in a manner contributing to the consumer's quality of life. Objective CWB associated with product maintenance reflects experts' assessment that the maintenance of the product is easy (or convenient), not costly (affordable), and safe to the people who are doing the maintenance, the maintenance or repair facility, the general public, and the environment.

Finally, in relation to *product disposal*, this subjective CWB dimension signifies consumer satisfaction with the disposal (junking, trading-in, or re-selling) of the product in a manner contributing to the consumer's quality of life. On the other hand, objective CWB means experts' assessment that the disposal of the product is easy (or convenient), not costly (or affordable), and safe to the person doing the disposal, the disposal facility, the general public, and the environment.

COMPARING ETHICAL FOUNDATIONS OF WELL-BEING MARKETING WITH TRANSACTIONAL MARKETING AND RELATIONSHIP MARKETING

In this section, we will contrast the ethical foundations of well-being marketing with two other forms of marketing, namely transactional marketing and relationship marketing. We will do so to show how well-being marketing can be distinguished from traditional marketing (as captured in transactional and relationship marketing). We argue that well-being marketing is based on a business ethics philosophy that is more adapted to contemporary society. To make this argument, we do the following in this section. We argue that the ethics supporting *transaction marketing* is based on the concept of *consumer sovereignty* of business ethics. We will then argue that consumer sovereignty falls short in several ways, and therefore is not well-suited to contemporary society. Then we will focus on *relationship marketing* and argue that this approach to marketing is grounded in *stakeholder theory* of business ethics. We will then argue that stakeholder theory serves society better than transaction marketing, but nevertheless it also falls short. Finally, we will define *well-being marketing* and show how this approach to marketing is grounded on business ethics concepts of duty of beneficence and non-maleficence, deontological ethics, normative ethics, and moral idealism. Our goal is to convince the reader that well-being marketing is most ethical in serving the business community, consumers at large, and society overall.

Table 2 summarized the comparison of ethical foundations of well being marketing vis-à-vis relationship marketing and transactional marketing.

Table 2. Well-Being Marketing vis-à-vis Transactional Marketing and Relationship Marketing

	Transactional Marketing	Relationship Marketing	Well-being Marketing
Ethical philosophy	• Consumer sovereignty	• Stakeholder theory	• Duty of beneficence and non-maleficience • Deontological ethics • Moral idealism • Normative ethics
Major strategic objectives	• Financial goals (short term)	• Financial goals (long-term)	• Financial and societal goals (long-term)
Strategy	• Developing marketing programs designed to enhance brand preference and purchase	• Developing marketing programs designed to enhance customer satisfaction, trust, and commitment	• Developing marketing programs designed to enhance consumer well being
Target market	• Focus on developing brand preference and purchase intentions of new customers	• Focus on developing satisfaction, trust, and commitment of current customer	• Focus on developing well being of consumers whose quality of life can be significantly enhanced through product adoption, and doing this safely to consumers, other publics, and the environment
Consumption/product life cycle	• Product purchase	• Product purchase, preparation, use, ownership, maintenance, and disposal	• Product purchase, use, ownership, maintenance, and disposal
Importance of social responsibility in marketing practice	• Low	• Moderate	• High

The Ethics of Transaction Marketing

Transaction marketing is marketing practice guided by neo-classical economic theory and consumer sovereignty. It focuses on maximizing profit by recruiting more and more customers to purchase the firm's product. Sales reflect the notion that the firm serves society by marketing a product that consumers need or want. A firm meeting market demand for consumer goods is a firm that serves society. Furthermore, the more sales, the more the firm prospers financially. Financial prosperity translates into more jobs and economic security for the firm's employees. The firm's financial prosperity also benefits society through taxation—the more the firm sells, the more it is taxed, the more the tax revenues are used by government to provide public services that benefit society at large. Similarly, the more people are employed, the more tax revenues are generated through personal income taxation, which in turn serves society at large.

Competition among firms to generate higher levels of sales is the motivating force that drives firms to develop higher quality products and selling them at low prices. Thus, the drive to sell serves society by motivating the business enterprise to innovate and develop new and better quality products, and market those products at lower prices than the competition. When consumers purchase high quality products at low prices, they reward firms that develop better products at lower prices. Thus, firms that are able to meet consumers' needs and wants for better products at lower prices significantly benefit (financially speaking), and those that cannot compete fall by the way side (e.g., Friedman 1962, 1970; Scherer 1971; Smith 1776).

The main goal of transactional marketing is profit maximization. Transactional marketers focus on product efficiency and thus there is only limited interaction with customers and the degree of customization to the customer needs.

Consumer sovereignty theory posits that society benefits when consumers vote with their pocketbooks (e.g., Nelson, 1970; Smith and Quelch 1993, pp. 30-34; Stigler 1971; Thorelli and Thorelli 1977). To do so, consumers have to be informed about the product's quality and price. Consumer behavior is based on the assumption that consumers shop around and buy the highest quality product at the lowest price. Consumer sovereignty reflects the idea that consumers can serve society by engaging in "rational decision-making" and exercising their economic votes wisely. By selecting products that provide best value, consumers reward manufacturers that best serve consumers. Much of today's business laws (e.g., anti-trust laws, consumer protection laws) are designed to ensure that consumers are well-informed about their market choices. Because if they are well-informed, they serve society by rewarding efficient firms that deliver "a better mousetrap at a lower price" and weed out inefficient firms that cannot deliver on the same terms.

Nevertheless, market inefficiencies do occur in the form of sales that do not reflect market demand and the fulfillment of consumer wants. For example, Galbraith (1956, 1973, 1977, and 1985) has argued that many firms survive and prosper not because they market higher quality products at lower prices. They survive and prosper because they have countervailing power. They overwhelm their competitors through massive advertising and marketing communications campaigns. They also may control the channels of distribution, thus restricting consumer access to competitors. Furthermore, it has been argued that consumer sovereignty is increasingly becoming *less relevant* in the age of high tech, and that it fails to sufficiently guide ethical marketing practice (Sirgy and Su 2000). This is due to the fact that many consumers lack the opportunity to be exposed to objective information about the quality and prices of competing high-tech products, and consumers also lack the ability and motivation to process this information

The Ethics of Relationship Marketing

Relationship marketing is an emerging paradigm in marketing thought that focuses on the development and maintenance of quality relationship between exchange partners for mutual benefit. Relationship marketing refers to all marketing activities directed towards establishing, developing, and maintaining successful relational exchanges (Morgan and Hunt 1994). That is, relationship marketing is an integrated effort to identify, maintain, and build up a network with customers for mutual benefit over a long time. The conceptual domain of relationship marketing includes concepts such as trust, commitment, and satisfaction (e.g., Ganesan 1994; Parvatiyar and Sheth 1994; Morgan and Hunt 1994).

The main goal of relationship marketing is long-term profit maximization. Marketers with relationship marketing focuses on development and maintenance of long term relationship and there are certain degree of interactions with customers especially in the acquisition and disposition stage. The degree of customization is moderate and there is also some degree of socially responsible marketing practices and environments (see Table 2).

According to the stakeholder view of the firm (Freeman 1984), a firm operates in a network of relationships. That is, a firm engages in various exchange relationships with many exchange partners including suppliers, customers, competitors, other functional departments within the organization, and various stakeholders in the society (e.g., Carroll 1989; Evan and Freeman 1988; Goodpaster 1991; Morgan and Hunt 1994; Robin and Reidenbach 1987; Wheeler and Sillanpaa 1997). Stakeholder theory is a grounded in the literature of business ethics and corporate social responsibility (e.g., Caroll 1989). Stakeholders are typically classified as external stakeholders, internal stakeholders, and distal stakeholders (e.g., Sirgy 2002). *Internal stakeholders* are other functional departments and business units within the firm—other than the marketing department. *External stakeholders* refer to stakeholders outside of the firm, which survival and growth of the firm depends on (e.g., customers, shareholders, distributors, and suppliers). *Distal stakeholders* refer to stakeholders that influence the survival and growth of the firm indirectly through external stakeholders (e.g., legal groups, consumer advocacy groups, government agencies).

One can argue that the ethics of relationship marketing can be justified by stakeholder theory. A firm serves society well by establishing positive relationships with its various stakeholders. The firm does this by meeting the demands of stakeholders leading to trust and commitment. By the same token, if the primary stakeholders of marketing are customers and distributors, then stakeholder theory advocates that the marketing department within the firm should make every effort to cater to customers and distributors in ways to elicit their trust and commitment. Doing so necessitates ethical marketing practice, which in turn serves society as a whole. Relationship marketers focus on developing long-term relationship with customers. Relationship marketing concentrates on generating repeated sales from customers by providing satisfaction and establishing trust.

Although one can argue that relationship marketing is considered to be on a higher ethical plane than transaction marketing, it still falls short. Establishing positive relationships with customers based on trust and commitment does not ensure that the firm's marketing decisions enhance consumer and society well-being. For example, consider the automobile industry. Many automobile manufacturers do a good job trying to establish positive relationships with customers. Customers are happy with their cars and the service provided by the warranty and dealer network. Customers end up trusting their automobile manufacturers and their dealers. They feel a sense of loyalty and commitment to manufacturers and dealers. Paradoxically, the same automobile manufacturers might design their cars by cutting corners on safety measures. The same manufacturers might design more fuel-efficient cars to minimize toxic gas emissions and air pollution but choose not to. Relationship marketing based on stakeholder theory fails to guide marketing decision-making in areas concerning consumer safety, the safety of other publics, as well as the safety of the environment (see Table 2).

The Ethics of Well-Being Marketing

In this section we will argue that the ethics of well-being marketing is guided by duties of beneficence, duties of non-maleficence, deontological ethics, normative ethics, and moral idealism.

Duties of Beneficence and Non-maleficence

One can argue that well-being marketing is grounded in duty ethics, especially the duty of beneficence and non-maleficence. Well-being marketing focuses on the enhancement of CWB. This is the essence of the *beneficence* component of well-being marketing (e.g., Beauchamp 1999). The principle of beneficence refers to a general group of duties that include a negative injunction to refrain from harming customers and a positive injunction to assist customers. The principle of beneficence argues that four criteria should be used to judge the ethical nature of an action. First, one ought not to inflict evil or harm. Second, one ought to prevent evil or harm. Third, one ought to remove evil or harm. Fourth, one ought to promote good (Frankenna 1973, p. 47).

Well-being marketing also focuses on preserving the well being of stakeholders. This is the essence of the moral duty of *non-maleficience*. The principle of non-maleficience refers to the injunction not to inflict harm on others (Beauchamp 1999; Fisher 2001). Thus, well-being marketing is grounded in the ethics concepts of duty of beneficence and non-maleficence in that the focus is not only on serving consumers safely in a manner that contributes to their quality of life but also the preservation of well being of the firm's other stakeholders.

Fisk's (1971) argument is a case in point on the applicability of the duty of non-maleficence for a marketing institution that is gentler and more ethical. He proposed that the social performance of marketing can be assessed using five criteria: (1) biological survival or environmental habitability, (2) consumer sovereignty, (3) business interests, and (4) government. These criteria take into account the major publics whose goals are typically served by marketing.

Deontological Ethics

Deontological moral philosophy is typically distinguished from teleological moral philosophy. Deontological moral philosophy focuses on specific actions or behaviors of an individual and the inherent rightness of an action rather than its consequences (Ferrell and Grasham 1986; Hunt and Vitell 1986; Tsalikis and Fritzsche 1989).

Examples of rules that reflect deontological moral philosophy include the golden rule, the categorical imperative, and prima facie duties. The golden rule states, "treat others as one would like others treat us." Kant's categorical imperative states that the action with good intention or goodwill is ethical. When an act is carried out driven by a moral duty to be fair and honest, the act is considered ethical. One should act in such a way that we could wish the maxim or principle of our action to become a universal law.

In contrast, teleological moral philosophy focuses on consequences of an action. This philosophy is based on the notion that the amount of good and bad are embodied in the consequences of the action. Teleologists determine what is right by examining the ratio of good to bad that action produces. They focus on the consequences of an action based on the probable consequences, the desirability of those consequences, and the relative importance of various stakeholders.

Examples of rules reflecting teleological moral philosophy include egoism and ethical utilitarianism. Egoism reflects the notion that one should strive to promote one's greatest good. Egoism states that an act is ethical if the consequences of the act for an individual are more favorable for that individual than the consequences of any other act. Ethical universalism or utilitarianism reflects the notion that an act is ethical if it produces for all people a great balance of good consequences than other available alternatives. Utilitarianism posits that an act is ethical when it produces the greatest ratio of good to bad for everyone *relative to other possible actions*. Here the end justifies the means (Hunt and Vitell 1986; Vitell 1986).

We argue that the ethics of well-being marketing is grounded more in deontological than teleological ethics. In other words, well-being marketing is conceptualized not only in terms of end-states (e.g., enhancement of CWB and the preservation of the well-being of other stakeholders), but also in terms of a set of axioms about marketing practices designed to achieve these ends. It is those marketing axioms related to actual marketing practice that lead to those desirable end states. Actual marketers cannot and should not be placed in a position to make judgments about the ultimate consequences of their actions. Such judgments belong to social science experts who can assess the overall effect of certain marketing actions on the many publics (e.g., the quality of life of customers, the distributors, the suppliers, the environment, the economy at large, and other societal institutions). Thus, marketers in embracing the ethical philosophy of well-being marketing have to be guided by specific marketing axioms (ethical do's and don'ts).

In contrast to well-being marketing, one can argue that stakeholder theory (theory guiding the ethics of relationship marketing) is teleological in nature. In other words, marketers are encouraged to meet the demands of their customers as one of their key stakeholders. Doing so enhances customer retention and therefore long-term profitability. Furthermore, relationships marketers are encouraged to meet the demand of other stakeholder because not doing so may adversely affect customer retention.

The ethics of transaction marketing is also teleological. The goal here is consumer sovereignty. Any action (marketing or otherwise) that adversely affects competition and consumers' ability to choose is considered unethical. Conversely, actions that promote competition and consumers' right to choose are ethical. Note how actions are judged by consequences related to consumer sovereignty.

Normative Ethics

Much of the literature in marketing ethics can be grouped in two major camps: descriptive (positive) versus prescriptive (normative) models of marketing practice. Descriptive or positive models of marketing ethics focus on explaining actual behaviors in an ethical situation (e.g., Hunt and Vitell 1986, 2006; Ferrell and Grasham 1986; Trevino 1986; Wortuba 1990). The focus of these models is to describe how marketers behave in ethical dilemmas. These models attempt to capture the ethical decision-making process and all the organizational, social, cultural, situational, and personality related factors that influence the various components of the decision-making process.

Normative marketing ethics, on the other hand, is designed to advocate and establish guidelines for ethical marketing practice rather than attempt to report what practitioners say or do (Smith 2001). Much has been written about prescriptive or normative models of marketing. However, the vast majority of what has been done in this camp has focused on narrow topics such as design and manufacture of poor quality products, failure to ensure product safety, misleading advertising, among others (e.g., Cespedes 1993; Mattsson and Rendtorff 2006) and the prescriptive standards that marketers should adhere "minimize the damage." With respect to general or overarching models of normative marketing ethics, Dunfee, Smith, and Ross (1999) found only four models that are distinctively normative. These are: Laczniak (1983), Williams and Murphy (1990), Reidenbach and Robin (1990), and Smith (1995). More recently, Laczniak and Murphy (2006) developed seven normative perspectives for ethically and socially responsible marketing.

An example of seminal work on normative marketing ethics is that of Fisk (1982). Fisk argued that ethical marketing can be characterized by five principles, namely (1) trade, (2) non-coercion, (3) fairness, (4) independent judgment, and (5) marketing. The principle of *trade* states that marketing can be considered ethical when there is an exchange of value (i.e., something valued by one party exchanged for another thing of value with another party). The principle of non-coercion means that marketing can be considered ethical when it rejects all forms of coercive behavior. The principle of *fairness* communicates the notion that one should treat others as independent equals (i.e., the power is distributed equally among competitors, between firm and customers, and between a channel member and another channel member). The principle of *independent judgment* posits that all parties involved exercise independent judgment and expect the same for their trading partners. Finally, the principle of marketing states that satisfying customer needs is the key to the needs of marketer. Profits are maximized by satisfying customer needs.

One can argue that well-being marketing is a business philosophy grounded in normative ethics. Well-being marketing has been translated in terms of a set of normative principles guiding marketing practice reflecting two super-ordinate goals: enhancing CWB and decreasing the adverse impact of marketing practice on the firm's stakeholders (e.g., customers, employees, distributors, suppliers, the local community, and the environment).

Moral Idealism

Moral idealism refers to the degree to which individuals assume the desirable consequences can always be obtained with the right action (Forsyth 1992). Marketers with moral idealism express concern for the well being of others and think harming others is always avoidable. Those with high moral idealism think that one should strive to produce positive consequences and harming others is always avoidable (cf. Lee and Sirgy 1999b).

Studies have found that those who are more idealistic and the less relativistic tend to exhibit higher levels of honesty and integrity (Vitell, Rallapalli, and Singhapakdi 1993). Studies also found that those scoring high on deontological norms score highly on moral idealism and low on moral relativism (Vitell and Singhapakdi 1993).

Drucker (1969) has long maintained that business can have a significant impact on society. Therefore, business managers should accept the responsibility to preserve and enhance consumer and society well being. The concept of well being should be built into the firm's mission and mindset of senior executives. This is most significant for large corporations since they tend to impact society more significantly than small firms. Drucker argued that executives should incorporate the concept of well being in their mission statement, business strategies, and daily operations for three reasons. First, the society's costs for neglecting to do this are very high. Second, business is part of society, and not doing something about the preservation and enhancement of quality of life in society will ultimately affect business in adverse ways. That is, healthy business and a sick society are not compatible. Third, improving consumer and society well being should be a tremendous business opportunity. Drucker's view of business in society is moral idealism *par excellence*.

Other business scholars have expressed their moral idealism of business (e.., Kelly 1974; Kotler 1987). Specifically, Kelley (1974) argued the goal of the firm is service to society-- providing a social purpose for the business enterprise beyond simple profit. Kelley referred this concept of marketing as "sociomarketing." *Sociomarketing* has six major elements. These are:

1. The mission of the business is defined in social system terms of long-run profitable service to the consumer-citizen.
2. The firm recognizes that service to the consumer-citizen requires fulfilling societal and environmental concerns as well as the satisfaction of traditional economic goods and services.
3. Products are defined as sociomarketing products, not just economic goods.
4. Profit concepts are recognized in their full complexity.
5. Organizational commitment to sociomarketing is reflected in prioritized action programs in each area of sociomarketing performance.
6. The firm acknowledges that its sociomarketing performance should be evaluated by external groups.

Kotler (1987) is the most prominent scholar who formally introduced well-being marketing to the marketing discipline. He referred to this concept as "societal marketing". The *societal marketing* concept calls for a consumer orientation backed by integrated marketing activity aimed at generating consumer satisfaction and long-run consumer well being as key to achieving long-run profitability. He developed a set of axioms for societal marketing. Examples include "Outside parties should be represented in seller decision-making" and "Sellers will be effective to the extent that they attempt to serve consumers' interests in addition to their desires." Kotler (1986) defined marketing effectiveness in terms consumer and society well-being: "The organization's task is to determine the needs, wants, and interests of target markets and to deliver satisfaction more effectively and efficiently than competitors in a way that preserves or enhances the consumer's and society's well-being" (p. 16).

Kotler (1987) also suggested three stages of evolution of marketing. The first stage is the *marketing concept*. He argued that the marketing concept had emerged as a result of movement from a product orientation to a sales orientation to a marketing orientation. The marketing concept focuses on consumer wants. Marketers adhering to the marketing concept make no judgments about whether consumer wants are consistent or inconsistent with society's well being. The second stage of marketing evolution is the *humanistic marketing concept*. This concept posits that marketers consider both consumer wants and consumer interests. Thus, humanistic marketers do not tell people what they should have. Instead they market "better" goods and services and subsequently attempt to "educate" consumers about the benefits of the new and improved "products." The third stage of the evolution of the marketing concept is *societal marketing*. This concept is designed to address the concerns of the humanistic marketing concept (i.e., some marketing practices may serve consumer wants and interests and yet hurt society's interests).

Built on these earlier conceptualizations of societal marketing concepts, we conceptualize well-being marketing as a business philosophy that guides the development, pricing, promotion, and distribution of consumer goods to individuals and families for the purpose of enhancing CWB at a profit (in the long run) in a manner that does not adversely affect the public, including the environment. Because customers are considered to be the primary external stakeholder, marketers' primary responsibility is to meet the demand of their customers safely and enhance their quality of their life. But, because the firm's marketing decision may adversely impact the well being of other external stakeholders, it is vital that marketing decisions are made in ways to minimize possible adverse effects impacting the well being of employees, distributors, suppliers, stockholders, etc. (Sirgy 2002).

The main goal of well being marketing is enhancement of consumer well being and happiness. Marketers with well-being marketing orientation focus on customer needs. They focus on need satisfaction throughout the entire consumption cycle. The degree of customization is highest for this marketing orientation. Emphasis on socially responsible marketing practice is also highest for this marketing orientation. Thus, we believe that the ethics of well-being marketing is based on the norms of moral idealism. The ethics of well-being marketing is placed on a higher plane than transaction and relationship marketing. Well-being marketing is more comprehensive in the way it accounts for both consumers' and society's well-being.

CONCLUSION

We strongly believe that firms engaging in well-being marketing are likely to prosper in the long run than firms practicing transactional marketing. Well-being marketing serves to help establish long-term relationships with customers and develop company goodwill (cf. Collins 1993). Studies have identified that long-term relationships and positive corporate image help business firms achieve higher financial performance (e.g., Collins 1993; Kalwani and Narayandas 1995; Jap 1999; Naidu, et al 1999). But then the reader would say: and so do firms guided by relationship marketing. The difference, of course, is that well-being marketing is a business philosophy grounded in business ethics. That is, consumer goods companies are urged to practice well-being marketing not only because this philosophy translates into a business strategy that leads to higher financial returns in the long run; companies should practice well-being marketing because it is the right thing to do. It is the moral thing to do. It is most ethical.

One can argue that marketing paradigms have evolved to culminate in well-being marketing. At early stages of marketing thought and practice, marketing performance was judged in terms of sales and profit. Much research was generated focusing on competition and marketing performance was judged mostly by market share. In time, the competition paradigm was overshadowed by much research on customer satisfaction. That research has shown that customer satisfaction leads to brand loyalty and repeat purchase, and therefore high levels of profitability. Much of the research dealing with the marketing concept, customer orientation, and marketing orientation reflect that paradigm. The focus of customer relationship marketing here has been on how to establish long-term relationships with customers to secure repeat business and therefore ensure the survival and growth of the firm. Satisfying customer needs is the key to satisfying the needs of the marketer. We believe that well-being marketing is the next paradigm in this evolution and progression of paradigms. Well-being marketing builds on relationship marketing by bringing marketing and business ethics into the picture. Well-being marketing strives to enhance the quality of life. Thus, well-being marketing can be regarded as an ethical extension of relationship marketing.

REFERENCES

Armstrong, Gary and Philip Kotler (2002), *Marketing*, 6th Edition, Prentice Hall: Upper Saddle River, NJ.

Barry, V. (1979), *Moral Issues in Business*, Belmont CA: Wadsworth.

Beauchamp, T. L. (1999), "Ethical Theory and Bioethics," in *Contemporary Issues in Bioethics*, 3rd Edition, edited by T. L. Beauchamp and L. Walters. Belmont CA: Wadsworth Publishing Company.

Carroll, Archie B. (1989), *Business and Society: Ethics and Stakeholder Management.* Cincinnati, Ohio: South Western Publishing.

Cespedes, Frank V. (1993), "Ethical Issues in Distribution," in *Ethics in Marketing*, edited by N. C. Smith and J. A. Quelch. Homewood, Illinois: Irwin, pp. 473-490.

Collins, Marylyn (1993), "Global Corporate Philanthropy-Marketing beyond the Call of Duty?" *European Journal of Marketing*, 27 (2), 46-58.

Drucker, Peter F. (1969), *Preparing Tomorrow's Business Leaders Today.* Englewood Cliffs, NJ: Prentice-Hall.

Dunne, Patrik M., Robert F. Lusch, and David A. Griffth (2002), *Retailing*, 4th Edition. Mason OH: South-Western.

Evan, William M. and R. Edward Freeman (1988), "A Stakeholder Theory of the Modern Corporation: Kantian Capitalism," in *Ethical Theory and Business,* edited by Thomas L. Beauchamp and Norman E. Bowie. Englewood Cliffs, NJ: Prentice-Hall, pp. 97-106.

Ferrell, O. C. and Larry G. Grasham (1986), "A Contingency Framework for Understanding Ethical Decision-making in Marketing," *Journal of Marketing*, 49 (Summer), 87-96.

Fisher, Josie (2001), "Lessons for Business Ethics from Bioethics," *Journal of Business Ethics*, 34, 15-24.

Fisk, George (1971), "New criteria for Evaluating the Social Performance of Marketing," in *New Essays in Marketing Theory*, edited by George Fisk, Boston: Mass.: Allyn and Bacon, pp. 440-441.

Fisk, Raymond P. (1982), "Toward a Theoretical Framework for Marketing Ethics," in *Southern Marketing Association Proceedings*, pp. 255-259.

Forsyth, Donelson R. (1992), "Judging the Morality of Business Practices: The Influence of Personal Moral Philosophies," *Journal of Business Ethics*, 11, 461-470

Frankenna, W. (1973), *Ethics*, 2nd Edition. Engelwood Cliffs, NJ: Prentice-Hall.

Freeman, R. Edward (1984), "The Politics of Stakeholder Theory: Some Future Directions," *Business Ethics Quarterly*, 4 (4), 409-21.

Friedman, Milton (1962), *Capitalism and Freedom*. Chicago: University of Chicago Press.

_____ . (1970), "The Social Responsibility of Business Is to Increase Its Profits," *The New York Times Sunday Magazine*, September 13.

Galbraith, John Kenneth (1956), *American Capitalism: The Concept of Countervailing Power*, Revised Edition. Boston: Houghton Mifflin.

_____ . (1973), *Economics and the Public Purpose*, Boston: Houghton Mifflin.

_____ . (1977), *The Age of Uncertainty*, Boston: Houghton Mifflin.

_____ . (1985), *The New Industrial State*, 4th ed. Boston: Houghton Mifflin.

Ganesan, Shankar (1994), "Determinants of Long-term Orientation in Buyer-Seller Relationships," *Journal of Marketing*, 58 (April), 1-19.

Goodpaster, Kenneth E. (1991), "Business Ethics and Stakeholder Analysis," *Business Ethics Quarterly*, 1 (1), 53-73.

Hunt, Shelby D., and Vitell, Scott. C. Jr. (1986), "A General Theory of Marketing Ethics," *Journal of Macromarketing*, 5-16.

Jap, Sandy D. (1999), "Pie-Expansion Efforts: Collaboration Processes in Buyer-Supplier Relationships," *Journal of Marketing Research*, 36 (November), 461-75.

Kalwani, Manohar U. and Narakesari Narayandas (1995), "Long-Term Manufacturer-Supplier Relationships: Do They Pay Off for Supplier Firms?" *Journal of Marketing*, 59 (January), 1-16.

Kelley, Eugene J. (1974), "Integrating Social Feedback into Business Decisions: Value System Conflicts and Corporate Planning," in *Social Indicators and Marketing*, edited by Robert L. Clewett and Jerry C. Olson, Chicago: American Marketing Association, pp. 129-145.

Kotler, Philip (1979), "Axioms for Societal Marketing," in *Future Directions for Marketing*, edited by George Fisk, Johan Arndt, and Kjell Gronharg, Boston: Marketing Science Institute, pp. 33-41.

_____ . (1986), *Principles of Marketing,* 3rd edition. Engelwood Cliffs, NJ: Prentice-Hall.

_____ . (1987), "Humanistic Marketing: Beyond the Marketing Concept," in *Philosophical and Radical Thought in Marketing*, edited by A. Firat, N. Dholakia, and R. Bagozzi, Lexington, MA: Lexington Book, pp. 271-288.

_____ and Nancy Lee (2005). *Corporate Social Responsibility: Doing the Most Good for*

Laczniak, Gene R. (1983), "A Framework for Analyzing Marketing Ethics," *Journal of Macromarketing*, 3(1), 7-18.

_____ and Patrick. E. Murphy (1993), *Ethical Marketing Decisions –The Higher Road.* Boston MA: Allyn and Bacon.

_____ and _____ . (2006), "Normative Perspective for Ethical and Socially Responsible," *Journal of Macromarketing*, 26(2), 154-177.

Lee, Dong-Jin and M. Joseph Sirgy (1999a), "International Marketers' Quality-of-Life Orientation: A Measure and Validational Support," *Journal of Business Ethics*, 18 (January), 73-89.

_____ and _____ . (1999b), "The Effects of Moral Philosophy and Ethnocentrism on Quality-of-Life Orientation: A Cross-Cultural Comparison," Journal of Business Ethics, 18 (1), 73-89.

_____ and _____ . (2004), "Quality-of-Life (QOL) Marketing: Proposed Antecedents and Consequences," *Journal of Macromarketing*, 24 (June), 44-58.

_____ and v(2005), *Well-Being Marketing: Theory, Research, and Applications*, Seoul, Korea: Pakyoungsa Publishing.

_____ , _____ , and Chenting Su (1998), "International Marketer's Quality-of-Life Prientation: The Construct, Its Antecedents and Consequences," *Research in Marketing*, 14, 151-184.

Mattsson, J. and J. D. Rendtorff (2006), "E-marketing Ethics: A Theory of Value Priorities," *International Journal of Internet Marketing and Advertising*, 3(1), 35-45.

Morgan, Robert M. and Shelby D. Hunt (1994), "The Commitment-Trust Theory of Relationship Marketing," *Journal of Marketing*, 58 (July), 20-38.

Naidu, G. M., Atul Parvatiyar, Jagdish N. Sheth, and Lori Westgate (1999), "Does Relationship Marketing Pay? An Empirical Investigation of Relationship Marketing Practices in Hospitals," *Journal of Business Research*, 46 (3), 207-219.

Nelson, Phillip (1970), "Information and Consumer Behavior," *Journal of Political Economy*, 78 (March-April), 311-329.

Parvatiyar, Atul and Jagdish N. Sheth (1994), "Paradigm Shift in Marketing Theory and Approach: The Emergence of Relationship Marketing," in *Relationship Marketing: Theory, Methods, and Applications*, edited by Jag Sheth and Atul Parvatiyar, Atlanta, GA: Center for Relationship Marketing, Emory University.

Robin, Donald P. and R. Eric Reidenbach (1987), "Social Responsibility, Ethics, and Marketing Strategy: Closing the Gap between Concept and Application," *Journal of Marketing*, 51 (January), 44-58.

Reidenbach, R. E. and D. P. Robin (1990), "Toward the Development of Multidimensional Scale of Improving Evaluation of Business Ethics," *Journal of Business Ethics*, 9(8), 639-653.

Samli, A. Coskun (1992), *Social Responsibility in Marketing: A Proactive and Profitable Marketing Strategy*. Westport, CT: Quorum Books.

Scherer, Frederic M. (1971), *Industrial Market Structure and Economic Performance*. Chicago: Rand McNally.

Sirgy, M. Joseph (1986), "A Quality-of-Life Theory Derived from Maslow's Developmental Perspective," *The American Journal of Economics and Sociology*, 45 (July), 329-342.

_____ . (1991a), "Quality-of-Life Studies in Marketing and Management: An Overview," *Journal of Business and Psychology*, 6 (Fall), 3-8.

_____ . (1991b), "Can Business and Government Help Enhance the Quality of Life of Workers and Consumers?" *Journal of Business Research*, 22 (June), 327-334.

_____ . (1996), "Strategic Marketing Planning Guided by the Quality-of-Life Concept," *Journal of Business Ethics*, 15 (March), 241-259.

_____ . (2001), *Handbook of Quality-of-Life Research: An Ethical Marketing Perspective,* Dordecht, The Netherlands: Kluwer Academic Publishers.

_____ . (2002), "Measuring Corporate Performance by Building on the Stakeholders Model of Business Ethics," *Journal of Business Ethics,* 35 (3), 143-162.

_____ and Dong-Jin Lee (1991), "Setting Socially Responsible Marketing Objectives: A Quality-of-Life Approach," *European Journal of Marketing,* 30(2), 20-27.

_____ and _____ . (1994), "Relationship Marketing and Beyond: A Quality-of-Life Approach to Consumer Marketing," in *Relationship Marketing: Theory, Methods, and Applications,* edited by Jagdish N. Sheth and Atul Parvatiyar, Atlanta, GA: Center for Relationship Marketing, Emory University.

_____ and _____ . (2006), "Well-Being," in *Encyclopedia of Business Ethics and Society,* edited by Robert W. Kolb, Thousand Oaks, CA: Sage Publications.

_____ , _____ , and Nora Reilly (2006), "Highlighting the Concept of Well-Being in Business," *Die Unternehmung—Swiss Journal of Business research and Practice,* 60(1), 61-76.

_____ , H. Lee Meadow, and A. Coskun Samli (1995), "Past, Present, and Future: An Overview of Quality-of-Life Research in Marketing," in *New Dimensions of Marketing and Quality-of-Life Research,* edited by M. Joseph Sirgy and A. Coskun Samli, Westport, CT: Greenwood Press, pp. 335-361.

_____ and Tamara Fox Mangleburg (1988), "Toward a General Theory of Social System Development: A Management/Marketing Perspective," *Systems Research,* 5(2), 115-130.

_____ and Michael Morris (1986), "The Growth of the Marketing Discipline in Relation to Quality of Life: A General Systems Perspective," in *Marketing/Quality-of-Life Interface,* edited by A. Coskun Samli, Westport, CT: Greenwood Press, pp. 312-333.

_____ , _____ , and A. Coskun Samli (1985), "The Question of Value in Social Marketing," *The American Journal of Economics and Sociology,* 44 (April), 215-228.

_____ , A. Coskun Samli, and H. Lee Meadow (1982), "The Interface between Quality of Life and Marketing: A Theoretical Framework," *Journal of Public Policy and Marketing,* 1, 69-84.

_____ and Chenting Su (2000), "The Ethics of Sovereignty in the Age of High Tech," *Journal of Business Ethics,* 28, 1-14.

Smith, Adam (1776, 1971), *The Wealth of Nations.* London: Everyman.

Smith, N. Craig (1995), "Marketing Strategies for the Ethics Era," *Sloan Management Review,* 36 (Summer), 85-97.

_____ . (2001), "Ethical Guidelines for Marketing Practice: A Reply to Gaski and Some Observations on the Role of Normative Marketing Ethics," *Journal of Business Ethics,* 32(1), 3-18.

_____ and John A. Quelch (1993), *Ethics in Marketing.* Homewood, IL: Irwin Publishers.

Stigler, George J. (1971), "The Theory of Economic Regulation," *Bell Journal of Economics and Management Science,* Spring.

Thorelli, Hans B. and Sarah V. Thorelli (1977), *Consumer Information Systems and Consumer Policy.* Cambridge, Massachusetts: Balinger.

Trevino, L. (1986), "Ethical Decision Making in an Organization: A Person-Situation Interactionist Model," *Academy of Management Review,* 11, 601-617.

Tsalikis John and David J. Fritzsche (1989), "Business Ethics: A Literature Review with a Focus on Marketing Ethics," *Journal of Business Ethics,* 8, 695-743.

Vitell, Scott J. Jr. (1986), "Marketing Ethics: Conceptual and Empirical Foundations of a Positive Theory of Decision Making in Marketing Situations Having Ethical Content," Unpublished Dissertation, Texas Tech University.

_____ , Kumar Rallapali, and Anusorn Singhapakdi (1993), "Marketing Norms: The Influences of Personal Moral Philosophies and Organizational Ethical Culture," *Journal of the Academy of Marketing Science*, 21 (Fall), 331-337.

_____ and Anusorn Singhapakdi (1993), "Ethical ideology and Its influence on the Norms and Judgments of Marketing Practitioners," *Journal of Marketing Management,* 3 (Spring/Summer), 1-11.

Wheeler, David and Maria Sillanpaa (1997), *The Stakeholder Corporation: A Blue Print for Maximizing Stakeholder Value.* London: Pitman Publishing.

Williams, O. F. and Patrick E. Murphy (1990), "The Ethics of Virtue: A Moral Theory for Marketing," *Journal of Macromarketing*, 10(1), 19-29.

Wotruba, Thomas R. (1990), "A Comprehensive Framework for the Analysis of Ethical Behavior, with a Focus on Sales Organizations," *Journal of Personal Selling & Sales Management*, 10 (Spring) 29-42.

In: Contemporary Issues in Business Ethics ISBN: 978-1-60021-773-9
Editors: M. W. Volcox, Th. O. Mohan, pp. 67-106 © 2007 Nova Science Publishers, Inc.

Chapter 3

CLIMATE CHANGE, PUBLIC POLICY PRODUCTION, AND THE ETHICS OF CORPORATE GOVERNANCE STRUCTURE

David Burress
Ad Astra Institute, Lawrence Kansas, USA

ABSTRACT

Newly emerging evidence suggests that global warming could endanger human existence itself, unless there is quick, effective, and worldwide collective action. In particular, runaway global warming mechanisms have been identified that in past eons apparently replaced much of atmospheric oxygen with hydrogen sulphide, causing the Permian (and perhaps other) mass extinctions of most of the world's land and water species. Accepted climate models suggest that anthropogenic global warming is capable of triggering those mechanisms [Ward, 2006]. Even assuming less catastrophic scenarios, human institutions have ethical responsibilities to support, or at least not impede, solutions to global warming. Yet many major corporations contribute adversely to global warming through two channels: first, by actively producing products and services that emit a major part of all greenhouse gas emissions; and second, by exerting political power via lobbying and other means that impede governments from appropriately regulating those emissions. With respect to the second channel, Burress [2005] contrasts two major ethical frameworks, showing that the stakeholder approach recommends that corporations should support corrective government action, while the neoclassical profit-maximizing approach sometimes recommends opposition to corrective action. In practice, major corporations have lobbied heavily against environmental regulation. A straightforward interpretation is that these corporations are in fact motivated by systematic incentives to maximize profits, even when this entails considerable damage to the common world we inhabit. These corporate choices are inconsistent with ordinary ethical facts accepted by most individuals. Therefore both internal incentive structures and external controls on corporate political action are matters of considerable ethical importance. This paper raises the following question: should incentive structures regulating corporate business be reformed to reduce ethically dubious lobbying on climate change? The stakeholder and neoclassical frameworks suggest rather specific, and contrasting, ethical criteria for incentive structures. This Chapter considers how these criteria are, or might be, operationalized. It suggests for example that representation for non-shareholder interests on a Board of Directors are forbidden by neoclassical ethics, but obligatory under stakeholder ethics. Perhaps surprisingly, the neoclassical approach provides considerably more support than the stakeholder approach for limitations on the lobbying and political activities of major corporations.

1. INTRODUCTION

The Ethics of Structural Choice

Ethics refers to reasoning about right choices when goals are in conflict. Yet human behavior is influenced by many factors other than ethics. First, while most human beings have innate motives to behave ethically, they have other motives that may be in conflict. Second, human behavior depends not only on internal motives, but also on external circumstances. In particular, human beings respond to material incentives. These responses are not necessarily mechanical, because human beings have the power to choose right behavior even in the face of strong material incentives to the contrary. Yet, at least on average, increases in the relative weight of incentives to do wrong (however wrong is defined) do lead to increases in the likelihood that people will make wrong choices. Moreover, the incentives faced by individuals are heavily influenced by socially-defined incentive structures.

Therefore "second-level" choices concerning design or modification of incentive structures can have far-reaching effects on numerous subsequent "first-level" choices made by human beings. And therefore choices concerning incentive structures would seem to be among the most important ethical choices human beings can make. Certainly this follows from the consequentialist perspective assumed in this Chapter: a change in incentive structure that affects many outcomes is likely to be more important than a changing factor that affects only one of those outcomes. But even from deontological and virtue-ethics perspectives, it would be hard to deny that choices about incentive structure, like all other choices, are subject to ethical considerations.

A practical obstacle to such consideration is that incentive structures are widely perceived as "given" rather than chosen; very often, no one takes responsibility for them. Even though these structures are built up by an accumulation of small human choices over time, the contribution of any one individual choice seems too small to be worthy of notice. But whether or not this perception of existential irresponsibility is justified in general, it is clearly not justified in the case of government legislation. Legislation is in fact an act (*inter alia*) of consciously producing incentive structures.

The production of legislation is affected by many actors in addition to legislators; to simplify the discussion I will refer to these additional actors collectively as "lobbyists," and to all of their political activities as "lobbying" (but see below for a summary of activities intended to affect legislation that go well beyond conventional lobbying). It is important to subject both the methods and goals of lobbying activities to ethical criticism [see *inter alia*,

Goldman, 1980; Grant, 1991; Keffer and Hill, 1997; OECD, 2000; Paladino and Willi, 2002; Derber, 2003; Burress, 2005].

Lobbyists are subject to their own incentive structures. Indeed, there are "third level" ethical choices that need to be made about the incentive structures that affect the lobbyists who join in the production of second level incentive structures.

The previous comments address very general questions about the ethics of incentive structures, independently of particular conceptions of the good, particular laws or incentives, or particular issues or ethical problems. This Chapter addresses much more specific questions. We will be concerned with regulation of the emission of greenhouse gases by businesses, and with the incentive structures that affect the production of those regulations. And we will focus on second and third level choices (i.e. what incentive structures should we have?) rather than first level choices (i.e. what volume of green house gases should we produce?) Although the problem is global, our data and examples will refer primarily to the US–a country which is both the largest single source of greenhouse gases, and also the most powerful international opponent of effective remedial action.

The Empirical Context

For purposes of argument this Chapter will assume a number of factual and theoretical conditions without detailed discussion.

1. Anthropogenic global warming is an established scientific fact. In other words, the climate is being changed by excessive amounts of carbon dioxide and other gases that trap the earth's heat (greenhouse gases), being emitted by human activities. For the most recent United Nations consensus scientific statement, which is accepted by nearly all relevant active researchers throughout the world, see Intergovernmental Panel on Climate Change [2007].[1]

2. Anthropogenic global warming imposes a severe and relatively near term risk of eliminating a substantial fraction of human wealth, productivity, and even human life. For the most recent of many such assessments, see Stern [2006].

3. There is a credible threat that the costs of global warming could be much higher, possibly leading to collapse of civilization or even human extinction. In particular, runaway global warming mechanisms have been identified that in past eons apparently replaced much of atmospheric oxygen with hydrogen sulphide, causing the Permian (and perhaps other) mass extinctions of most of the world's multicelled land and water species. Accepted climate models suggest that anthropogenic global warming is capable of triggering those mechanisms [Ward, 2006].

4. The largest anthropomorphic sources of carbon dioxide are concentrated in a relatively few industrial sectors, especially transportation, energy, and buildings. These sectors are substantially controlled by major corporations throughout the world. I will use the term "corporate emitters" for these corporations (including

---

[1] See below for a description of the role of major corporations in falsely persuading majorities of Americans that this statement is scientifically controversial.

corporations that do not directly emit greenhouse gases, but do produce equipment or fuel that in turn produces greenhouse gases).

5. There is a scientific consensus that timely action is essential, and that the window of opportunity for effective action to avert serious catastrophe may be little more than ten years [Socolow and Pacala, 2006].

6. Identification of a range of workable policy reforms is not especially controversial among experts [Bierbaum, *et al.*, 2007]. A steep and increasing "carbon tax" (i.e. a tax on carbon dioxide emissions) would the single most useful reform, although similar results can be accomplished using other methods such as tradable emission quotas, production subsidies, and regulation of production technology. Other policy changes are needed to mitigate the political and economic shocks a carbon tax would impose on society. I will refer to any sufficiently effective package of reforms generically as a "carbon tax."

7. Any package of reforms that is chosen will have strong and controversial distributional consequences. Some who oppose those consequences have led an intense opposition to policy changes. Consequently, government responses to this threat have been completely inadequate. Short term economic interests have played a central role in this political failure.

8. Any helpful policy change must override positions that heretofore have been successfully defended by major corporate emitters. Corporate lobbying and other exercises of corporate political power are certainly not solely responsible for our policy failures. However, they are in fact deeply implicated [Gelbspan, 1998, 2004].

I believe the above statements fairly represent an existing expert consensus. But even if some of these statements should later turn out to be incorrect, they still make a strong case for precautionary steps to reduce greenhouse gas emissions. While reforming the political behavior of major corporations is not a *sufficient* condition for effective action against climate change, I will suggest below that it could be a *necessary* condition. That is, major polluting countries such as the US, India, and China may fail do what desperately needs to be done unless they reign in the political influence of those corporations that, at least in the short run, benefit from inaction

Morever, as pointed out in Section 6, the example of global warming is only one among a number of environmental problems that lead to similar dilemmas. Consequently, the general ethical issues raised in this Chapter are important and germane even if some of its empirical premises are incorrect.

The Ethical Context

The changes in the outcomes of corporate power we assume are needed could come about through one or more of three socio-political processes:

1. Countervailing power organized and exerted by private organizations and an informed citizenry could offset the power of corporate emitters, without any structural changes

2. Internal corporate governance structures could be changed so that corporate emitters reduce their opposition to needed reforms.

3. Changes in external laws and regulations concerning lobbying and political action could reduce the power of corporate emitters to block needed reforms.

These three processes are compliments as well as substitutes–that is, any process might, if strong enough, be sufficient by itself to establish policies equivalent to a carbon tax, but two or three processes working together would be swifter and more effective than any one operating alone. Since each process has social costs as well as social benefits, the selection of political processes is in part an ethical choice.

If a process of countervailing power had already prevailed, then the ethical dilemmas analyzed here would not arise. However while a successful uprising of citizenry remains possible in the future, citizen action has heretofore proven inadequate, and time appears to be short. Hence the fate of the earth could well depend on changes in the political behavior of major corporate emitters. For purposes of this Chapter we assume there will be unacceptable social costs unless corporate emitters moderate their opposition to a carbon tax (and to equivalent policies). This suggests three plausible propositions in business ethics:

(I) Major corporate emitters should not oppose a carbon tax.

(II) The structure of corporate governance should be changed in such a way that corporate emitters would be less likely to lobby against a carbon tax.

(III) The structure of lobbying rules should be changed to reduce the effectiveness of corporate lobbying against the carbon tax.

The first proposition is addressed in Burress [2005]. That paper compares two standard frameworks for business ethics, the neoclassical approach [Friedman, 1970] and the stakeholder approach [Donaldson and Preston, 1995], as applied to a corporation's stance on the regulation of globally significant emissions (including but not limited to greenhouse gases). According to that paper, the stakeholder approach implies a corporate obligation to support corrective government action such as a carbon tax (implying Proposition I), while the neoclassical approach can sometimes imply an ethical obligation for corporations to actively oppose corrective action (negating Proposition I). The paper more briefly develops two additional frameworks I will refer to as "Marxian ethics" and "the common ethics," both of which would support Proposition I.

The present Chapter addresses the second and third propositions using the same general approach.

The plan of the Chapter is as follows:

- Section 2 shows that the various frameworks lead to conflicting recommendations about internal corporate incentive structures and external regulation of corporate lobbying, and discusses their relative plausibility.

- Section 3 argues that existing incentive structures of typical corporations are much closer to the neoclassical recommendations than to those of alternative frameworks.

- Section 4 suggests that actual lobbying behavior of corporate emitters is close to the neoclassical recommendation and contrary to the shareholder recommendation, but the existing regulation of lobbying is in some degree contrary to any recommendation.

- Section 5 describes some criteria for reform of incentive structures and lobbying regulations suggested by the various frameworks.
- Section 6 makes concluding remarks and generalizes the arguments being presented.

2. ETHICAL ANALYSIS OF INCENTIVE STRUCTURES

This section applies ethical theory to corporate governance and the regulation of lobbying.

Four Normative Frameworks for Business Ethics

The neoclassical ethical model [Friedman, 1970] posits that the sole ethical duty of the corporation is maximize profits returned to shareholders, limited only by a duty to remain within the law. The stakeholder ethical model [Donaldson and Preston, 1995] posits that corporations should seek to reconcile the interests of major stakeholders of the corporation, which is say all individuals whose well-being is substantially affected by corporate actions. These contrasting ways of characterizing business ethics focus clearly on goals and speak directly to incentive structures. The ethically appropriate incentive structure for a neoclassical corporation is one that leads managers and workers at all levels to maximize profits within the law. The ethically appropriate incentive structure for a stakeholder corporation is one that leads managers and workers at all levels to reconcile the interests of all major stakeholders.

Similarly, what I will call "Marxian ethics" posits an ethical duty of corporations to solely advance the interests of workers as a class[2]–supporting an incentive structure that leads managers and workers at all levels to advance the interests of all workers. Also, what I will call "the common ethics" posits a duty of concern for all human beings and therefore supports an incentive structure that leads workers and managers to advance the interests of all human beings.

A Meta-model

Burress [2005] develops a meta-model which compares and contrasts the four frameworks for business ethics by placing them within a common utilitarian framework. Each approach is assumed to posit that ethical business behavior consists in maximizing an aggregate of welfare (or happiness or utility) for individual human beings. However, the four frameworks differ with respect to the weights placed on the utilities of different persons, the conceptualization of utility, and the identity of the agent who is being given ethical advice.[3]

---

[2] While I am aware of no Marxist source that directly makes such a statement, it seems reasonable to infer this position from the Marxist theory of exploitation, which implies that all profits are exploitative. Note that managers are also viewed as workers, to the extent that they perform "socially necessary" labor.

[3] A static version of the meta-model can be made economically precise as follows:

the firm "j" is ethically obligated to maximize social welfare $V_j = \Sigma_i \, w_{ij} \, (E_i(u_i, p))^\alpha$, where:

i runs over all persons;

$w_{ij} \geq 0$ is the utility weight the firm applies to person "i";

Utility Weighting

The frameworks differ most importantly in the weights that are placed on different categories of human beings, as explained below. In addition to the explicit effect of utility weighting, we assume that maximization is limited by available or affordable information. Information costs will often lead to an implicit additional weighting on the utilities of persons closely associated with firm–because it easier predict impacts on them of actions by the firm, as well what interests they view as being affected by the firm, than it is to predict more distant effects. Thus, there is considerable merit to the point that society cannot maximize utility unless individuals focus differentially on their own needs. However the emphasis in this Chapter largely ignores information costs.

The neoclassical ethical approach can be described quite precisely as recommending that the corporation should, while remaining within the law, maximize the aggregate utility of its shareholders, with the utility of each shareholder calculated in money metric and weighted by the ownership shares of individual stockholders. It is further assumed that impacts on shareholder utility are mediated solely by profits. (This is actually a literal restatement of Friedman [1970] in economic language, rather than a model of Friedman's position. "Money metric" means that the marginal utility of money is constant for all individuals, or in other words makes a "one dollar-one vote" welfare assumption.)

The stakeholder approach can be modeled as recommending that the corporation should maximize the weighted utility of its stakeholders. The precise utility metric chosen for individual utilities will not be important for our purposes, except that we will assume a declining marginal utility of money – i.e., a dollar is more socially valuable when given to a poor person than to a rich person. Moreover, the exact nature of the weights applied variously to specific stakeholders, and in particular how those weights can be justified, measured, and applied, would be of considerable importance in quantitative applications of stakeholder theory. However these issues are not crucial for the present application and will not be addressed here.

The "common ethics" approach will be modeled as recommending that the corporation should maximize the equally-weighted utility of all human beings. We will assume a utility metric with a declining marginal utility of money.

The Marxian approach is modeled as recommending that the corporation should maximize the equally-weighted utility of all workers. We again assume a declining marginal utility of money.

In this Chapter I will use the term "interests" to refer to concrete expressions of utility or preference for a particular person or group, to the extent that they are known and understood by managers and other persons making ethical judgments.

---

u_i is the level of utility achieved by person i (using any utility function that correctly describes that person's system of preferences);

$E_i(u_i, p)$ is the total expenditure that person i would require in order to achieve the level of utility u_i if all goods were purchased at prices and shadow prices p;

p is a fixed vector of prices for market goods and shadow prices for non-market goods. Because p is normatively somewhat arbitrary, let p equal world average prices and shadow prices in some fixed reference year; and

α is a normative parameter that determines the marginal utility of money. For the neoclassical model, $\alpha = 1$. For the other models, $1 > \alpha > 0$.

The Nature of Utility

In the neoclassical approach, the utility of shareholders is equated with profits. The intuition behind this assumption is that profit is the only strong linkage through which the corporation can affect an individual shareholder's well-being. In the other three frameworks, individuals are assumed to have "thick" utility functions. In particular, all human beings are assumed to have a significant personal interest in avoiding global catastrophe within the lifetime of the next generation. This interest has to be weighed against short term material interests also held by individuals, but the former interest is assumed to be strong enough to influence the ethical decisions of corporations.

The Identity of the Advisee

All four theories address managers of corporations. As I will argue below, the neoclassical model shifts much ethical responsibility away from business managers and onto government; as a result, it offers advice to government policy-makers separate from, and very different than, its advice to managers. Because stakeholder theory places considerable emphasis on corporate self-regulation, it places little or no emphasis on external regulation by government, and does not offer strong advice to policymakers. The other two theories are focused more on society than on the firm, and give generalized ethical advice that could be taken to apply either to managers or policy-makers.

Neoclassical Recommendations

In the neoclassical framework for business ethics, the sole goal of the corporation should be to maximize profits while following the law. Logically, if there are profit-maximizing corporate behaviors that are legal and yet contrary to the good of society, the problem lies in the law and not in corporate structure. Government is responsible for all larger questions, including controlling any negative externalities of corporate behavior and ensuring social survival.[4] Therefore from time to time society may need reforms which discourage or limit socially negative corporate behaviors by means of new laws and external incentives. However, as long as corporations continue to maximize profits within the law, government should not attempt to modify their internal incentives.

It follows that:

(II-N) Neither government nor corporation should attempt to change any internal corporate governance structures that lead to maximizing profits within the law (a negation of Proposition II).

In cases where corporations can affect government policy, the neoclassical approach leads to a nice conundrum. Thus, in the case of global warming, the first instance of socially

---

[4] This point is not emphasized in most accounts of neoclassical ethics, yet it is clearly implicit. This point is much more explicit in the literature of welfare economics, which was well-known to Friedman and provided the background intuition for all of his work. In particular, a version of the First Theorem of Welfare Economics (in common language, an "invisible hand" argument) shows that (under certain technical conditions) social aggregate utility in money metric is maximized if firms maximize profits while externalities are prevented by government regulation [see e.g. Little, 2002, Chapter 3].

negative corporate behavior consists in the emission of greenhouse gases. Given our technical assumptions about global warming, neoclassical ethics recommends government action to control that behavior:

(IV)   Government should take necessary steps to control greenhouse gases–i.e. it should pass a carbon tax.

However, corporate emitters emit greenhouse gases because it is profit maximizing. The carbon tax will reduce their corporate profits, at least in the short run. It can be shown that:

(I-N)   A neoclassical emitting corporation is ethically obligated to lobby against the carbon tax (the negation of Proposition I, as developed in Burress [2005]).

It may seem counterintuitive to claim that a neoclassical corporation could be ethically required to lend political support to socially catastrophic policies. In particular, it seems counter-intuitive that a rational profit-maximizing organization might pursue activities that ultimately destroy the society that makes those profits possible. Nevertheless that conclusion follows logically from neoclassical assumptions.

In particular, and briefly summarized, Burress [2005] argues as follows. In the received economic theory accepted by Friedman, "maximizing profits" is shorthand for a more complex idea: maximizing the present value of an expected future stream of profits. It can be shown through the mathematics of discounting that, with usually accepted discount rates and with socially sustainable growth rates in profits, profits expected far in the future (e.g. 50 years out) have no significant impact on the present value of profits–and hence no significant impact on corporate decisions made in the present. In particular, even an expected collapse of civilization leading to the end of all profits 50 years from now would have no significant impact on decisions made in the present. Therefore a corporation obligated to maximize profits is logically obligated to oppose any regulation of emissions that would reduce short term profits, independently of any possible long term consequence.

Thus the second instance of socially negative corporate behavior consists in lobbying (inclusive of all related political activities) by corporate emitters against the carbon tax. If that lobbying is successful, then (by hypothesis) catastrophe will follow. According to neoclassical ethics, it is government's job to prevent catastrophe. In this case that can only be accomplished through a reduction in the effects of corporate lobbying. By proposition II-N, that reduction cannot ethically be accomplished through reform of corporate governance structures. Logically, therefore, neoclassical ethics recommends:

(III')   Government should take necessary external regulatory steps to control any corporate lobbying that allows the carbon tax to blocked (a partial instantiation of Proposition III).

However, it is important to understand that any lobbying restrictions are likely to reduce the profits of corporate emitters. How do we know that? Quite simply, according to the neoclassical ethical framework corporate lobbying should be done solely to increase profits;[5] therefore if lobbying is limited then profits are likely to be reduced. It follows that neoclassical ethics recommends:

> (III'-N) Emitting corporations should lobby to impede any new restrictions on lobbying (a partial negation of Proposition III).

Thus, the third instance of socially negative corporate behavior consists in lobbying by corporate emitters against lobbying reform.

If that lobbying is successful, then, logically, society needs to reform the laws of lobbying that allowed lobbying reform to blocked:

> (III'') Government should take necessary external regulatory steps to control any corporate lobbying that allows lobbying reform to blocked (a second partial instantiation of Proposition III).

But how could this change be brought about? According to the neoclassical model, it is not the business of corporations to establish appropriate external incentive structures. In fact, by Proposition III'-N they should block reform if they can.[6] The obligation to support reform rests on other parties; exactly who is not addressed in the neoclassical model. The model simply assumes that someone will pick up the slack.

And if, as an empirical matter, corporate emitters happen to hold a preponderance of political power, then there is no recourse. Regulation of lobbying would not change, corporate lobbying activities would not change, global warming reforms would not be adopted, and (by assumption) a global warming catastrophe would follow.

If one believes that, as an empirical matter, corporations presently lack sufficient power to block the carbon tax, or to block the needed lobbying reforms, the cutting edge of this contradiction will not be not reached, and neoclassical ethics can be defended as a contingently acceptable system.

But if (as assumed in this Chapter) corporate lobbying has already slowed governmental responses sufficiently to cause significant real damage to the planet, and stands ready to cause more, then neoclassical ethics is an unsustainable system that, in practice, is aiding the destruction of its own conditions for existence.

More generally, we have shown that neoclassical ethics may be contingently acceptable but cannot constitute an acceptable complete or self-contained system of business ethics.

---

[5] Moreover, according to the neoclassical descriptive framework accepted by most Anglo-American economists, lobbying *is* in fact done solely to increase profits. Moreover, corporations have a profit motive to invest in obtaining better information than other actors have about which lobbying activities would be most profitable.

[6] This conundrum is fundamental to Friedman's thought, as witnessed by Charles H. Brunie, chairman of Oppenheimer Capital Corporation:
"William Simon in his book, A Time for Truth, keeps castigating businessmen for running down to Washington and looking for handouts, as opposed to sponsoring the free market. Ralph Leach, the retired Vice-Chairman of Morgan Guaranty, and Milton Friedman have each told William Simon they disagree with him. They maintain that is exactly what a businessman should do; he should run to Washington for all the help he can get; it is the politician's job to say no." (quoted. in Wilcke [1983], as cited by Wilcke [2004]).

Stakeholder Recommendations

The stakeholder approach generates no such conundrums. As argued in Burress [2005], the stakeholder corporation is obligated to support the interests of its stakeholders in regulating harmful emissions. In the case of global warming, that implies supporting a carbon tax (implying Proposition I).

By an extension of the same argument, if some emitting corporations (presumably, non-stakeholder corporations) are lobbying effectively to block a carbon tax, then the stakeholder corporation is obligated to support reforms to overcome this problem. But which reforms should the stakeholder corporation support: changes in internal governance (Proposition II), or changes in external regulation of lobbying (Proposition III)?

The stakeholder corporation has strong reasons to support changes in internal governance. In many cases, it has good reasons to oppose changes in the regulation of lobbying.

The Case for Governance Reform

In a world inhabited by competing stakeholder corporations and neoclassical corporations, stakeholder corporations have two very general reasons to support governance reforms, provided those reforms would make corporate incentives more similar to the stakeholder ideal and less similar to the neoclassical ideal.

First, and more obviously, neoclassical corporations sometimes act in ways that are contrary to stakeholder corporate interests. In the present application, as we have seen, neoclassical emitters oppose the carbon tax, while stakeholder firms support it. To the extent that neoclassical corporations are successful in blocking the carbon tax, they have done a serious injury to the stakeholders of stakeholder corporations. More generally, neoclassical corporations are likely to contribute to a rather rough market place that is not naturally congenial for stakeholder corporations. The point isn't that stakeholder corporations can't be tough competitors, but rather that behaviors the stakeholder corporations view as unethical may give neoclassical corporations what, at least in the minds of stakeholders, is an unfair advantage.

There is a second and less obvious reason for stakeholder corporations to support governance reform in some cases. Just as an ethical person who, being aware of her own susceptibility to temptation, tries to arrange the incentives in her life to avoid being subjected to temptation, so (other things being equal) an ethical corporation should welcome changes in its own internal incentive structures that would support ethical behavior. Imposition of these changes by external law would not necessarily be unwelcome, since it would reinforce internal goals while creating an external level playing field.

The Cases for and against Lobbying Reform

A stakeholder corporation might well oppose many (though not all) efforts to regulate its lobbying activities. The stakeholders of the corporation have numerous interests (including, but not only, maximizing profit) that are heavily affected by actions of government. Reducing the range of lobbying tools available to a given corporation would reduce its ability to maximize the utility of its stakeholders.

The main situation where a stakeholder corporation is obligated to support lobbying reform would be cases where the gain to that corporation's stakeholders from limitations on lobbying activities of other corporations outweighed the loss from limitations on its own lobbying activities. For example, because bribery leads to a corrupt and inefficient marketplace, it might gain more than it would lose from additional laws preventing corporate bribery. Other such situations are often intensely fact-sensitive and hard to analyze in general. In the particular case of global warming, if the carbon tax could be successfully supported through governance reform, there would seem to be no remaining basis for lobbying reform. However if governance reform proved impractical or insufficiently effective or politically infeasible, the stakeholder firm should support some degree of lobbying reform.

It can also be argued that the US and western system of lobbying is innately corrupt, or close to it [Khera, 2001]. If so, the stakeholder corporation should support fundamental reforms simply out of the various stakeholder's unanimous desire to live in an honest society.

Marxian and Common Ethics Recommendations

Marxian and common ethics would agree with stakeholder ethics on the general need for governance reform. Both frameworks focus on the interests of ordinary people, though with different weightings, and those interests (under the technical conditions assumed in this Chapter) support the carbon tax. Appropriate governance reform could undercut corporate opposition to the carbon tax.

The two theories would tend to agree further that stakeholder incentive structures are to be preferred over neoclassical incentive structures. The reasoning is that stakeholder goals are more closely aligned than neoclassical goals with the goals recommended by the two theories.

However, neither theory would agree that stakeholder incentive structures are ideal, because those structures do not accurately align corporate incentives with the weighting of utility that is favored by either theory.

Marxian and common ethics are considerably less sympathetic than stakeholder ethics to the corporate need for a public lobbying voice. The stakeholder approach has a special sympathy for the interests of persons whose well-being is closely associated with a particular corporation, leading it to place a high derived value on corporate success, and hence on any lobbying that advances it. In contrast, the Marxian and common ethics frameworks place no value on persons associated with particular corporations beyond that due to them as general members of society. Therefore those frameworks would tend to support much more extensive lobbying reforms. This Chapter will not work out the details of these alternative positions.

3. OBSERVED CORPORATE INCENTIVE STRUCTURES

This section examines the existing incentive structures of actual public corporations in general terms, without much reference to the specific case of corporate emitters.

Profit Maximization

Profit-making is the sole stated end-purpose in the articles of incorporation of most profit-making corporations. Incentives in a typical publicly-traded profit-making corporation are primarily structured to maximize profits and not to reconcile stakeholder interests. This has both internal and external aspects.

Internal Structures

Ultimate corporate authority usually rests with a Board of Directors who are directly responsible only to shareholders; moreover they are generally elected by votes weighted in proportion to ownership shares (though some shares may be non-voting). The fiduciary duty of the Board is to advance the interests of those shareholders, and shareholder interests are conceptualized in law and practice purely in terms of their financial gain from holding or selling stock. Financial gain is a complex notion that has dimensions of time, uncertainty, and control, so that, at least in principle, the Board may need to reconcile differences among shareholder interests. Nevertheless the Board has a very focused duty which does not, for example, include advancing interests of non-shareholders, or nonfinancial interests of shareholders, or any financial interests of shareholders that aren't based on ownership of stock in this particular company. Rather its duty is to maximize financial gain of this company, subject only to the law.

The Board hires and fires a management team that, in practice, is nearly always expected to make profits that constantly increase over time. Practically speaking, a demand for constantly increasing profits can be met only by a constant search for, and persistent exploitation of, new opportunities for profit. To the extent that there is likely to be an ever-increasing cost of locating ever-more elusive profit opportunities, a demand for constant increase in profit has almost the same force as a demand for profit maximization–and yet is much easier to monitor. Conversely, "profit-maximization" would seem to be an effective heuristic for managers who are conducting a constant search for new profit opportunities.

The management team controls the workforce and resources of the business. Its main job might be described as the creation and maintenance of incentive structures that lead individual employees to help maximize profits.

In summary, the internal governance and incentive structure of a typical corporation is explicitly designed to advance neoclassical behavior and not stakeholder behavior.

Structural Failures

It is true, however, that there are many opportunities for this (or any) system to fail to deliver the profit maximization demanded by shareholders, mainly because employees are tempted to divert business resources from organizational goals to their own personal goals, while the span of management control is finite. This is referred to in the literature as the "principal-agent problem" [Milgrom and Roberts,1992]. That literature focuses on the design of incentive systems that can minimize the diversion of resources and maximize the achievement of organizational goals. In other words, the design and implementation of mechanisms to ameliorate or solve the principal-agent problem is itself part of the profit maximization process.

Perhaps the most important example of structural failure in the literature is the partial or complete capture of loyalties of the Board of Directors by top management [Hermalin and Weisbach, 1998]. Such capture supports the diversion resources from stockholders to top managers, but typically does not affect profit-maximizing incentives in the rest of the organization. Top managers would logically prefer for the rest of the organization to continue to maximize profits so that larger sums become available for diversion to their own use.

External Structures

The strong internal profit-seeking incentives of a typical corporation are reinforced by the structure of capitalist financial markets. If any public corporation fails to maximize profits, and if this becomes known to outside capitalists, there is a strong incentive for them to impose a merger or acquisition, leading to new management that does maximize profits. In particular, in equilibrium the market value of the firm consists in the present value of its expected future profits [Cook and Holtzman, 1976]; therefore the firm will have a higher market value if its profits can be increased; therefore the firm is worth more to new owners who will maximize profits, than it is to existing owners whose hired management is failing to maximize profits. Moreover, because of the improved market value the new owners will ordinarily be able to pay off the full costs of acquisition by selling shares in the reformed company, and still retain some positive remaining value in the firm as their reward. While there are a variety of reasons why this mechanism may not always work as advertised (e.g. costs of obtaining information about failures to maximize profits; poison pill defenses; etc.), smoothly functioning capital markets very often do work this way. The main reason it works is that the current shareholders, who do in fact own the company, generally stand to gain financially from these takeovers.

A related external structure is the ethical and lobbying positions taken by major business organizations that support neoclassical profit-maximizing ethics and oppose stakeholder ethics. For example, the Business Roundtable [1997, p.3], an organization of CEOs of major corporations, has declared that "the paramount duty of management and the board is to the stockholders; the interests of other stakeholders are relevant as a derivative of the duty to stockholders."

Summary

There are good reasons to expect that widely-traded public corporations will have extremely strong (though not entirely perfect) internal incentives to maximize profits. However there may be room for improved structures to limit diversion of profits from shareholders to top managers.

Obedience to Law

To what extent are profit-making incentives limited by obedience to law? The above discussion included little reference to law, except with respect to the legal structures that define the corporation as a profit-seeking organization. In many cases obedience to the law may well reduce profits. For example, prior to passage of the US Foreign Corrupt Practices Act of 1977 it was widely argued that obeying foreign laws against bribery would put

American corporations at a disadvantage and reduce their profits. In such cases, law-abiding behavior can logically be viewed as a diversion of business resources that (in principle) could be prevented by improved incentive design.

All corporate activities are highly entwined with the law—labor law, tax law, consumer law, contract law, corporation law, environmental law, antitrust law, criminal law. Every department of a corporation makes innumerable routine and non-routine decisions that are molded by an accommodation to the law. Obeying the law is often the path of least resistance. Many routine actions automatically leave a paper trail that makes the law relatively easy to enforce. While the paper trail can be falsified, doing so requires significant planning, effort, and risk. In such cases, unless the risks are relatively low and the expected gains relatively high, breaking the law would fail to maximize expected profits.

However, in cases where rewards are large and expected penalties relatively small, law breaking can become widespread, as in corporate income tax noncompliance [Duffel, 2006] and unfair labor practices [Rose and Chaison, 2001].

So why do corporations obey the law? To the extent that they do obey the law, there are two possible explanations: external constraint, and internal motivation. In the latter case, corporations could have internal incentive structures that encourage law-abiding behavior, or lacking such structures they might rely on the consciences of individual employees to keep them out of trouble.

Opportunistic Law-abiding Behavior

In many cases external conditions and opportunities are such that obeying the law actually helps the corporation maximize profits. For example, strong government enforcement of the law can make law-breaking a money-losing strategy. Alternatively, in a law-abiding culture, actors in goods and service and labor markets might be reluctant to do business with a corporation that had a reputation for law-breaking. This reluctance can sometimes be re-enforced by voluntary and non-profit organizations that promote adverse publicity or support boycotts.

But note that law-abiding behavior as a rational response to external pressure is purely contingent—it would change if external conditions changed. To believe in perfect law-abiding behavior in such a case is to believe in perfect law-enforcement (possibly due to a combination of public police action plus private social pressure). Yet nearly all academic theories of law enforcement stress its incomplete and secondary nature [Vold and Bernold, 1986]. The front-line source of legal order rests in the simple willingness of most actors to obey the law. In an amoral world, law and order fails.[7]

Innate Law-enforcement Structures

Historically, there typically were no *innate* incentive structures within the corporation to control unlawful behavior. As suggested above, the laws of incorporation explicitly encourage incentive structures that support profit maximization, but there is nothing comparable in the laws of incorporation requiring internal structures to repress unlawfulness. Historically, most of the internal policing structures that did exist showed every sign of being

---

[7] It is true however that a certain kind of order can be created among amoralized individuals by terroristic surveillance regimes in which all spy on all (as analyzed in Arendt [1958]). Such totalitarian regimes are not lawful, and in the long run not stable.

purely contingent profit-maximizing responses to external conditions such as successful law enforcement. These structures were not innate, in the following sense: they would be likely to decay over time if law-enforcement and other external pressures ceased to be effective.

Over time, however, laws and regulations were passed that require some degree of internal policing structures on a permanent basis. Most importantly, the Securities and Exchange Act of 1934 (and its amendments over time) led to numerous controls on corporate bookkeeping and required a degree of public accountability for those controls. Many of these laws are unpopular among corporate leaders, and some are viewed as an alien intrusion. Nevertheless, these laws represent important steps towards internalizing incentive structures in support of the neoclassical proposition that corporations should obey the law.

Currently most corporations have auditing and financial control units that do exercise some internal police powers, but these units focus most heavily on the protection of business assets from employee diversion. Some but not all corporations do have internal ethics programs. Most large corporations do have a legal department. However, legal departments are not usually tasked as internal police units, but rather as advisers on how to use (or in some cases avoid) the law in pursuit of profit.

The Role of Conscience

Social science research has not been sympathetic to the idea, or hope, that lawful corporate behavior can be enforced by an unaided individual conscience. If an individual following her conscience presents an obstacle to profit maximization beyond what is imposed through external and internal regulation, then, according to the logic of profit-making, that constitutes a diversion of resources from profit maximization that needs to be controlled through mechanism design. In other words, profit-making incentive systems dictate that such an employee should be fired, neutralized, or at least removed from any position with power to obstruct.

Whistle-blower laws are an extremely important external palliative, but research by the Government Accountability Project and others shows that these legal initiatives have a very long way to go before they will be broadly effective. Advice from GAP's legal director to both public and private sector whistle-blowers amounts to this: even though anonymous whistle-blowing may have limited effectiveness, you personally are better off doing it anonymously. Otherwise we can't protect you very well. Don't do it publicly unless you are prepared to retire early and also withstand intense pressure that may include slander and threats [Devine, undated].

But even where whistle-blower laws are ineffective and open obstruction to law-breaking is ruthlessly crushed, there remains some scope for the individual conscience to resist law-breaking using means such as anonymous tipoffs, sabotage, or quiet foot-dragging. While these behaviors aren't capable of producing a regime of total legality, they could at least reduce the amount of illegality.

The Internal Evolution of Competing Incentive Structures

Profit-seeking incentive structures such as asset markets and the voice of demanding shareholders occupy the commanding heights of power within a profit-seeking corporation. Therefore they have great influence over the process of change in internal incentive structures. In some cases internal law-enforcement structures are strongly reinforced by external law enforcement and public pressure. Where this is not the case, it seem reasonable to predict that internal law enforcement structures will gradually be degraded over time in favor of increased profits.

The External Evolution of Law

A more sinister hypothesis could be that corporations obey the law simply because they have written the laws in the forms they want to obey. In a world rationally dominated by the political power of large corporations, laws would purely reflect the agreed-on collective interests of those corporations. Nevertheless, such a world would still face law-enforcement problems, because there would still be opportunities for specific corporations to advance their private interests by cheating on public agreements with other corporations. Therefore collective corporate dominance of the production of law can neither explain nor predict law-abiding behavior on the part of individual corporations.

Summary

At present the modern corporation has an incentive to remain within the law to the extent that the law is strictly enforced by police or custom; in addition, internal structures to encourage lawfulness are gradually being developed. However, in cases where they can get away with it, many corporations continue to have strong incentive structures that can encourage maximization of profits quite irrespective of the law.

Responding to Stakeholder Interests

Internal corporate incentive structures for responding to stakeholders are less developed than incentive structures for obeying the law–with the important exception of those stakeholders whose interests are in fact protected by law enforcement structures. We will refer to the residual interests unprotected by law-enforcement structures as "residual stakeholders."

Internal Structures

Many corporations do have internal institutions that respond to particular residual stakeholders; examples include ombudsmen, the anonymous grievance box, and complaint manager.

Stakeholder Organizations

Some institutions are established by stakeholders of a specific corporation to protect their own interests. Even though they are formally external to the corporation, since they are attached to a specific corporation they could be regarded as quasi-internal incentive structures of that corporation. Examples include labor unions, supplier organizations, franchisee organizations, and customer organizations. These organizations can use methods such jawboning, adverse publicity, strikes, boycotts, and lawsuits to advance stakeholders' interests.

External Structures

At a further remove, there are organizations that may defend particular stakeholder classes for multiple corporations or entire industries, such as consumers unions, professional organizations, buying coops, nonprofit think tanks, and advocacy groups.

Summary

Incentive structures to respect the needs of residual stakeholders do exist but tend to be weaker than structures supporting profit maximization and obedience to law.

Regulation of Lobbying

This Chapter will not review the large literature describing the effectiveness of US regulation of corporate lobbying and limitations on corporate political power. For a survey suggesting that effectiveness is rather limited see Bartels, Heclo, Hero, and Jacob [2004].

Interpretation of Corporate Incentives

This section has discussed five types of incentive structures:

- internal governance and management structures;
- financial market incentive structures;
- labor, goods and service market incentive structures;
- voluntary and non-profit incentive structures; and
- government regulatory structures.

We suggest that the internal structures and asset market structures of typical public corporations are dominated by profit-making motives, but constrained to a limited extent by independent legal-compliance motives, and constrained to an even smaller extent by motives to respect residual stakeholder interests. The main burden of constraining an otherwise unbridled profit motive rests on external pressures exerted by goods and service markets, private and non-profit organizations, and government regulation. Moreover such internal constraints as do exist are themselves largely a contingent profit-seeking response to external pressure.

This account is not very supportive of the stakeholder model. It says that any stakeholder-respecting behavior is contingent on the external societal pressures that happen to exist in a particular time and place, rather than innate to the corporate form. Or to put the case in strongest terms, given the clear strength of profit-seeking incentive structures and the diffuseness of incentive structures that represent the interests of stakeholders, the stakeholder approach might seem almost fecklessly naive. Nevertheless several considerations suggest that the stakeholder model may be defensible in a wide range of particular cases. Thus:

1. In some cases, obeying stakeholder ethics might in fact be profit-maximizing. That is, the network of external law enforcement and sources of public pressure could in

some cases be sufficient to force a profit-maximizing corporation to take stake-holder interests fully into account.

2. Even if not, the combination of external pressures, plus the growing set of internal structures intended to accommodate those pressures, plus the impact of individual consciences as protected by whistle-blower laws, could produce complex behaviors in public corporations that can be understood more simply under the stakeholder rubric than under the profit-maximizing rubric.

3. Even if not, the stakeholder model may be appropriate for some privately-held corporations, as well as some closely-held public corporations, in which the owners happen to be personally motivated by a deep concern for the stakeholders.

Note that each of these cases is hard to dismiss empirically, in part because we haven't clearly specified who are the stakeholders and what are the relative weights the stakeholder corporation should place on their various interests. Also, these possibilities suggest that profit-maximizing behavior (in both law-abiding and lawless variants) and stakeholder behavior are alternatives that can occupy separate or even overlapping niches within the same industry. Therefore incentive structures alone can't tell us how best to characterize the ethics of corporations. We also need to look at actual behavior.

But even if stakeholder-respecting behavior were never observed in the real world, it can still be argued that stakeholder ethics lead to more defensible recommendations for managers than neoclassical ethics, whether or not corporations are willing to follow those recommendations. In particular, stakeholder ethics supports autonomous managerial steps toward environmental sustainability, and neoclassical ethics does not.

4. Observed Behavior of Corporate Emitters

This section examines the specific behavior of major corporate enablers and emitters of greenhouse gases.

Corporate Emitters and Corporate Lobbying

Throughout the world, the production chain for every human source of emissions is touched by corporations from multiple industries at multiple points. Conversely, every corporation (and every other organization and every individual person) contributes to the production of greenhouse gases. This Chapter is concerned with a much smaller class of corporate emitters that are heavily engaged in lobbying against a carbon tax and equivalent laws. This lobbying can take place at all levels of government and can involve corporations of all sizes. While the most significant lobbying is done at the national level by very large corporations, smaller corporations are having important effects at the state and local level.

Corporate Emissions of Greenhouse Gases

Fuel Companies

Most of the production of greenhouse gases is directly caused by combustion of fuels for the purpose of capturing free energy. The main exceptions are deforestation (no longer important on net in the US) and animal husbandry (which releases methane). Indeed global warming can be said to be 100% caused by fuel uses, in the sense that all other sources combined are not large enough by themselves to cause threshold global warming.

In the US nearly all combustible fuel comes from mined hydrocarbons, and in particular from petroleum, natural gas, and coal, generally produced or distributed by mid-sized to major corporations [Socolow and Pacala, 2006]

Electrical Generation Companies

About 40% of US fuel by carbon content is used to create electrical power, mostly by regional power companies. Power generation is regulated jointly by state and national regulators. Generating companies tend to be small to mid-sized regional rather than national companies.

Transportation Equipment Companies

About 33% of US fuel by carbon content is used in the course of motorized movement of people and things. Transportation equipment is typically produced by very large corporations, but used by much smaller corporations, businesses, and households.

Buildings

Around 27% of fuel by carbon content is used to directly heat buildings and run industrial processes, not including electrical power. Building construction is typically done by small regional corporations. Building materials and heating equipment are typically produced by national corporations.

Lobbying and other Corporate Political Action against the Carbon Tax

Lobbying by corporations implicated in environmental damage has a bad reputation, evidently for good reasons: as shown by Cho, Patten, and Roberts [2006] the worst polluters are also the heaviest spenders on political action. In other words, political power is an economic substitute for good behavior. This pattern is fully borne out in the case of corporate emitters of greenhouse gases.

The Anti-carbon-tax Coalition

While the particular actors have shifted somewhat from time to time, the leading forces opposing a carbon tax have been coal, petroleum, and gas companies, automobile and heavy equipment manufacturers, and electricity generating companies–i.e., most of the leading corporate emitters. Building materials and equipment manufacturers are lesser players. (Somewhat out-of-date political analyses are given by Gelbspan [1998] and Leggett [2001].)

The coalition channels financial resources through a number of organizations as sketched below. Their leading organization during 1989-2002 was the Global Climate Coalition [Sourcewatch, 2007], whose secret funding totaled several tens of millions. Its members made at least $63m in contributions to political candidates during1989-1999.

Petroleum companies have maintained powerful Washington lobbies since the 1920's. Many of their very formidable successes in achieving subsidies, tax breaks, public land concessions, abating environmental regulation, and influencing American foreign policy are not directly relevant to global warming, but they have also devoted major resources for opposing regulations that directly or indirectly limit greenhouse emissions. They have worked closely with coal and gas companies.

Automobile companies have effectively blocked change in CAFE fuel economy standards.

Electricity generating companies have been most active in lobbying against state and local regulation of carbon dioxide emissions.

Global Warming Denial

The leading tactic of the anti-carbon tax coalition has been denial of existence of any problem [McCright and Dunlap, 2000]. (For an exemplary denial website, see Cooler Heads Coalition [2007].) That denial takes a layered form, allowing for sequential fallback positions when older positions become increasingly untenable. Put in a logical sequence, these positions are:

- there is no global warming
- global warming is only a short term fluctuation
- long term global warming has not been proven
- long term global warming is no worse than other long term warming events in the past
- long term global warming is not caused by human beings
- global warming is not sufficient in amount to cause important climate changes
- it has not been proven that global warming will cause important climate changes
- human contribution to global warning has not been proven
- human contribution to global warming is only a small share of the cause
- it has not been proven that human contribution is a large share of the cause
- there is a long window of opportunity for mitigating global warming
- it hasn't been proven that the window of opportunity for mitigation is short [8]
- the benefits of global warming will exceed the costs
- human economies will readily adapt to global warming at low cost
- it hasn't been proven that human economies can't adapt at low cost
- the costs of mitigating global warming would exceed the costs of adapting
- the optimal mix of mitigation and adaptation requires that mitigation proceed slowly.

---

[8] The complete and utter scientific indefensibility by c. 1993 of every claim higher on the list than this one was demonstrated by a review of 928 abstracts from articles on global warming published in refereed physical science journals between 1993 and 2003 [Oreskes, 2004]. Not a single article denied the existence of massive anthropogenic global warming Items lower on this list have a social science component, but have been attested to by a number of scientific organizations.

Even when it becomes necessary to introduce new fallback positions into public discourse, all of the older positions remain in play and continue to appear in *Wall Street Journal* editorials or on Fox News or in letters to the editor in local newspapers. Some of the overriding (and contradictory) meta-messages are:

- global warming is highly controversial
- global warming is highly complex
- global warming is scientifically unsettled
- global warming is a partisan issue
- global warming apostles have ulterior motives
- there is a conspiracy to defund scientists who oppose the alleged consensus
- elitist experts should not be taken as face value
- we should criticize "extremists" on both sides
- the truth lies somewhere in the middle
- ordinary people cannot hope to understand global warming
- ordinary people have just as good a grasp on global warming as so-called experts.

For detailed documentation on global warming denial, see Gelbspan [2004].

Junk Science

Global warming denial is supported by a quasi-scientific establishment parallel to the real scientific establishment. This establishment is highly subsidized by interested corporations (much of the funding comes from coal companies and Exxon-Mobile Corporation) [9] and receives little or no peer-reviewed funding. Whenever possible, this school of junk science makes heavy use of:

- real science that is out of date
- endorsements by individuals with scientific credentials but without expertise in a relevant field.
- endorsements by fringe scientists who were once in the mainstream but continue to hold on to older views that the scientific consensus now views as discredited
- quasi-scientific conferences that produce seemingly authoritative working papers lacking any mainstream scientific participation or review.
- quasi-scientific think tanks. [10]

---

[9] For example:
> ...in spring 2003 [a] study by lead authors Sallie Baliunas and Willie Soon at the Harvard-Smithsonian Center for Astrophysics and published in an obscure journal, Climate Research, concluded that the 20th century is neither the warmest century, nor the century with the most extreme weather, of the past 1,000 years. Both researchers had previously contended that the recent warming was due, almost entirely, to solar variations -- a finding long since disproved by peer-reviewed scientific studies. ... the report by Baliunas and Soon was funded in part by the American Petroleum Institute. It was also coauthored by Craig Idso and Sherwood Idso, whose Center for the Study of Carbon Dioxide has been funded by the coal industry and Exxon-Mobil. .... Three editors of the journal that published the skeptics' study resigned in protest after they were forbidden from writing an editorial pointing out the methodological errors. [Gelbspan, 2004].

The Baliunas and Soon study is widely cited in global warming denial literature.

[10] Thus:

However, some of the most successful junk science publicists have been writers with no relevant expertise at all, such as Crichton [2004] (a science fiction writer) and Lomborg [2001] (a statistician with no training or experience in environmental research).

No doubt, many of the involved scientists and writers are sincere in their beliefs. However it is important to understand that every major scientific field includes left-behind supporters of outmoded or quack ideas. These fringe ideas are unlikely to achieve mainstream public credibility–except when they are backed by strong outside funding or organization, as in global warming denial and creation science.

The Rogue PR Industry

Stauber and Rampton [1995] document the existence of a large public relations industry skilled at the secret use of unethical and illegal techniques for sabotaging unwelcome policy-related messages, e.g. preventing their publication through threats. While a full study of that industry's role in global warming denial has not yet been written, two signature techniques are "astroturf" organizations (industry funded groups posing as spontaneous grassroots organizations) supporting denial, such as Cooler Heads Coalition [2007] and strategic lawsuits against public participation ("SLAPPS"), such as a Western Fuels Association suit against environmental groups that pointed to "coal" as a cause of global warming in a New York Times ad [Progressive Wire, 2001]. For a condemnation of global warming denial by a respected mainstream PR professional, see Hoggan [2005].

The Right Wing Communications Machine [11]

In the last 20 years a right wing coalition within the Republican Party has established an effective and highly disciplined communications machine that produces simple, unified, and highly amplified public messages, artfully coordinating short-run message goals with long-run message themes. Actors in the machine include public officials, party leaders, coalition faction leaders, media companies, right wing think tanks, columnists, cartoonists, and grass roots leaders who write letters to the editor.

The anti-carbon-tax coalition has substantial financial connections with the right-wing Republican coalition. For that and other reasons outside the scope of this Chapter, the communications machine has fully embraced and publicized the claims of global warming denial.

Oligopolistic Media

A number of major media corporations such as Fox News and The Wall Street Journal closely aligned with the communications machine have actively support global warming denial.

At the same time, most of what are commonly called "mainstream media" corporations have passively supported this campaign. In particular, they generally treat global warming as

---

By 2003, Exxon-Mobil was giving more than $1 million a year to an array of right-wing organizations opposing action on climate change -- including the Competitive Enterprise Institute, Frontiers of Freedom, the George C. Marshall Institute, the American Legislative Exchange Council, and the American Council for Capital Formation Center for Policy Research. [Gelbspan, 2004].

[11] "Noise machine" [Brock, 2004], "Republican propaganda machine" [Conason, 2003] and "Echo chamber" [Rampton and Stauber, 2004] are the most common names given to the communications machine by its

an unresolvable "he said, she said" controversy, rather than as a serious problem in which the truth can be discovered and made known through aggressive investigative journalism [Boykoff and Boykoff, 2004].

Tracing the detailed incentives that lead main-stream media corporations to passively support the goals of emitting corporations is beyond the scope of this essay, but see Bagdikian [1997] for a relevant analysis of the role of media concentration. Whatever those incentives may be, the end result has helped block the formation of a unified public demand for action–and made possible the very considerable successes of the anti-carbon-tax lobby.

Campaign Contributions and Conventional Lobbying

Corporate emitters are heavy contributors to national and state-wide political campaigns and support a heavy lobbying presence in Washington DC and in state capitals [Gelbspan 1998, 2004].

Two Bush Administrations

It is well known that many of the highest officials in both Bush administrations had stints of highly paid employment in the petroleum industry, including both Presidents and (in the second Bush administration) Vice President Richard Cheney, Secretary of State Condoleezza Rice, and Secretary of Defense Donald Rumsfeld. Continued close contacts between the administration and energy company executives and lobbyists are well documented [Gelbspan, 2004]. The firm opposition of both administrations to the carbon tax and equivalent policies is also well known.[12]

The Democratic Party

While most of the national officials who support action on global warming are in the Democratic Party, it is not the case that the Democratic Party as a whole is committed to action. Corporate emitters are careful to contribute to candidates on both side of the aisle. The Clinton Administration negotiated and signed the Kyoto Treaty but (in the face of overwhelming bipartisan opposition in the Senate) did not submit it for ratification. Al Gore, now the most prominent supporter of action against global warming, failed (on advice of his handlers) to make the issue visible in his 2000 Presidential campaign. The Democratic Party failure can perhaps be best understood as resulting from political timidity in the face of corporate power rather than direct financial interest.[13]

---

analyzers and detractors. Its potential defenders do not admit to its existence and haven't suggested a preferred name.

[12] A full discussion of this political history would need to take into account changes in scientific evidence and understanding over time as they have influenced policymakers. However, note that as early as the UN's first World Climate Conference in 1979, many experts believed the case for precautionary action had already been made. That conference issued a Declaration [WMO, 1979] stating that human activity was increasing atmospheric CO_2 at a rate of .4% per year and that climate change would occur on a time scale comparable to that needed to redirect the world economy–but then merely called for more research and urged governments "to foresee and to prevent potential man-made changes in climate that might be adverse to the well-being of humanity."

[13] Which is not intended to defend the seriously flawed Kyoto treaty. While the principle that developed countries should take responsibility for most of the existing excess stock of greenhouse gases is ethically sound, the principle that developing countries should accept no emission limits at all is ethically unsound. Deciding whether such a treaty is better than no treaty is a pragmatic question.

Summary of Lobbying and PR Successes and Failures

Among the major successes of the coalition in staving off a carbon tax or equivalent policies, as of this writing we have:

- failure of the environmental protection agency to define greenhouse gases as a regulatable pollutant
- failure of the US and Canada to sign the Kyoto accords
- failure to increase CAFE milage standards after 1985
- effective relaxation of CAFE mileage standard after 1985 through failure to appropriately regulate SUVs and minivans and light trucks
- failure to adopt national efficiency standards for heating and cooling of buildings
- public policy focus on distractions such as ethanol and research on the hydrogen economy [14]
- public acceptance of the conventional wisdom that a carbon tax as such is not politically feasible.

At the same time, the coalition lobby is not all-powerful. Their noteworthy policy defeats have included:

- original adoption of CAFE standards in 1975
- adoption of air quality standards for nitrogen oxides, sulphur oxides, and ozone
- adoption of energy standards for home appliances
- increasing efforts to regulate auto mileage and air pollution at the state and local level.

However, these policies were primarily aimed at energy independence or healthy air and provided no impetus for efforts directly against global warming. More recently, California and many other state and local governments have begun to agree to regulate greenhouse gases as such [see, e.g., Eilperin, 2007], a movement that represents the first direct defeat the US anti-carbon-tax coalition has ever experienced.

It is also significant that some petroleum companies are backing away from extreme forms of global warming denial. Exxon-Mobile is detaching itself from some of the astroturf groups it funded, and Shell and BP have made public statements supporting the need for policy action on global warming. However in 2007 Exxon-Mobile apparently funded efforts to attack the latest UN consensus scientific statement on global warming [Sample, 2007].

The coalition's successes were enabled for well over a decade by thoroughly mistaken public opinion [see e.g., Saad, 2002]. However, increasingly large majorities of Americans have recently come to believe that global warming really is happening, and are prepared to support unspecified action–but they remain confused and divided on the urgency and desirability of specific policy proposals [Trei, 2007]. Finally, it is significant that in 2005 Fox news ran a one hour scientifically-accurate documentary on global warming (albeit with an initial disclaimer pointing out its "one-sided" nature).

---

[14] See Socolow and Pacala [2006]. Ethanol-based fuels have not been shown to reduce net emission of greenhouse gases; hydrogen is not a fuel source but rather an intermediate fuel that won't be technologically ripe within our window of effective action.

Countervailing Corporate Power

Some corporations that stand to gain from effective action against global warming have provided limited support for a carbon tax. For example, several major insurance companies have expressed concern about impacts of global warming on costs of hurricane damage, and have sponsored scientific study of the issue. Also number of small corporations take an active interest in energy conservation or in developing energy sources that don't produce greenhouse gases [Hartman and Stafford, 1997].

Public choice theorists beginning with Olson [1971] have given several reasons why countervailing lobbying efforts by profit-seeking corporations would be unlikely to prevail. The data given above suggests that these theorists are correct. They argue:

First, because lobbying requires substantial threshold costs to be effective, it is mostly done by disproportionately large corporations that can afford to spread those costs over large profits. Established firms invested in successful existing technologies and regulatory regimes are nearly always larger than startup firms gambling on untried new technologies and proposed new regulations. This leads to bias in favor of established, more polluting technologies and against newer, less polluting technologies.

Second, while it is theoretically feasible for smaller corporations to band together to support lobbying on major policy issues, because of free-ride problems it is not profit-maximizing to do so. Small corporations typically lobby on very small issues, such as getting their next government contract.

Third, as argued in Section 2, profit-maximizing corporations heavily discount the future and consequently have relatively short planning horizons. Since the costs of corrective action against greenhouse gases must be incurred now, paid in part by actually existing corporations, while the benefits will be enjoyed later, at a time beyond the planning horizons of many corporations, corporations are more likely to gain from opposing than supporting corrective action.

The Regulation of Lobbying

In effect, lobbying and campaign finance reform is opposed by corporations and business organizations almost across the board. Whatever their individual opinions on lobbying and campaign practices, large numbers of businesses participate in a system of lobbying whose interlocking internal incentives make the system highly resistant to reform.

In contrast to the carbon tax, opposition to lobbying reform is largely carried out in secret. Only limited efforts are being made to convince either the electorate or public interest groups that corporate lobbying and campaign contributions are in the public interest, or that they are being adequately controlled. Indeed, there is a long-standing and widely shared public opinion that lobbying and campaign finance practices in the US are corrupt and unfair [Persily and Lammie, 2004]. In US experience, existence of unified public opinion by itself does not lead to reform (though it can block reform).

Instead of making major public relations efforts, supporters of the existing system make an implicit (and, behind closed doors, quite possibly an explicit) appeal to the self-interest of elected officials. Nearly every elected officials holding a major office in the US has received large sums of campaign contributions from business interests. Once officials are elected, they tend to have a substantial fund-raising advantage over out-of-office opponents. This advantage, combined with the increasingly effective electoral advertising and campaign techniques that large sums of money can buy, helps create a high degree of job security for incumbent politicians. In US House of Representatives, for example, even in the bell-weather election of 2006, some 95% of incumbents were re-elected. Consequently, supporting genuine reform in lobbying and campaign finance rules is contrary to the self interest of most incumbent politicians. (Of course other factors support the incumbency advantage as well; see e.g. Romeo [2006].)

A large majority of all national campaign contributions and lobbying expenditures come from business interests, largely associated with corporations [see e.g. La Raja and Hoffman, 2000]. The system works well for many businesses, because they have assured access to politicians who will give them a sympathetic hearing. Also, politicians who receive substantial contributions are generally known in advance to be sympathetic to the businesses that support them. There is no direct material incentive for most corporations to support reform, and strong material incentives to oppose it.

As an offsetting consideration, corporations in general might gain from a system of government with less perceived corruption. More concretely, campaign contributions can be seen as a shake-down operation, with an implied threat that politicians will turn against companies that do not contribute. However, as public choice theorists point out, the costs for an individual corporation of bucking the system could be high, while the benefits of any resulting changes in the system (e.g. reductions in coercive power exerted against donors by the campaign finance system) would be shared broadly across all corporations. That calculus suggests that bucking the system is rarely a profit-maximizing act.

In any case, it seems likely that most corporations stand to lose more from lobbying reform (in the coin of reduced political power) than they stand to gain (in the coin of reduced campaign contributions). One important point to understand is that campaign contributions that are extremely large from any politician's point of view (e.g. $1M) are insignificant from the point of view of a corporation like Exxon-Mobile–which in 2006 had some $40B in profits out of $378B in revenues. From a corporate point of view, political expenditures can have extremely high benefit-cost ratios.

Citizen efforts to reduce the political power of US corporations through regulatory reform have a long history [Corrado, 2003]. There is no reason to expect major breakthroughs in a time frame relevant to action on global warming.

An Interpretation of Corporate Behavior

There is strong evidence that major emitting corporations have followed neoclassical recommendations much more closely than stakeholder recommendations. In particular, their opposition to the carbon tax has been open, intense, and thus far successful—a success that depends on partly on a profit-motivated false discourse, as modeled by le Menestrel and de Bettignies [2002]. While there are emerging signs of strong public support for action, in the

US public support doesn't guarantee public action.[15] It seems reasonable to predict a long battle.

Existence of widespread and successful corporate lobbying to prevent or delay effective action on global warming, and against lobbying reform, suggests that regulatory mechanisms are not in place, or not sufficiently strong, to protect us from the consequences of socially destructive corporate lobbying. There are few signs that that will change during the window of opportunity for action against global warming.

5. CRITERIA AND OPTIONS FOR REFORM

Both the incentive structure of major corporate emitters, and their actual behavior in the case of public policy on greenhouse gases, approximates the neoclassical norm rather than stakeholder or other norms. Under the assumptions of this Chapter that behavior is socially destructive. How can that behavior be altered, and what particular structures need to be changed? That is, what can ethical theory tell us about detailed structural reform?

We have been considering three possible sources of social control: internal incentive structure, external regulation of lobbying, and countervailing lobbying power. The four frameworks give conflicting answers:

- Countervailing power is the only form of social control fully acceptable to all ethical theories, but by assumption in the case of global warming that form has been inadequate.
- Internal incentive reform is strongly discouraged by neoclassical theory. (Exception: the theory could support reforms to reduce diversion of profits from shareholders to managers.) However the other three frameworks could support internal incentive changes designed to reduce corporate opposition to the carbon tax. Those changes could be voluntarily adopted by shareholders, or could be imposed by government regulation.
- Lobbying reform tends to be discouraged by stakeholder theory. Since corporate managers are expected to pursue broad ethical ends, presumably they can also be trusted with a substantial degree of political power. However the other three frameworks support lobbying reforms.

Incentive design, organizational design, mechanism design, and implementation theory have large, complex, and mostly non-empirical literatures that are relevant to these possible reforms. This Chapter will not attempt to either to apply those literatures or provide specific recommendations. What we can do here is develop ethical criteria for acceptable structures, as well as suggestions for possible structural reforms that might be explored in the future.

---

[15] A comparison with health insurance may be instructive. Strong majorities of Americans have supported national health care ever since polling on the topic began in the 1930s [Steinmo and Watts, 1995].Yet because of the opposition of a major industry (coupled no doubt with political errors on the part of its proponents) the US still doesn't have it. As a share of GNP, the anti-carbon-tax coalition is comparable in size to the private health care industry.

Many of the reform options for corporations discussed below could be extended as well to organizations that contest corporate power, including labor unions and environmental groups, but we will not address those possible extensions.

Criteria for Reform in Internal Corporate Incentive Structures

Each of the four ethical theories makes recommendations concerning the internal incentive structure of corporations. While the theories are not so specific as to require particular structures, they do specify general lines of responsibility and general criteria for what constitutes a good structure. In particular, each theory implies that governance and incentive structures should lead corporations to respond to the interests of particular classes of individuals. The theories differ only with respect to who those individuals are. To recap:

- Neoclassical corporate structures should respond to the narrow profit interests of shareholders of that corporation while remaining within the law.
- Stakeholder corporate structures should respond to the broad interests of stakeholders of that corporation.
- Marxian corporate structures should respond to the broad interests of all workers.
- Common ethics corporate structures should respond to the broad interests of all human beings.

Structural Reform Examples

Some structural reforms can be adopted voluntarily by the Board of Directors or by stakeholder groups; others would need to be imposed by government.

Stakeholder Representation on the Board of Directors
The most clearcut structural implication of stakeholder theory is that each significant stakeholder group should have direct representation on the Board of Directors. Stakeholder representatives will be ineffective unless they are selected independently by the stakeholder groups themselves, and have full access to the powers and information available to other Directors.

Any such proposal raises complex issues of social incentive. A web of supplier or customer representatives creates significant opportunities for anti-competitive collusion. Labor representation is hard to reconcile with management's strategic need for confidentiality in the course of collective bargaining. The stakeholder approach is vacuous until the relevant stakeholder groups have been defined, and there is no agreement on how this should be accomplished. Also, stakeholder representatives are a minority voice that may be ineffective.

In contrast, the most clearcut structural implication of neoclassical theory is that only shareholders should be represented on the Board.

Marxian and common ethics frameworks are potentially supportive of experiments in stakeholder representation on Boards of Directors, but not clearly in favor of stakeholder representation as a settled principle. Because both frameworks treat large classes of persons equally, they provide no clear basis for singling out particular stakeholder groups or organizations for representation. The Marxian theory in particular focuses on the interests of all workers, not the interests of workers in a given corporation. While providing corporate employees with representation might seem an attractive idea, acting in the narrow interests of the relatively small group of workers at any one firm is far different from acting in the broad interests of all workers.

Ethics Officers and Ombudsmen

In all ethical frameworks, it makes theoretical sense for the Board of Directors to appoint an independent officer with the power to seek out ethical violations within the firm, attempt to correct them, and report on such cases to the Board of Directors. These officers should have the power to see any documents of the corporation, to question any employees in private, to promise confidentiality, and to provide full reports to all members of the Board of Directors. Ideally they would have a specific term of office and be very difficult to remove. In larger corporations they need an independent staff.

A majority of large corporations do in fact have such officers, though they not always given the full powers they need. It is an open question as to whether ethics officers are effective in practice. They are unlikely to have much effect unless the Board itself is committed to ethical behavior [Weaver, Treviño, and Cochran, 1999].

Ethics Codes

The Board should make its intended concept of ethics as explicit as possible. Ethics codes accomplish that goal and are a supplementary form of social control [Thompsen, 2004]. About 90% of Fortune 500 do have ethics codes [Reichert,. Webb, and Thomas, 2000].

The concept of ethical behavior ethics officers and codes should enforce depends of course on the assumed ethical framework. The most forgiving ethical concept is the neoclassical notion that all is allowed except law breaking and inefficient use of company resources. The most restrictive ethical concept comes from the common ethics, which forbids any action that erodes the common good.

Stakeholder Representatives

A narrower form of ethics officer would a corporate officer charged with protecting the interests of a defined stakeholder class. To be fully effective, they would need the same kinds of powers and institutional position as an ethics officer.

There are theoretical reasons to expect that stakeholder representatives might be more effective than ethics officers. The stakeholder representative has a narrower and much clearer charge and a well defined constituency. The representative can consult with the constituency for guidance on what priorities really matter, while the constituency can help defend the power and effectiveness of its representative.

Stakeholder Organizations

A labor union is an example of an independent organization protecting the interests of a particular stakeholder group within a particular corporation. On the face of it, stakeholder corporations should welcome the existence of organizations to articulate and protect stakeholder interests that the corporation itself recognizes as important. Such an organization is likely to be considerably more effective than an ethics officer or stakeholder representative, because it is backed by the power of collective action.

In fact however most US corporations strenuously oppose the organization or recognition of new labor unions [Rose and Chaison, 2001]. It seems likely that, to the extent that other types of stakeholder organizations were effective, corporations would tend to oppose them as well. This could be taken as additional evidence that corporations fit the neoclassical mold much better than the stakeholder mold.

Alternatively, it could be argued that stakeholder organizations create too much conflict and undercut the interests of the corporation as a whole; and that it is better to rely on top managers to make a good faith effort to reconcile stakeholder interests. In response, it has to be noted that the interests of competing stakeholder groups really are, at least in part, in conflict with each other. Since top managers themselves are one of these competing groups, saying that managers should be the ultimate arbiters has the effect of putting their interests above all others.

Another possibility would be to charge the Board of Directors with harmonizing interests. However, the Board is not in a good position to make the kinds of operational decisions that are needed. The Board's job is setting over-all policy, while top managers necessarily make the day to day decisions.

Job Tenure

Traditional employment is at the will of the employer. Creating job rights, especially the right not be discharged without good cause, increases the power of individual workers to act on their conscience. Moreover, having job rights is in fact a very important interest of one particular stakeholder class–namely, employees. However job rights may also increase an employee's power to obstruct profit maximization and other legitimate stakeholder interests.

Whistle-Blower Laws and Rules

Whistle-blower protection is explicitly linked to acts of conscience. Therefore it is targeted much more precisely than is job rights on encouraging individual workers to act on conscience. Managers often argue that particular claims for whistle-blower protection are opportunistic and insincere, but journalistic literature suggests that is rarely the case. In particular, existing laws in the US have proven too weak to provide much protection to whistle-blowers, so it is hard to imagine rational reasons other than conscience (or possibly as a self defense of last resort) for a whistle-blower to go public with information that is embarrassing to that individual's organization.

On the other hand, if whistle-blower statutes are strengthened sufficiently to provide real protection, then undoubtedly there will be cases where employees use that protection opportunistically. In general, any form of legal rights or protection creates opportunities for exploitative behavior, but that is hardly an argument against the existence of rights. The creation of new rights does need to be subjected to benefit-cost tests, but it hard to imagine any right more clearly linked to the general public good than whistle-blower protection.

Whistle-blower protection is supported by all four ethical frameworks. However the detailed recommendations would differ between frameworks. All frameworks would be seem consistent with:

- legal protection for employees who take evidence of corporate law breaking to top managers or the Board of Directors
- legal protection for employees who take evidence of corporate law breaking to government authorities, after top management is notified and fails to take action
- internal corporate rules and employment agreements providing protection for employees who take evidence of diversion of corporate resources to the Board of Directors.

All except the neoclassical framework would seem consistent with:

☐   internal corporate rules and employment agreements providing protection for employees who take evidence of corporate actions contrary to stakeholder interests to the Board of Directors.

The Marxian and common ethics frameworks would seem consistent with:

☐   legal protection for employees who take evidence of corporate law breaking directly government authorities, without consulting management.

At the same time, it has to be recognized that whistle-blowers almost always alienate their immediate superiors, and no amount of protection is likely to reinstate a comfortable set of working relationships. Whistle-blowing is a useful social control technique only for extreme cases.

Criteria for Reform of Lobbying and Political Action

All four frameworks accept at least the possibility that lobbying reforms might be needed to reduce the effectiveness of opposition to the carbon tax (with stakeholder theory standing out as the most skeptical). The four theories provide little guidance about how lobbying practices might be reformed, but it is possible to reason from general principles.

Provision of Information
Corporations possess a major share of all private information on how the economy actually operates. Much of that information is needed by policymakers when they make decisions. To the extent possible that information needs to be provided voluntarily, if only because involuntary means of acquisition are both costly and distorting of the information. Moreover all four frameworks recognize corporate activities as valuable and necessary parts of the economy that need to be supported by appropriate government policies. It is important that corporations provide feedback to government on the effects of laws and regulation. It follows that corporations should have the freedom to volunteer information for use in policy-making.

In the global warming case, the power of large corporations to block the carbon tax has not hinged on honest sharing of private information, but rather on convincing a broad public of the truth of false statements. (See Hertz [2003] for similar examples.) Reforms are needed that somehow encourage the direct provision of honest information to policy-makers, but discourage the wide dissemination of false information.

Influence on Elections

There is no obvious ethical justification for major corporations to have great influence over the outcomes of political elections.

The neoclassical framework includes no explicit explanation of how government should be motivated to control externalities and protect the common good, but it's hard to speak to modern ears of benign government as an achievable goal without appealing to the ideals and procedures of democracy. One-person one-vote democracy really is not consistent with a one-dollar one-vote system in which large corporations have major power over elections.

Marxian and common ethics are even less sympathetic to corporate electoral power than the neoclassical approach.

The stakeholder framework, however, does have some features that tend to support preservation of corporate electoral power. First, since managers are expected to reconcile stakeholder interests without government help, the framework does not provide any explicit rationale for government action. Second, since the framework is corporate-centered, it does tend to legitimate some degree of corporate political power. However, if faced with electoral outcomes that are unacceptable to its stakeholders and caused by the unbridled electoral power of corporate emitters, managers governed by stakeholder ethics should be willing to support a reigning in of that corporate power.

Influence on Well-being and Careers of Public Officials

There is no obvious ethical justification for corporations to have any power over the personal utility of public officials. Officials are expected to respond to the voters and the law, not to personal inducements.

An efficiency argument for allowing the revolving door between government and industry is that in some cases public officials may need expertise that can only be learned in the private sector, and vice versa. But to whatever extent that claim may be true, there is no obvious basis for opposing elaborate sanitizing procedures that would so far as possible reduce or eliminate incentives for public officials to act against the public interest.

Free Speech Issues

Limitations on corporate political activities raise two Constitutional free speech issues: first, whether corporations should have some of the same speech rights as natural persons; second, whether natural persons should have unlimited rights to spend money on behalf of candidates. Any lobbying reform effort will have to grapple with these questions–questions on which business ethical frameworks do not provide any simple guidance.

In the utilitarian meta-model assumed in this Chapter, corporations are not persons, meaning that they do not have their own utility functions and are not the subjects of anyone's ultimate concern. They are simply instrumentalities for improving human welfare. The argument for the legal fiction of corporate personhood is that human welfare might be improved on average if we grant certain rights to corporations. That is a complex question of social design we can't address here.

Lobbying and Political Reform Examples

Transparency

Public officials could be required to log and publish all contacts with corporate representatives. Such meetings could be recorded and/or covered by open meetings laws. Public officials could be required to make public all of their financial holdings and transactions, plus those of their immediate family. Corporations could be required to give a full and unified accounting of all of their advocacy activities, stating specific policy goals and categorizing funds by goals. Media companies could be required to reveal financial connections with non-media companies. Media companies could be required to disclose all content-related communications with advertisers and business partners.

Conflicts of Interest

Public officials above a certain level and their immediate families could be required to divest all holdings in specific companies or in industry-specific investment funds (as opposed to allowing so-called blind trusts).

Gifts to Officials

Existing limits could be tightened.

The Revolving Door

Transition between related positions in government and the private sector could be limited by a lengthy cooling off period. Former public officials could be limited from lobbying or contracting with government for a significant period of time. It could be presumed that an official who takes an action notably favoring a particular corporation and later takes a job with that corporation acted out of corrupt self-interest.

Direct Campaign Contributions

Corporations could be forbidden from making campaign contributions. Corporate executives could be forbidden from bundling or coordinating their contributions or contributing in equal amounts.

Dirty PR

Specific criminal penalties could be provided for threats or harassment designed to prevent publication or dissemination of adverse messages. Full disclosure of funding could be required in all public attacks on individual persons.

Indirect Campaign Contributions

Corporations could be forbidden from making contributions to political issue advertising.

Astroturf Organizations and Biased Think Tanks

Corporations could be forbidden from contributing to issue-oriented nonprofits. Issue-oriented organizations could be required to be fully transparent about their funding sources.

Biased Research

Issue-oriented organizations that publish research claims could be covered by specific fraud statutes. Tax exempt organizations that perform research could have their research data subject to open information laws (with suitable personal privacy protections). Scholarly journals could require full disclosure of possible conflicts of interest by authors.

Media Oligopolies

Financial transactions of major media companies could be subjected to transparency rules. Cross-ownership of media firms could be restricted. Stronger antitrust rules could be applied within or between media modes of delivery. Equal time rules could be reimposed.

6. CONCLUSION

Even though the potential consequences of global warming are immense, the arguments presented here are in some respects much too weak to support the large political reforms being suggested. Only a handful of corporations are leading the charge against the carbon tax. Without their leadership and resources, there is every likelihood that global warming could have been handled much like the hole in the ozone layer–a problem which, although not entirely solved, has been substantially ameliorated through ordinary national and international political processes, accomplished within about 20 years once scientists were in agreement on the problem. What distinguishes the two cases is the fact that production and use of chlorofluorocarbons constitutes a relatively small share of world product, while emission-dependent petroleum companies and automobile producers are among the largest corporations in the world. Nevertheless, it may be hard to see why a problem caused mainly by a small number of large corporations needs to be solved by fundamental legal changes that would affect millions of smaller corporations. If changes in corporate governance or regulation really are needed, one might want to limit them to major emitters.

Moreover, making large changes in fundamental corporate governance and free speech structures seems on the face of it an even tougher political sell than simply adopting a carbon tax. Thus one searches for a less drastic solution. Pragmatically, it would seem to make better political sense to focus political energies on the carbon tax itself rather than on power relationships.

Several points should be made in response. First, the main argument in this Chapter has been ethical, not pragmatic. If one does accept the premises of stakeholder ethics, then one should accept the rightness of changes in corporate governance to make corporations more responsive to stakeholders–whether or not those changes are politically feasible at the present time. But if on the contrary one accepts the premises of neoclassical ethics, then one should accept the rightness of making changes in government regulation to offset the negative externalities of profit-maximization–even if those changes involve curtailing the lobbying power of major corporations.

Second, while the case of global warming is important, it is also merely an example that raises larger issues of structure and governance. The analysis of observed incentive structures given in Section 3 was very general and not limited to the case of global warming. It suggests that actually existing incentive structures can't be fully justified by *any* major theory of business ethics. That fact by itself makes a significant case for change. Moreover the analysis in Section 4 of lobbying against the carbon tax shows that these misaligned incentive structures can have very important negative consequences.

Third, global warming cannot reasonably be viewed as an isolated example. Instead, it is one example from a rather long list of environmental problems, most of which have helped cause the collapse of entire civilizations in the past, and all of which now constitute an interacting set of live threats to our own civilization. Jared Diamond's *Collapse* [2005] lists those threats as follows:[16]

- Accelerating loss of natural habitats
- Overexploitation and destruction of fisheries
- Mass extinction and loss of genetic diversity
- Soil loss from erosion, salinization, acidification or alkalinization, and nutrient exhaustion
- Increasing costs of fossil fuel extraction
- Depletion of fresh water
- Full bio-utilization of solar energy (limiting the expansion of crops)
- Toxic emissions
- Transfer of destructive alien species
- Atmospheric modification, leading to loss of lowlands to rising seas
- Population growth
- Growth in resource demand per person.

As Diamond argues, all of these threats can be managed if human beings work together and make reasonable compromises in favor of the common good. However, because corporations are deeply embedded in every corner of our life, every useful effort to address these threats already does or soon will conflict with the narrow profit-making interests of particular corporations. These conflicts occur at all levels of government and involve corporations of all sizes and in all industries. Therefore it is reasonable to assume that self-interested corporate lobbying will continue to be an impediment to solving problems that, at this point in our history, need to be solved relatively quickly. That lobbying would not be important if corporations had only minimal power. But, as illustrated here, large corporations can be immensely powerful political actors. Dealing successfully with environmental threats depends on dealing successfully with the internal incentives and/or external power of corporations.

REFERENCES

Arendt, Hannah. 1958. *Origins of Totalitarianism, second enlarged edition*, Cleveland OH: Meridian Books.

Bagdikian, Ben H. 1997. *The Media Monopoly*, New York NY: Beacon Press.

Bartels, Larry M.; Hugh Heclo; Rodney E. Hero; and Lawrence R. Jacob. 2004. *Inequality and American Governance*, Task Force on Inequality and American Democracy,

American Political Science Association (available at http://www.apsanet.org/imgtest/ governancememo.pdf, accessed March 3, 2007).

Bierbaum, Rosina M.; John P. Holdren; Michael C. MacCracken; Richard H. Moss; and Peter H. Raven (eds.) 2007. *Confronting climate change: Avoiding the unmanageable and managing the unavoidable*, Scientific Expert Group Report on Climate Change and Sustainable Development; Prepared for the 15th Session of the Commission on Sustainable Development, Washington DC: United Nations Foundation.

Boykoff, Maxwell T.; and Jules M. Boykoff. 2004. "Balance as bias: global warming and the US prestige press," *Global Environmental Change-Human and Policy Dimensions* 14, July, pp. 125-136.

Brock, David. 2004. *The Republican Noise Machine: Right-Wing Media and How It Corrupts Democracy*, New York NY: Crown Publishers.

Burress, David. 2001. "Modeling Global Catastrophe," Presented to the University of Kansas Hall Center for the Humanities Faculty Colloquium on Globalization, Ethics, and Culture; September (available at http://www.people.ku.edu/~dburress/globalmodel.pdf).

Burress, David. 2005. "What global emission regulations should corporations support?," *Journal of Business Ethics* 60(4), September, pp. 317-339 .

Business Roundtable. 1997. *Statement on Corporate Governance*, September (accessed May 30, 2003 at http://www.brtable.org/document.cfm/11).

Cho, Charles H.; Dennis M. Patten; and Robin W. Roberts. 2006. "Corporate Political Strategy: An Examination of the Relation between Political Expenditures, Environmental Performance, and Environmental Disclosure," *Journal of Business Ethics* 67(2), August, Pages 139-154.

Conason, Joe. 2003. *Big Lies: The Right-Wing Propaganda Machine and How It Distorts the Truth*, New York NY: St. Martin's.

Cook, John S.; and Oscar J. Holzmann. 1976. "Current Cost and Present Value in Income Theory," *The Accounting Review* 51(4), October, pp. 778-787.

Cooler Heads Coalition. 2007. *Global Warming*, website. (Available at http://www. globalwarming.org/; accessed March 1, 2007).

Corrado, Anthony. 2003. "Money and Politics: A History of Federal Campaign Finance Law," Chapter 2 in *The New Campaign Finance Sourcebook*, Washington DC: Brookings Institution, (available at http://www.brookings.edu/gs/cf/sourcebk/chap2.PDF, accessed March 3, 2007).

Crichton, Michael. 2004. *State of Fear*, New York NY: HarperColllins.

Derber, Charles. 2003. *People before Profit: The New Globalization in an Age of Terror, Big Money and Economic Crisis*, New York: St. Martin's Press.

Devine, Tom. undated. *Courage Without Martyrdom: The Whistleblower's Survival Guide*, Washington DC: Government Accountability Project (available at http://www. whistleblower.org/template/page.cfm?page_id=43, accessed March 3, 2007).

Diamond, Jared. 2005. *Collapse–how societies choose to fail or succeed*, New York NY: Viking.

Donaldson, Thomas; and Lee E. Preston. 1995. "The Stakeholder Theory of the Corporation: Concepts, Evidence, and Implications," *Academy of Management Review* 20(1), pp. 65-91.

---

[16] For an alternative catalog of catastrophic threats, see my working paper [Burress, 2001].

Duffel, Mike. 2006. "National Issues Affecting State & Local Tax Administration," presented to New York City Department of Finance – TAXRAPP Conference, October 26 (available at www.nyc.gov/html/dof/downloads/taxrapp_filing.ppt, accessed March 4, 2007).

Eilperin, Juliet. 2007. "Western States Agree to Cut Greenhouse Gases," *Washington Post,* Tuesday, February 27, page A08.

Friedman, Milton. 1970. "The Social Responsibility of Business Is to Increase Its Profits," *New York Times Magazine,* September 1, 1970. Reprinted in Tom L. Beauchamp and Norman E. Bowie, eds., 1993, *Ethical Theory and Business,* Englewood Cliffs N.J.: Prentice-Hall.

Gelbspan, Ross. 1998. *The Heat is On* (revised edition), Reading MA: Perseus Books.

Gelbspan, Ross. 2004. *Boiling Point,* New York NY: Basic Books.

Goldman, Alan H. 1980. "Business Ethics: Profits, Utilities, and Moral Rights," *Philosophy and Public Affairs* 9(3), Spring, pp. 260-286.

Grant, Colin. 1991. "Friedman fallacies," *Journal of Business Ethics* 10(12), December, Pages 907-914.

Hermalin, Benjamin E.; and Michael S. Weisbach. 1998. "Endogenously Chosen Boards of Directors and Their Monitoring of the CEO," *The American Economic Review* 88(1), March, pp. 96-118.

Hartman, Cathy L.; and Edwin R. Stafford. 1997. "Green Alliances: Building New Business with Environmental Groups," *Long Range Planning* 30(2), pp. 184-196.

Hertz, N. 2003. *The silent takeover,* New York NY: Harper Business.

Hoggan, Jim. 2006. "Slamming the Climate Skeptic Scam," (availble at http://www.desmogblog.com/slamming-the-climate-skeptic-scam; accessed March 2, 2007).

Intergovernmental Panel on Climate Change. 2007. *Climate Change 2007: The Physical Science Basis–Summary for Policymakers–Contribution of Working Group I to the Fourth Assessment Report of the Intergovernmental Panel on Climate Change* (available at http://www.ipcc.ch/SPM2feb07.pdf; accessed March 1, 2007).

Keffer, Jane M.; and Ronald Paul Hill. 1997. "An Ethical Approach to Lobbying Activities of Businesses in the United States," *Journal of Business Ethics* 16(12-13), September, pages 1371-1379.

Khera, Inder P. 2001. "Business Ethics East vs. West: Myths and Realities," *Journal of Business Ethics* 30(1), March, Pages 29-39.

Leggett, Jeremy. 2001. *The Carbon War: Global Warming and the End of the Oil Era,* London UK: Routledge.

Little, Ian M.D. 2002. *Ethics, Economics, and Politics: Principles of Public Policy,* New York: Oxford University Press.

Lomborg, Bjørn. 2001. *The Skeptical Environmentalist – Measuring the Real State of the World,* Cambridge UK: Cambridge University Press.

Marc Le Menestrel; and Henri-Claude de Bettignies. 2002. "Processes and Consequences in Business Ethical Dilemmas: The Oil Industry and Climate Change," *Journal of Business Ethics* 41(3), December, Pages 251-266.

McCright, Aaron M.; and Riley E. Dunlap. 2000. "Challenging Global Warming as a Social Problem: An Analysis of the Conservative Movement's Counter-Claims," *Social Problems* 47(4), November, pp. 499-522.

Milgrom, Paul; and John Roberts. 1992. *Economics, Organization and Management*, London UK: Prentice-Hall.

OECD. 2000. *Guidelines for Multinational Enterprise, Revision 2000*, Organization for Economic Cooperation and Development (accessed March 24, 2004 at http://www. oecd.org/document/28/0,2340,en_2649_34889_2397532_1_1_1_1,00.html).

Olson, Mancur. 1971. *The Logic of Collective Action – Public Goods and the Theory of Groups*, revised, Cambridge MA: Harvard University Press.

Oreskes, Naomi. 2004. "Beyond the Ivory Tower: The Scientific Consensus on Climate Change," *Science* 306(5702), December 3, p. 1686 .

Paladino, Marcelo; and Alberto Willi. 2002. "Business Managers: Leaders in Society?," *Journal of Corporate Citizenship* 5, Spring, pp. 37-55.

Persily, Nathaniel; and Kelli Lammie. 2004. "Perceptions of Corruption and Campaign Finance: When Public Opinion Determines Constitutional Law," *University of Pennsylvania Law Review* 153, pp.119-180 (available at http://lsr.nellco.org/ cgi/viewcontent.cgi?article=1033&context=upenn/wps, accessed March 2, 2007).

Progressive Newswire. 2001. "Environmental Organizations Defeat Coal Industry Global Warming SLAPP Suit – Federal Judge Dismisses Coal Industry Suit," Common Dreams NewsCenter, April 6 (available at http://www.commondreams.org/news2001/ 0406-02.htm, accessed March 4, 2007).

La Raja, Ray; and Alana Hoffman. 2000. "Who Benefits from Soft Money Contributions?", Institute of Governmental Studies and Citizens' Research Foundation Working Paper 2000-14, July (availabe at http://www.igs.berkeley.edu/publications/workingpapers/ WP2000-14.pdf, accessed March 3, 2007).

Rampton, Sheldon; and John Stauber. 2004. *Banana Republicans--How the Right Wing Is Turning America into a One-Party State*, New York NY: Jeremy Tarcher/Penguin.

Reichert, Alan K.; Marion S. Web; and Edward G. Thomas. 2000. "Corporate Support for Ethical and Environmental Policies: A Financial Management Perspective," *Journal of Business Ethics* 25(1), May, Pages 53-64.

Romero, David W. 2006. "What They Do Does Matter: Incumbent Resource Allocations and the Individual House Vote," *Political Behavior* 28(3), September, pp. 241-258.

Rose, Joseph;. and Gary Chaison. 2001. "Unionism in Canada and the United States in the 21st Century: The Prospects for Revival," *Relations Industrielles* 56, pp. 34-65.

Saad, Lydia. 2002. "Poll Analyses: Americans Sharply Divided on Seriousness of Global Warming – Only one-third consider the problem grave," Gallup News Service, March 25.

Sample, Ian. 2007. "Scientists offered cash to dispute climate study," Friday, February 2 (available at http://www.guardian.co.uk/print/0,,329703480-103681,00.html, accessed March 4, 2007).

Socolow, Robert H.; and Stephen W. Pacala. 2006. "A Plan to Keep Carbon in Check," *Scientific American* 295(3), pp. 50-59.

Sourcewatch. 2007. "Global Climate Coalition," at http://www.sourcewatch.org/index. php?title=Global_Climate_Coalition (accessed March 2, 2007).

Stauber, John C.; and Sheldon Rampton. 1995. *Toxic Sludge is Good for You: Lies, Damn Lies and the Public Relations Industry*, Monroe ME: Common Courage Press.

Steinmo, Sven; and Jon Watts. 1995. "It's the Institutions, Stupid!: Why the United States Can't Pass Comprehensive National Health Insurance" *Journal of Health Politics Policy and Law*, 20(2), pp. 329-372 (reprinted in *Health Policy*, James Warner Bjorkman and Christa Altenstetter, eds. Cheltenham: Edward Elgar Publishing Limited, 1998, pp. 255-298; earlier draft available at http://stripe.colorado.edu/~steinmo/stupid.htm, accessed March 4, 2007).

Stern, Nicolas. 2006. *Stern Review: The Economics of Climate Change*, Cambridge UK: Science Marketing (available at http://www.hm-treasury.gov.uk/independent_reviews/ stern_review_economics_climate_change/sternreview_index.cfm; accessed March 1, 2007).

Thomsen, Steen. 2001. "Business Ethics as Corporate Governance," *European Journal of Law and Economics* 11(2), March, Pages 153-164.

Trei, Lisa. 2007. "Public agrees global warming exists but also divided over severity of problem," *Stanford News–Stanford Report*, February 21 (available at http://news-service.stanford.edu/news/2007/february21/gwaaassr-022107.html, accessed March 4, 2007).

Vold, George B.; and Thomas J. Bernard. 1986. *Theoretical Criminology, Third Edition*, Oxford: Oxford University Press.

Ward, Peter D. 2006. "Impact from the Deep: Overview/Mass Extinctions," *Scientific American*, October, p. 64-71.

Weaver, Gary R.; Linda Klebe Treviño; and Philip L. Cochran. 1999. "Corporate Ethics Practices in the Mid-1990's: An Empirical Study of the Fortune 1000," *Journal of Business Ethics* 18(3), February, pp. 283-294.

Wilcke, Richard W. 1983. "Business on the Take—Whose Fault?," *Competition* 4(5), September–December, p. 2.

Wilcke, Richard W. 2004. "An Appropriate Ethical Model for Business and a Critique of Milton. Friedman's Thesis," *The Independent Review* IX(2), Fall, pp. 187–209.

World Meterological Association. 1979. *The Declaration of the World Climate Conference*, Geneva: WMA (available at http://unesdoc.unesco.org/images/0003/000376/037648eb. pdf, accessed March 4, 2007).

In: Contemporary Issues in Business Ethics   ISBN: 978-1-60021-773-9
Editors: M. W. Volcox, Th. O. Mohan, pp. 107-117   © 2007 Nova Science Publishers, Inc.

Chapter 4

BUSINESS ETHICS AND THE CORPORATE WORLD

Almerinda Forte[*]

St. John's University, Division of Administration and Economics, Jamaica, NY, USA

Business ethics, especially among top managers, has become a topic of concern to the public and business community. As a result, much attention has focused on the development of moral reasoning in corporate individuals. Past research examining individual and business decision behavior, indicates that several variables such the level of moral reasoning, perceived ethical climate, education, age, management level, work tenure, industry types and gender have a significant impact on individual decisions. The following outlines the major findings by researchers investiaging these variables.

James Rest developed the Defining Issues Test (DIT) from Kohlberg's six stages of moral judgment. The reasoning and the level of one's moral evelopment can be determined by this test (Rest, 1979). The DIT seeks the reasons behind the decisions and is used to determine the level of the respondent's oral development. The DIT presents the test-taker with a series of scenarios and offers the test-taker solutions based on different rationales. Even though two individuals may arrive at the same answer, their reasoning can reflect a substantial difference in moral development and level of critical thinking, which the DIT reveals. The scenarios and responses present fundamental, underlying structures of social thought instead of the fine descriptions of specific concepts and ideas. The long form of the DIT contains six moral dilemmas, each with a set of forced choice questions. An index measures the relative importance placed on principled moral thinking. The scores are computed to indicate the placement of the respondent on a scale analogous to Kohlberg's six stages. The short form of the DIT contains three ethical scenarios, each accompanied by a set of questions. A Likert-type scale records the scores on the test. The subject ranks different issues presented for each dilemma or scenario by level of importance. This ranking provided the researcher with the subjects' preference for certain modes of thinking or stage structure. The higher stage preferences are weighted and averaged by the researcher A "P-Score," i.e., a principled score, calculated from the averages, indicates the extent to which a subject reasons in terms of

[*] St. John's University, Associate Professor and Chairperson, Division of Administration & Economics, 8000 Utopia Parkway. Jamaica, NY 11439, (718) 990-2039 (voice).....fortea@stjohns.edu

principled ethical stages. The higher the P-score (which ranges from 0-90), the more moral reasoning the individual uses. The DIT also has an index of overall moral judgment development, consisting of a composite of all stage scores. Rest (1982, 1988) believed that the first three stages are not as significant as the latter three, and that each of the latter three stages operate with different importance for different individuals

Principled moral reasoning as measured by "P" scores was the dependent variable used in Forte's (2001) study. Forte's (2001) study found a mean "P" score of 35 with a standard deviation of 14.8. What should be noted is that this score is below the "P" score of 40 that Rest (1979) records as the average adult score. No definite reason can be given as to why the "P" scores of this sample fell slightly below the average adult "P" scores. Perhaps the results reflect the business environment. Bigel (1998) and Pennino (2001) found similar results in "P" scores researching business individuals.

In 1968, Harvard University's research division of the Graduate School of Business published two books on organizational work climates: Tagiuri and Litwin's *Organizational Climate, Exploration of a Concept,* and Litwin and Stringer's of *Motivation and Organizational Climate.* Litwin constructed a questionnaire to measure organizational climate. Working independently, Tagiuri investigated how executives perceived the environment in which they functioned. Litwin and Tagiuri reached the same conclusion: organizational climate influences the behavior of people in an organization (McKenna, 1993, p. 37).

Litwin and Stringer developed an instrument to collect perceptions of organizational environment. They contended that the realities of an organization are understood only as they are perceived by members of the organization (p. 42). Litwin and Stringer defined organizational climate operationally as the sum of perceptions of individuals working in the organization (p. 66).

Of importance to this research was their conclusion that organizational climate properties can be perceived by members of an organization and reported on by them through an appropriate questionnaire (p. 187).

Climate, according to Litwin and Stringer, influences organizational decisions by creating certain kinds of beliefs about what kind of consequences will follow from various actions (Litwin & Stringer 1968, p. 188). These authors conclude that members of organizations can offer an accurate perception of their firms' ethical climate.

Victor and Cullen in 1987 and 1988 studied the linkage between corporate ethical standards and organizational behavior. They designed an instrument that measured perceptions of ethical climate by members of an organization. Victor and Cullen prototyped organizations into categories of distinct ethical climate types (Caring, Law and Code, Rules, Instrumental, and Independence). The instrument they developed is a 36 statement survey questionnaire. Victor and Cullen not only concluded that corporations have distinct ethical climate types, but they also found that climate types influence managerial behavior and that climate types influence what ethical conflicts are considered and the process by which the conflicts are resolved.

Rest found that many studies "revealed that increased education is associated with higher levels of moral judgment" (Rest and Narvanez, 1994, p. 28). Years of formal education is a greater predictor of ethical reasoning and moral development than chronological age (Rest, 1986, p. 33). Rest summarized that "the evidence at hand suggests that adults in general do not show much advance beyond that accounted for by their level of education" (Rest, 1979, p.

113). Rest continued, "It is not specific moral experience as much as a growing awareness of the social world and one's place in it that seems to foster development in moral judgment. The people who develop in moral judgment are those who love to learn, who seek new challenges ... are reflective ... set goals ... take risks. ...(Rest, 1986, p. 57).

Mature managers may have more positive attitudes toward moral issues in business because of their more developed moral awareness. This explanation seems to be in accordance with Kohlberg's model of moral reasoning suggesting that individuals develop their capacity for moral reasoning over time. (Kuyala, 1995, p. 72) Touche Ross (1988) and Kelley et al. (1990) also reported a positive relationship between age and ethical behavior.

Lewin and Stephens (1994) state that post-conventional individuals are particularly likely to become leaders (Kohlberg et al., 1983), and as such have a special opportunity for organizational impact. Post-conventional or principled individuals believe that principles outweigh specific rules and interests, and view principles as universal, generalizable, and compelling. Principled individuals are very much concerned with right and wrong and with the dignity of the individual. Therefore, principled CEOs leaders at the highest levels will establish a climate of ethicality throughout their organizations and develop policies and processes that embody principles of respect for the individual. They will attempt to prevent wrongs committed in the name of the organization and not merely crimes of the organization (Lewin and Stephens, 1994, p. 198).

Drucker emphasizes that managers are responsible for the development and implementation of ethical decision making. He states, that "no one should ever become a manager unless he or she is willing to have his character serve as the model for subordinates" (David, Anderson, Lawrimore, 1990, pp. 31 & 32).

Sacasas and Cava (1990) state that good ethics requires that leadership become convinced of and committed to the notion that successful corporate governance requires more than just profit maximization.

Kelley, Ferrell, and Skinner in 1990 surveyed 1,500 marketing researchers. They found that respondents in their present positions for at least ten years reported their behavior to be more ethical than employees in their present positions for three to five years. Kelly, Ferrell, and Skinner suggested that employees after three to five years on a job may experience work frustrations. This may cause them to compromise their ethical values to advance their careers.

Posner and Schmidt (1984, 1987) suggested that the distinction between personal and organizational values of an employee becomes fuzzy over time. This happens not only the higher one advances up the organizational ladder, but also the longer one is employed by a particular organization. Posner and Schmidt alluded to a socialization process which influences this behavior. Harris in 1990 surveyed 148 individuals employed by the same organization at different management levels. He found that managers employed by the organization for at least ten years, which also included senior managers, were less tolerant of fraudulent practices than other employees.

On the other hand, Bigel (1998) investigated the ethical orientation of financial planners. Bigel hypothesized in his study that ethical orientation would increase with career tenure. This study showed a statistically significant decrease in ethical orientation from experienced (5-10 years) to established (10.1 + years). This finding was contrary to his hypothesized direction.

Numerous studies have been conducted on various professional fields such as accounting, nursing, teaching and medicine. These studies found that some of the service professions are prone to different levels of moral reasoning. This might suggest that there is something inherent in the industry's process that causes individual thought mechanisms to develop or not to develop to higher modes of moral development.

Forte (2001) did not find a statisical significance between industry types and the moral reasoning of individual managers.

Armstrong (1984, 1987) explored accountants' ethical reasoning and moral development. The results of Armstrong's research showed that CPAs and accounting students tended to be at lower levels of ethical reasoning than comparable groups of college-educated adults or college-age students.

Lampe and Finn (1992) studied accounting and CPAs in public firms but excluded partners. They compared subjects' DIT results to responses on a questionnaire containing seven short ethical scenarios. The results of Lampe and Finn's research found that both accounting students and practitioners tend to have lower DIT P scores than college-aged students, college-educated adults, and other professional groups such as law and medicine.

Studying the development of moral reasoning in nurses are Crisham, 1981a; Felton & Parsons, 1987; Gaul, 1987; Ketefian, 1981, 1989; Ketefian and Ormond, 1988; Mayberry, 1986. The moral reasoning of nurses was measured by the Defining Issues Test (DIT), or the Nursing Dilemma Test (NDT), developed by Crisham (1981b), which parallels the DIT. Crisham's research suggests that moral reasoning of nurses tends to increase with more formal education. The research showed that nurses' scores are usually equal to or sometimes higher than scores of other groups with similar academic credentials.

In the area of education, Diessner (1991) reviewed 30 studies and concluded that most teachers reasoned only at the conventional level. He used Kohlberg's interview format to measure the moral reasoning of teachers. Diessner found that most preservice and inservice teachers could recognize but were unable to produce postconventional thinking. The research also indicated that moral thinking is subject to change depending upon school leaders or the atmosphere of the schools in which the teachers serve.

Husted (1978) studied the moral reasoning ability of 488 medical students by utilizing the DIT test. The research found that medical students showed a preference for reasoning at stages 5 and 6.

While the mean "P" scores for females were higher than the mean "P" scores for males in Forte's (2001) study, no statistically significant correlations were found between gender and "P" scores. This finding is consistent with research conducted by Rest (1979) (1988), Derry (1989) and Harris (1990) and Pennino (2001). Rest found minimal differences between the moral reasoning scores of men and women. However, when differences did exist, females scored higher. Rest found that differences due to gender were not powerful when correlated with "P" scores. (Harris also found no differences between genders). Harris states, that with the exception of the self-interest construct, females, as a group, are not different from males in their degree of tolerance/intolerance to fraud, coercion, influence dealing, and deceit (1990, p. 744). Derry also found no moral reasoning differences between males and females. Derry's theory is that if general difference exist between men and women, they do not carry over into strong organizational cultures where both women and men are trained to think and judge as corporate members (Derry, 1989, p. 859). Pennino (2001) also did not find any difference between the moral reasoning of men and women.

Gilligan (1979, 1982) suggested that gender differences exist in the ways that men and women approach and solve ethical problems. She has argued that males typically take a justice orientation towards conflicts, emphasizing the importance of rights, justice, and obligations in the resolution of conflicts. Females, according to Gilligan, have a caring orientation, which emphasizes the importance of human relations and the welfare and well being of all parties involved. Gilligan also stresses that both males and females are capable of considering both perspectives, but one perspective or orientation predominates.

RECOMMENDATIONS

The following recommendations are divided into two sections: recommendations for the field and recommendations for future research.

RECOMMENDATIONS FOR THE FIELD

1. Managers and executive level employees of any age, especially older managers, may benefit from training devoted to shaping managers' ethical thought processes and decision making.

    Business education should continue to strongly emphasize business ethics in business curricula. All business subjects, such as accounting, management and marketing should challenge students with ethical dilemmas and situations requiring moral reasoning. Students should be made aware of the importance of ethical reasoning in corporate America.

2. Ethical soundness should be reinforced by engaging top management in social and ethical audits of the company. In addition, periodic ethical seminars should be organized to ensure ethical thought processes and decision making.

    Business educators must stress that a successful corporate leader has the ability to establish a climate of ethicality throughout their organization. They accomplish this by developing policies and processes that embody principles of respect for all individuals. Students can experience this through role playing and related activities.

3. Corporations should examine closely their perceived organizational work climate by analyzing the policies, code of ethics and all other processes that embody principles of respect for all individuals of their firms. These policies should be under continual review and dissemination.

4. Corporate leaders, as D'Aquila (1997) suggests, should always try to hire managers and staff employees who are well educated and well experienced in their field. Since managers, especially top managers, set the tone of the organization's ethical work climate, this hiring practice would insure a more ethically sound work climate.

5. Managers or executive level employees should keep in mind that gender and the industry experience of a new manager may have an impact on his/her moral reasoning; knowing this, firms should take measures to offer new hired managers an extensive orientation program which clearly outlines the policies, code of ethics and all other processes which they expect each manager to subscribe.

6. Based on the varied results between work tenure and the moral reasoning of individual managers, all executive and managerial level employees would benefit

from training to enhance their ethical sensitivity. However, dramatic intervention might be necessary if the actual culture of the organization encourages managers to think less ethically. In those cases, a change in management as well as training could be necessary.

7. Rest (1986) and Trevino (1992), however, claim that there is something inherent in the educational process that causes individual thought mechanisms to develop to higher modes of moral development. Education, whether through traditional schooling or training, enhances the ability of individuals to operate at higher levels of principled moral reasoning.

8. Rest (1979) (1980), Darry (1989), Harris (1990), Pennino (2001) and Forte (2001) did not find significant differences between males and females in strong organizational structures, perhaps because men and women are trained to think and judge as corporate members. Managers should therefore determine whether specific ethical dilemmas or decisions require solutions from managers with more of a justice or caring orientation.

9. Managers or executive level employees should keep in mind that gender and the industry experience of a new manager may have an impact on the potential success of the new manager's ability to help set or change the organizational ethical tone desired of that corporation.

10. Managers or executive level employees should keep in mind that age, work tenure, management levels, education and the five ethical climate types may have little or no impact on his/her moral reasoning.

RECOMMENDATIONS FOR FUTURE RESEARCH

Future research may be directed in addressing and answering the following issues and questions.

1. Forte's (2001) study should be replicated in order to ascertain whether there have been any changes in the moral reasoning of business managers of selected industries with a different sample as well as over a period of time.

2. A study should also be conducted to investigate this issue from a global perspective. A sample of business managers in selected industries drawn from a group of Canadian, British, Italian, German, or any other foreign country should provide interesting results.

3. An analysis should be conducted of other professional organizations and groups, such as accountants, lawyers, doctors, and educators in order to see if the results would be replicated or if these professions differ from the results found in Forte's (2001) study.

4. It would also be revealing to study individual managers from selected industries on a longitudinal basis to determine how changes in their levels, positions, and industries might impact their moral reasoning. Periodic examination over a number of years could prove insightful into determining how changes affect moral reasoning.

5. Further research is needed to investigate why the perceived ethical climate of some industries attract certain age groups while repelling others. For example, why is an individual in Forte's (2001) study with a mean age of 44 attracted to a Caring perceived organizational ethical climate type, and what experiences has a 55 year old individual experienced which may have affected his/her perception of their organizational ethical work climate causing a deviation from one perceived organizational climate type to another.

6. Additional research across industry types should be conducted to assess what, if any, differences occur in moral reasoning among those industries and identify possible characteristics and reasons.

7. Future research is needed to investigate further the relationship between tenure and perceived ethical climate type. Because of the different findings of Kelley, Ferrell, Skinner and Bigel a closer examination seems to be warranted.

8. Future research should investigate whether managers and executive level employees gravitate to the perceived ethical climate type of their ethical tendency. This is important since members of a corporation may move to a more comfortable ethical climate if they feel uncomfortable in one organization. On the other hand, if these members remain with the organization, they may change the ethical orientation of the organization.

9. Future research should investigate the relationship between industry types, gender, and moral reasoning. Managers who move from organization to organization travel with their professional baggage from previous positions, which may influence their moral reasoning. It would be beneficial to understand as much as possible the subtle variations that could affect a manager's moral reasoning.

10. Additional research dealing with age and the moral reasoning of individual managers is needed. A sample with more of a variance in age than Forte's (2001) study may be drawn to measure a statistical significance, if any, observed.

11. A sample with more of a variance in education than Forte's (2001) study may be drawn to measure a statistical significant between education and P scores.

12. Given the varied research between managerial and executive women and men exist or do not exist. As Morrison (1997) recommended, research should address specific factors and examine them from a qualitative approach rather than a quantitative approach. Interviews could also prove useful in enhancing the findings of this research. Further studies should be undertaken to ascertain whether corporate culture, the nature of the management position or other variables cause men and women to demonstrate similar or difference decision making processes when dealing with ethical dilemmas and moral reasoning in the work place.

13. Additional studies should be undertaken to assess if a relationship between management levels and moral reasoning might exist. A sample with more of a variance in management levels may be drawn to measure a statistical significance between managerial levels and P scores. A statistical significance between management levels and P scores did not result in Forte's (2001) study possibly because the majority of the respondents were upper management. Dun & Bradstreet provided the researcher with a list consisting of a proportional stratified random sample of Fortune 500 firms but the majority of the respondents came from upper management.

14. Additional research across perceived ethical climate types should be conducted to assess what if any differences occur in moral reasoning among these types.

15. Future research should investigate the relationship between tenure, education, gender and industry types and perceived organizational ethical climate types. It would be beneficial to understand as much as possible how these variables affect variations in perceived ethical climate types.

16. Future research should investigate the relationship between age, work tenure, management levels, education, and the five ethical climate types and moral reasoning. It would be beneficial to understand as much as possible how these variables affect the subtle variations in a manager's moral reasoning.

17. Future research should investigate the relationship between the perceived organizational ethical work climate type among individual industry types.

CONCLUDING COMMENTS

The value of ethical reasoning is that it is a premise upon which our country and our business enterprises are founded. High moral reasoning and the continued development of ethical standards are goals to which our government, businesses, and educational system must ascribe.

BIBLIOGRAPHY

Armstrong, M. (1984). *Internalization of the Professional Ethic by Certified Public Accountants: A Multidimensional Scaling Approach.* Unpublished: University of Southern California, Doctoral Dissertation.

Armstrong, M. (1987). Moral development and accounting education. *Journal of Accounting Education*, 27-43.

Bigel, K. (1998). *The Ethical Orientation of Financial Planners Engaged In Investment Activities: A comparison of Practitioners Based on Professionalization and Compensation Sources.* Unpublished doctoral dissertation, New York University.

Crisham, P. (1981a). *Moral Judgment of Nurses in Hypthetical and Nursing Dilemmas.* Unpublished doctoral dissertation, University of Minnesota..

Crisham, P. (1981b). Measuring moral judgment in nursing dilemmas. *Nursing Research.* 30 (2), 104-110.

D'Aquila, J. (1997). *Internal Control Environment Forces and Financial Reporting Decisions Made by Financial Accountants.* Unpublished doctoral dissertation, New York University.

David, F.R., Anderson L.M., & Lawrimore, K.W. (1990). Perspectives on Business Ethics in Management Education. *SAM Advanced Management Journal*, Autumn, pp. 26-32.

Derry, R. (1989). An empirical study of moral reasoning among managers. *Journal of Business Ethics*, 8, pp. 855-862.

Derry, R. and R.M. Green. (1989) Ethical Theory in Business Ethics: A Critical Assessment. *Journal of Business Ethics*, 8,521-533.

Diessner, R. (1991). *Teacher education for democratic classrooms: Moral reasoning and ideology critique.* 16th Annual Conference of the Association for Moral Education, Athens, GA.

Drucker, P. (1973). *Management,* New York, N.Y.: Harper & Row.

Felton, G.M., & Parsons, M.A. (1987). The impact of nursing education on ethical/moral decision making. *Journal of Nursing Education,* 26, 7-11.

Forte, A. (2001). *Business Ethics: A Study Of The Moral Reasoning Of Selected Business Managers.* Unpublished doctoral dissertation, New York University.

Gaul, A.L. (1987). The effect of a course in Nursing ethics on the relationship between ethical choice and ethical action in baccalaureate Nursing students. *Journal of Nursing Education,* 26, 113-117.

Gilligan, C. (1982). *In a different voice: Psychological theory and women's development.* Cambridge MA: Harvard University Press.

Gilligan, C., & Attanucci, J. (1988). Two moral orientations: gender differences and similarities. *Merrill-Palmer Quarterly,* 34(3), 223-237.

Gilligan, C. (1979). Women's place in man's life cycle. *Harvard Educational Review,* 29, 119-133.

Gilligan, C. (1977). *In a different voice: Women's conceptions of the self and of morality.* Cambridge, MA: Harvard Educational Review 47: Harvard University.

Harris, J.R. (1990). Ethical values of individuals at different levels in the organizational hierarchy of a single firm. *Journal of Business Ethics,* 9, 741-750.

Husted, S.D. (1978). *Assessment of moral reasoning in pediatric faculty, house officers and medical students.* Proceedings of the 17th Annual Conference on Research in Medical Education, 17, 439-441.

Kelley, S.W. Ferrell, O.C., & Skinner, S.J. (1990). Ethical behavior among marketing researchers: An assessment of selected demographic characteristics. *Journal of Business Ethics,* 9, 681-688.

Ketefian, S. (1981). Moral reasoning and moral behavior among selected groups of practicing nurses. *Nursing Research.* 30, 171-176.

Ketefian, S. (1989). Moral reasoning and ethical practice. In J. Fitzpatrick, R. L. Taunton, and J. Benoliel (Eds.), *Annual review of nursing research* (pp. 173-195). New York: Springer.

Ketefian, S., and Ormond, I. (1988). *Moral reasoning and ethical practice in nursing: An integrative review.* New York: National League for Nursing.

Kohlberg, L. (1981). *The Psychology of Moral Development Volume One.* Harper and Row.

Kohlberg, L. (1970). *Moral Stages and Moralization. Moral development and behavior* New York, N.Y.: Holt, Rinehart & Winston.

Kohlberg, L. (1984). *The Psychology of Moral Development Volume Two.* San Francisco: Harper & Row Publishers.

Kohlberg, L. (1969). Stage and sequence: the cognitive - developmental approach to socialization. *Handbook of Socialization Theory and Research.* Goslin D. (ed), Chicago, Rand McNally, pp 347-480.

Kohlberg, L. (1969). Stage and Sequence. *Handbook of Socialization Theory and Research Chicago,* IL: Rand McNally.

Kohlberg, L. (1976). Moral stages and moralization; the cognitive developmental approach. *Moral Development and Behavior.* Lickona, T. (ed). New York: Holt,Rinehart, & Winston, pp 31-55.

Kohlberg, L. (1984). *The Relationship of Moral Judgement To Moral Action, Morality, Moral Behavior and Moral Development*. New York: John Wiley & Sons.

Kohlberg, L. (1982). *Essays On Moral Development: The Philosophy of Moral Development*. San Francisco, CA: Harper & Row.

Kohlberg, L. (1958). The Development of Modes of Moral Thinking and Choice in the Years 10 to 16. Unpublished Doctoral Dissertation, The University of Chicago.

Kohlberg, L., Levine, C., and Hewer, A. (1983) *Moral stages: a current formulation and a response to critics*. Basel: Karger.

Kuhn, D., Langer, J. & Kohlbeg, L. (1971). *Relations Between Logical and Moral Development*. Recent Research In Moral Development. Holt: New York, NY.

Kujala, J. (1995). *Moral issues in business: Top managers' perceptions of moral issues in stakeholders relations*. University of Tampere, Finland, School of Business Administration.

Lampe, J., & Finn, D. (1992). A model of auditors' ethical decision process. *A Journal of Practice and Theory,* Supplement, 1-21.

Lewin, A.Y., & Stephens, C.U. (1994). CEO attitudes as determinants of organization design: An integrated model. *Organization Studies, 15* (2), 183-212.

Litwin, G.H. and Stringer, R.A. (1968). *Motivation and Organizational Climate*. Harvard Business School.

Mauro, N.J. (1987). *Business Ethics, Managerial Decision Making, and Corporate Culture and Values*. Unpublished doctoral dissertation, New York University.

Mayberry, M.A. (1986). Ethical decision making: A response of hospital nurses. *Nursing Administration Quarterly*, 10 (3), 75-81.

McKenna, J.N. (1993). *Ethical Dilemmas In Financial Reporting Situations and The Preferred Mode of Resolution of Ethical Conflicts As Taken By Certified and Noncertified Management Accountants In Organizations With Perceived Different Ethical Work Climates*. Unpublished doctoral dissertation, New York University.

Morrison, J. (1997). *Managerial Job Satisfaction: An Examination of the Impact of Selected Psychological, Personal, and Industrial Variables on the Job Satisfaction of Executive and Managerial Corporate Women*. Unpublished doctoral dissertation, New York University.

Pennino, C. (2001). *The Relationship Between Managerial Decision Style, Principled Ethical Reasoning, and Selected Variables in Business Organizations*. Unpublished doctoral dissertation, New York University

Posner, B.Z. & Schmidt, W.H. (1987). Ethics in 'American companies: A managerial perspective. *Journal of Business Ethics, 6,* 383-391.

Posner, B.Z. & Schmidt, W.H. (1984). Values and the American manager. *California Management Review, 20* (3), 202-216.

Rest, J.R. (1983). Morality. *Handbook of Child Psychology*, edited by P. Mussen, 4th Edition, Vol. 3 on Cognitive Development, pp. 556-629. New York, NY: John Wiley and Sons.

Rest, J.R. (1979). *Development In Judging Moral Issues*. Minneapolis, Minnesota: University of Minnesota Press.

Rest, J.R. (1982, February). *A psychologist looks at the teaching of ethics*. Hastings Center Report pp. 29-36

Rest, J.R. (1986a). *DIT Manual* (Third Edition, 8/90 Revision). Minneapolis, MN: Center for the Study of Ethical Development.

Rest, J.R. (1988). Why Does College Promote Development In Moral Judgement? *Journal of Moral Education, 17* (3), 183-193.

Rest, J.R. and Narvaez, D. (1994). *Moral development in the professions: Psychology and applied ethics.* Hillsdale, N.J. Lawrence Erlbaum Association, Publishers.

Rest, J.R. (1986). *Moral development: Advances in research and theory.* New York, NY: Praeger Publishers. Katholieke Universiteit Levven, Belgium Doctoral Dissertation.

Sacasas, R., & Cava, A. (1990). Law, ethics and management: Towards an effective audit. *Business Forum, 15* (1), 18-21.

Tagiuri, R. and Litwin, G.H. (1968) *Organizational Climate, Exploration of a Concept.* Harvard University Law School.

Touche Ross (1988, January). *Ethics in American Business: An Opinion Survey of Key Business Leaders on Ethical Standards and Behavior.*

Trevino, L.K. (1986). Ethical decision making in organizations: A person-situation interactionist model. *Academy of Management Review*, 11, 601-617.

Trevino, L.K. & Nelson, K.A. (1995). *Managing Business Ethics: Straight Talk About How To Do It Right.* New York: John Wiley and Sons.

Trevino, L.K. (1992). Moral reasoning and business ethics: Implications for research, education, and management. *Journal of Business Ethics*, 11, pp. 445-459.

Victor, B. and Cullen, J. B. (1987). A theory and measure of ethical climate in organizations. *Research In Corporate Social Performance and Policy* 9, 51-71.

Victor, B., & Cullen, J.B. (1988). The organizational basis of ethical work climates. *Administrative Science Quarterly March*, pp 101-125.

In: Contemporary Issues in Business Ethics   ISBN: 978-1-60021-773-9
Editors: M. W. Volcox, Th. O. Mohan, pp. 119-133   © 2007 Nova Science Publishers, Inc.

Chapter 5

THE RELATIONSHIP BETWEEN BUSINESS AND GOVERNMENT: AN EXAMINATION OF CORPORATE POLITICAL ACTION COMMITTEES (PACS) IN THE ENERGY AND NATURAL RESOURCES SECTOR

Charles H. Cho[*]

John Molson School of Business, Concordia University
1455, de Maisonneuve Blvd West, Montréal, Québec H3G 1M8, Canada

ABSTRACT

The passage of the Federal Election Campaign Act of 1971 and its subsequent amendments had a significant impact on the relationship between business and politics. With this piece of legislation, the U.S. Congress made available to corporate executives an ideal avenue to express themselves in the political arena through a newly legalized political tool, the corporate political-action committee (Shipper and Jennings, 1984). Since their allowed existence, these committees (hereafter, PACs) flourished as they increased in number from 89 in 1974 to over 1,600 in 2004 (Federal Election Commission, 2007). In addition, during the 2003-2004 election cycle, corporate PACs donated over $211 million to congressional candidates (Center for Responsive Politics, 2007).

In this chapter, I give an overview of the history behind corporate PACs; determine when, how and why such entities were created; examine their organizational and disclosure requirements; and analyze their operations. Second, I examine PACs related to specific industries subject to tighter regulation, thus greater public policy pressure, and study their spending behavior during recent election cycles. I select a cluster of business industries which activities are harmful to the natural environment, classified as the Energy and Natural Resources sector by the Center for Responsive Politics (CRP), and analyze their PAC contributions over the period 1998-2004. This research provides

---

[*] Tel: (514) 848-2424 ext. 2319; Fax: (514) 848-4518; E-mail: ccho@jmsb.concordia.ca

evidence that corporations from these industries generally hold a defined political agenda illustrated by the amount and allocation of their political contributions to legislators who are supportive (or not) of their business activities.

1. INTRODUCTION

"There is one commodity that scholars and journalists, plus the congressional candidates [...] universally agree is bestowed upon many contributors: *access*. Access means that during deliberations leading to relevant legislative decisions, corporate political-action committees (PACs) [...] get a respectful hearing from House and Senate members who have won election with the PAC's help. Corporations giving PAC contributions frequently receive 'face time' from members [...] and gain a valuable opportunity to present their perspectives" (Smith, 2000).

According to the theory of economic regulation, any business in search of political power will go to the appropriate political party, to which it will pay with votes and dollars because these will fulfill that party's needs (Peltzman, 1974; Stigler, 1971). The inherent domination of business in American politics (see, e.g., Eismeier and Pollock III, 1988; Smith, 2000) has motivated corporations to develop specific political strategies to maximize their political power (Suarez, 1998). Government becomes an essential factor for a entity's operations if corporate executives consider that decisions and regulations voted by government officials will affect profits (Humphries, 1991).

The passage of the Federal Election Campaign Act of 1971 (FECA) and its subsequent amendments in 1974, 1976 and 1979 had a momentous impact on the relationship between business and politics in the U.S. That is, the U.S Congress had just made available to corporate executives the ideal avenue to express themselves in the political arena (Shipper and Jennings, 1984). The core outcome espoused by this legislation was the birth of a newly legalized political tool; that is the corporate political action committee (PAC).

Progressive and rational-choice perspectives define PACs as "bloodless creatures, all of which purchase political power with the same calculations of advantage that they would purchase any other commodity" (Eismeier and Pollock III, 1988). Notwithstanding these views on PACs, the effectiveness and notoriety of PACs are far to be negligible. Since their allowed existence through FECA, the number of corporate PACs has sharply increased from 89 in 1974 to 1,469 in 1982 and shown progressive growth to reach approximately 1,622 in 2004. In addition, during the 2005-2006 election cycle[1], corporate PACs donated over $247 million to congressional candidates (Center for Responsive Politics, 2007). Thus, PACs are considered to be an efficient means to influence legislators. For example, Roberts et al. (2003) reported significant results when testing for effectiveness of PAC contributions from the U.S. public accounting profession; Luke and Krauss (2004) found a positive relationship between the amount of contributions made by the tobacco industry to a member of the U.S. Congress and the likelihood for him/her to vote in favor of tobacco-related bills. Given the overt power of PACs, one may then wonder what is it that corporate PACs are after and what

---

[1] In this chapter, contributions for the 2005-2006 election cycle for all sectors are based on the data released by the FEC on January 22, 2007. Campaign funds are still being transacted as the writing date of this chapter.

they receive from legislators in exchange for their hefty contributions. A direct answer to this question is given by the opening quote above: an *access* door to legislators.

The purpose of this chapter is twofold. First, it is to give an overview of the history behind corporate PACs; determine when, how and why such entities were created; examine their organizational and disclosure requirements; and analyze their operations. Second, I examine PACs related to specific industries subject to tighter regulation, thus greater public policy pressure, and study their spending behavior during recent election cycles. I select a cluster of business industries which activities are harmful to the natural environment, classified as the Energy and Natural Resources sector by the Center for Responsive Politics, and analyze their PAC contributions over the period 1998-2004.

The remainder of the chapter is organized as follows. Section 2 provides historical background information about PACs and corporate motivations to create such entities. Section 3 presents a technical discussion about PAC operations and functionality; it also provides with a brief overview on PAC research. In Section 4, I analyze corporate PACs sponsored by corporations operating in the Energy and Natural Resources sector in terms of their growth and spending behavior over the last several election cycles. Section 5 concludes the chapter.

2. CORPORATE POLITICAL ACTION COMMITTEES: BACKGROUND AND MOTIVATION

2.1. Historical Background

In 1943, a trade union under the name of Congress of Industrial Organizations (CIO) established the first political action committee to raise campaign funds for re-election of President Franklin D. Roosevelt. In order to comply with the Smith-Connally Act of 1943, the CIO ensured that contributions were individual and voluntary from union members and not coming from union dues. This type of PAC was commonly referred as "separate segregate funds" because a separate account was keeping campaign funds (Center for Responsive Politics, 2007). However, the origins and "officialization" of corporate and union PACs go back much earlier to a strong political battle.

During the 1902 elections, Senator Benjamin Tillman (D-SC) accused Theodore Roosevelt, who was seeking reelection, of running a campaign funded by wealthy people. After his victory, President Roosevelt reinforced his denial of such accusation by proposing a law that banned corporate political contributions in 1905. This piece of legislation was sponsored by Senator Tillman himself despite his differences with President Roosevelt (Shipper and Jennings, 1984). As a result, the Tillman Act of 1907[2] was passed and prohibited all corporate interest and political contributions during the federal electoral process (Ryan et al., 1987). Since then, constitutional issues associated with this ban have emerged and led to major reforms in this area. For example, the conflict between the "right of

---

[2] At first, the Act had a significant loophole as it only prohibited cash contributions. That is, other types of contributions such as goods or services in-kind were still allowed. The 1925 Federal Corrupt Practices Act eliminated this loophole by including other types of contributions in the ban.

Congress to regulate and control the federal election process" and the "right of individuals to participate in the electoral process free of Congressional control" was of foremost importance, especially because elections constitute the ultimate symbol and power of a democracy (Ryan et al., 1987). After sixty-four years of battles between the State and interest groups involving court cases that dealt with constitutional rights and amendments[3], Congress decided to permit corporate political involvement in the electoral process. It did so by overriding the Tillman Act of 1907 and passing the Federal Election Campaign Act of 1971 (FECA). This law brought a major overhaul in the way business and government interact. That is, the corporate political action committee[4], a "new statutory campaign contribution mechanism", was officially created and legalized (Ryan et al., 1987). To illustrate the high popularity and expansion of corporate PACs, Figure 1 shows the growth of corporate PACs registered with the U.S. Federal Election Commission (FEC) each election cycle shortly after the passage of FECA. The figures are self-explanatory; from 89 registered corporate PACs in 1974, the number rose to 1,206 in 1980, representing a nearly fourteenfold increase in six years. In 2004, the FEC reported over 1,600 registered corporate PACs.

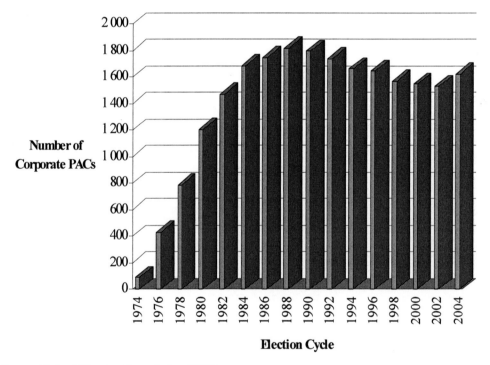

Source: Federal Election Commission (2007).

Figure 1. Number of corporate PACs registered with the FEC for election cycles 1973-1974 to 2003-2004.

---

[3] Article I, Section 4 of the U.S Constitution gives Congress the right to regulate and control the election of federal candidates. In contrast, the First and Fourteenth Amendments of the Constitution establish the right of individuals to participate in the electoral process unimpeded by the influence of the government (Ryan et al., 1987).

[4] In this chapter, I interchangeably use the terms "corporate political-action committee", "political action committee", "corporate PAC" and "PAC".

2.2. Motivations to Establish a PAC

Handler and Mulkern (1982) report five major motivations frequently mentioned by PAC officers when they were asked about the dominant consideration influencing their decision to create and sponsor a corporate PAC. First, management recognizes the central importance of government-business relationships. The growing government regulation in the 1970s accelerated the activities of PACs as they were viewed as one instrument that would reverse the trend to such overregulation. "A spirit of resentment of what perceived as government insensitivity to legitimate business concerns provides the animating energy behind such PACs" (Handler and Mulkern, 1982). Another consideration within this motive is the group of corporations which business depended on federal government contracts. This situation leaves almost no choice but make connections with politicians via PACs but also other channels. Second, corporate representatives lobbying in Washington are concerned about the need to respond to expensive fundraising invitations (high donations are expected at these receptions and dinners). With the increasing number of such fundraising events, Washington corporate lobbyists need access to adequate income which support can be obtained by a PAC. This issue by itself constitutes a key motivator to establish a corporate PAC. Third, PACs can enhance political involvement within the organization. That is, PAC activity is one way to better inform employees about corporate political issues but also "sensitize managers to their civic responsibilities and to develop awareness of government as the most significant external force affecting the enterprise" (Handler and Mulkern, 1982). Fourth, positive feedback from peers who have experienced PAC activity influence Chief Executive Officers (CEOs) to take initiatives towards the creation of a PAC. The CEOs usually hear such feedbacks when they serve on business roundtable task forces or as directors of other corporate boards. This motivation is sometimes referred as a result of bandwagon effect. Fifth, corporate PACs can be developed as a counterbalance to the political influence of adversary types of organizations such as labor unions. This defensive strategic motivation of PAC creation allows business to compete with labor on more equal ground in the political arena.

Overall, Handler and Mulkern (1982) note that the most significant motivation for corporations to establish PACs is the high frequency of PAC officers mentioning the theme of "government involvement in corporate affairs". Their study provides evidence that the higher government policies and actions affect the firm's operations, the higher the likelihood of PAC creation.

3. Corporate Political-action Committees: Functionality and Research

3.1. FEC Organizational and Reporting Requirements

The FEC is the federal agency in charge of administering federal electoral laws. As PACs became the key determinant for corporate involvement in the federal electoral process, they are subject of FEC oversight and jurisdiction. Although the FEC does not specifically mandate PACs to draft articles of organization or by-laws for operations, other rigorous organizational and reporting requirements are required. As part of organizational requirements, PACs must to file a Statement of Organization (FEC Form-1) with the FEC within ten days of its formation (Center for Responsive Politics, 2007; Dominguez, 1982). If campaign contributions will be made only to candidates for the U.S. House of Representatives (hereafter, House) or only to candidates for the U.S. Senate, PACs can file the Statement of Organization with the Clerk of the House or the Secretary of the Senate, respectively. Moreover, each PAC must have a distinct Chairman and Treasurer. This requirement is critical as no contributions can be received nor spent if any of these positions is left vacant. It is therefore recommended to appoint a Vice-Chairman and an Assistant Treasurer to immediately take office and avoid disruption should a vacancy occurs (Dominguez, 1982).

In addition to organizational requirements, the FEC also established specific reporting and disclosure requirements. As discussed above, the Statement of Organization is the first report filed by PACs. Other periodic reports on all campaign contribution monies transactions must be filed every year on FEC Form-3. These periodic reports are designed to list all receipts and disbursements from both the beginning of the calendar year and since the last report. Although requirements for election years and non-election years slightly vary, such data are made available to the public (Mizruchi, 1992). Other reports may include: (1) Modification of PAC Statement of Organization; (2) Independent Expenditure Report; (3) Special Election Reports; and (4) Termination Reports (Dominguez, 1982). It is interesting to note that despite these stringent regulations on organizational and reporting requirements[5], corporate PACs have still grown popular (see Figure 1) and become "an ever-growing phenomenon with increasing power and impact" (Shipper and Jennings, 1984).

3.2. Organization and Operations

With FECA, corporations became allowed to establish, fund and manage their own independent PACs. The sole purpose of a PAC is to collect campaign funds from members and disburse them to federal candidates (Mack, 1997; Ryan et al., 1987). From this, we can clearly identify the two "benefactors" of a political action committee. That is, the "parent" (or sponsor) company that created the PAC and "donors", without whose support the PAC would not be viable (Eismeier and Pollock III, 1988). Generally speaking, PACs function with one single committee - appointed by its contributors and represented by the sponsor corporation's shareholders and administrative personnel[6] - that decides the timing and method of solicitation as well as the selection of candidates to support. However, other PACs operate with more sophisticated committee structures, such as the creation of a parent committee and separate candidate-selection committee (Handler and Mulkern, 1982).

Groups solicited for PAC financial support and those represented in PAC board membership appear to be strongly correlated. For instance, shareholder representation is minimized or sometimes absent in most PACs because they simply do not solicit shareholders for contributions (Eismeier and Pollock III, 1988), mainly due to cost effectiveness issues

---

[5] These requirements are applicable to all types of PACs.
[6] The original 1971 law did not restrict membership of corporate PACs. However, the 1976 amendments imposed some limitations so that only executive or administrative personnel (i.e., policymaking, managerial, professional or supervisory staff) and shareholders could be members of corporate PACs.

(Handler and Mulkern, 1982). In contrast, PACs elect and solicit executive or administrative personnel with policymaking, managerial, professional or supervisory responsibilities and their families as often as it desires (Shipper and Jennings, 1984). PACs are also permitted to make no more than two annual written solicitations for contributions from employees paid hourly, other than executive or administrative personnel and families (Dominguez, 1982; Mizruchi, 1992; Shipper and Jennings, 1984). This rule, called the "twice-yearly option", is a compromising outcome of the 1976 amendments regarding the controversial issue of PAC solicitation access of the Sun Company's hourly employees[7] (Handler and Mulkern, 1982).

It is important to note two essential features of PAC contributions. First, there is a limitation on the dollar amount of contributions according to FEC regulations. Groups and individuals (each spouse in the case of single income family) may donate up to $5,000 to a single PAC per calendar year. In turn, PACs may contribute up to $5,000 to any candidate or his/her authorized committee per election (primary, general or special). They can also give up to $15,000 to any national party committee per calendar year (Center for Responsive Politics, 2007; Dominguez, 1982; Mack, 1997, 2001; Mizruchi, 1992; Shipper and Jennings, 1984). Second, contributions from any individual donor to a PAC must remain strictly voluntary. Because of the inherent asymmetry of the employer-employee or superior-subordinate relationship, Congress and the FEC have implemented laws to protect employees from coercion and pressure potentially exhibited by PAC solicitation practices. These laws also require confidentiality about employee contribution or complaint records as well as full disclosure on the purpose of PAC funds (Dominguez, 1982; Handler and Mulkern, 1982).

For each PAC, variations are substantial in terms of level of management solicited, method and frequency of solicitation, type of contribution and method of contribution collection. Methods of solicitation include mailing and variations of personal contact such as informal discussion or home-rule method. Contributions can be classified as earmarked, contributor-recommended, split given, in-kind or restricted. Single lump-sum payment and pledging are available methods of payment but the most commonly used is payroll deduction because of its numerous attractive features for PACs such as the stabilization of the number of contributors and consistency of contribution inflows (Dominguez, 1982; Handler and Mulkern, 1982).

3.3. PAC Giving Preferences

Handler and Mulkern (1982) identified two main streams of PAC giving. In general, corporate PACs portray either a predominantly pragmatic or ideological inclination. The motives and degree of their desire for political change constitute their primary difference. The ideological PAC is concerned about altering the political composition of Congress whereas the pragmatic PAC's precedence remains on access-seeking strategies or "cultivating access to incumbents" (Eismeier and Pollock III, 1986; Handler and Mulkern, 1982). Differences

---

[7] The Sun Company's PAC requested from the Federal Election Commission (FEC) an opinion about exactly whom it could solicit. The response from the FEC was "stockholders and all employees". Unions expressed their discontent because they felt that management could now compete with them in raising political-action funds from hourly employees. In the 1976 amendments, a compromise resulted in allowing corporate PACs to solicit hourly paid workers no more than twice a year by a letter addressed to their home, while a reciprocal right was extended to union PACs to solicit stockholders and management personnel twice a year as well.

emerging from these two types of PACs vary across industries because of their inherent ties with the form of regulatory environment in which they operate. After two eras of industry-specific regulation (i.e., securities, banking, transportation and communication), a new-style social regulation wave appeared in the 1960s and 1970s, notably with the creation of regulatory institutions such as the Occupational Safety and Health Administration (OSHA) and the Environmental Protection Agency (EPA). This broader type of regulation encompassed a wider range of social issues such as health and working conditions, environmental quality and highway safety (Eismeier and Pollock III, 1986). Although some results suggest that PACs from industries under the scrutiny of social regulation tend to pursue a more ideological approach than their counterparts subject to industry-specific regulation (see, e.g., Eismeier and Pollock III, 1986, 1988), corporate PACs still appear to operate "for the purpose of supporting the sponsoring organization's lobbying program, to promote goodwill, especially among incumbents, and enhance a particular legislative interest" (Mack, 2001). In fact, there is compelling evidence that corporate PACs as a whole have been contributing vastly to incumbent candidates since their creation. During the 1979-80 election cycle, 64 percent of the 280 Fortune 500 PAC contributions went to incumbents (Ryan et al., 1987). In 1982, 75 percent of all corporate PAC contributions to federal candidates helped incumbents win re-election (Eismeier and Pollock III, 1986) and this trend has continued since the 1980s to date. Table 1 presents the evolution of PAC contribution dollars and percentages allocations in relation to incumbents, challengers and open seats. Panel A indicates that the FEC reported an average incumbency ratio of 79.03 percent for PAC contributions to all candidates over the four election cycles 1993-1994 to 1999-2000. Panel B shows a ratio of 86.30 percent for PAC contributions to House members over the eight election cycles 1985-1986 to 1999-2000 (Federal Election Commission, 2007).

3.4. Research on PACs

The candidate selection process and its related expenditure of PAC contributions have been the core of much interest in government-business relationship research since the 1970s and 1980s (Conway, 1986; Dominguez, 1982; Eismeier and Pollock III, 1986, 1988; Handler and Mulkern, 1982; Ryan et al., 1987). Needless to say, social scientists, in particular political scientists, did not hesitate to jump on research using PAC contribution data – due to its public availability – to study corporate PACs' behavior. Economists, business scholars and sociologists joined the PAC research community (Mizruchi, 1992). Four main issues were of interest to social scientists involved in corporate PAC research: (1) the determinants of PAC formation and the size of their expenditures (e.g., Boies, 1989; Masters and Baysinger, 1985; Masters and Keim, 1985), (2) the determinants of PAC political strategies (e.g., Burris, 1987; Clawson and Neustadtl, 1989), (3) the effects of PAC contributions on election outcomes (e.g., Green and Krasno, 1988; Herndon, 1982), and (4) the effect of PAC contributions on the voting behavior of legislators (e.g., Jones and Keiser, 1987; Wright, 1989; Roberts et al., 2003; Luke and Krauss, 2004). Sociologists, however, have been more interested in employing PAC data to study theories related to the "extent of integration within the business community" and "the effects of corporate network structures on business political activity" (Mizruchi, 1992).

Table 1. Distribution of corporate PAC contribution dollar and percentage allocations according to incumbents, challengers, and open seat candidate status

Panel A. Corporate PAC contributions dollars and percentages allocation to all candidates for election cycles 1993-1994 to 1999-2000

	1999-2000		1997-98		1995-96		1993-94	
Incumbents	$ 70,539,805	82.18%	$ 59,334,927	83.43%	$ 52,994,672	75.98%	$ 47,972,418	74.53%
Challengers	$ 3,797,707	4.42%	$ 4,640,602	6.52%	$ 4,329,085	6.21%	$ 4,885,278	7.59%
Open Seats	$ 11,495,266	13.39%	$ 7,146,002	10.05%	$ 12,422,341	17.81%	$ 11,505,128	17.88%
Total	$ 85,832,778	100%	$ 71,121,531	100%	$ 69,746,098	100%	$ 64,362,824	100%
Average incumbency ratio	79.03%							
Average challenger ratio	6.19%							
Average open seats ratio	14.78%							

Panel B. Corporate PAC contributions percentages allocations to House candidates for election cycles 1985-1986 to 1999-2000

	1999-2000	1997-98	1995-96	1993-94	1991-92	1989-90	1987-88	1985-86
Incumbents	87.89%	87.78%	86.23%	83.74%	82.38%	86.86%	90.23%	85.26%
Challengers	3.75%	4.26%	3.74%	6.77%	6.42%	4.15%	3.94%	4.01%
Open Seats	8.36%	8.15%	10.03%	9.49%	11.20%	8.98%	5.82%	10.72%
Total	100%	100%	100%	100%	100%	100%	100%	100%
Average incumbency ratio	86.30%							
Average challenger ratio	4.63%							
Average open seats ratio	9.09%							

Source: Federal Election Commission (2007).

Table 2. PAC contributions for all economic sectors as defined by the CRP for election cycles 1997-1998 to 2005-2006 and ranking of the Energy and Natural Resources sector in relation to peer sectors

Election Cycle	1997-1998	1999-2000	2001-2002	2003-2004	2005-2006
Agribusiness	$ 15,500,607	$ 16,340,223	$ 16,522,947	$ 17,148,603	$ 19,769,010
Communication/Electronics	$ 11,886,064	$ 14,709,140	$ 15,889,736	$ 18,222,030	$ 20,959,471
Construction	$ 8,327,930	$ 8,922,488	$ 9,170,565	$ 12,024,090	$ 14,310,773
Defense	$ 5,898,162	$ 6,408,038	$ 7,620,741	$ 8,091,537	$ 9,702,837
Energy and Natural Resources	$ 15,174,274	$ 17,494,523	$ 19,395,298	$ 19,562,919	$ 21,914,018
Finance/Insurance/Real Estate	$ 35,044,842	$ 41,254,331	$ 41,839,282	$ 49,673,723	$ 57,890,371
Health	$ 18,364,480	$ 22,002,411	$ 25,448,526	$ 31,723,576	$ 39,256,062
Lawyers & Lobbyists	$ 7,644,169	$ 9,057,480	$ 9,888,048	$ 11,396,788	$ 14,243,681
Transportation	$ 14,241,178	$ 15,969,160	$ 16,235,934	$ 18,544,826	$ 20,203,073
Miscellaneous Business	$ 17,556,454	$ 21,658,761	$ 22,819,414	$ 24,916,489	$ 28,891,551
Total	$ 149,638,160	$ 173,816,555	$ 184,830,491	$ 211,304,581	$ 247,140,847
Ranking of the Energy and Natural Resources sector by PAC contributions	5th	4th	4th	4th	4th

* Contributions for the 2005-2006 election cycle for all sectors are based on the data released by the FEC on January 22, 2007. Campaign funds are still being transacted as the writing date of this chapter.

** This sector broadly includes diverse industries such as, for example, Beer, Wine and Liquor, Business Associations, Business Services, Food and Beverage, Retail Sales, Manufacturing.

Source: Center for Responsive Politics (2007).

Table 3. Total PAC contributions made from the Energy and Natural Resources sector to Senators and House members for election cycles 1997-1998 to 2005-2006

Election Cycle	1997-1998	1999-2000	2001-2002	2003-2004	2005-2006	Total
Total PAC Contributions	$15,174,274	$17,494,523	$19,395,298	$19,562,919	$21,914,018	$ 93,541,032
Donations to Democrats	$ 4,400,539	$ 5,073,412	$ 6,206,495	$ 5,281,988	$ 5,697,645	$ 26,660,079
% to Democrats	29%	29%	32%	27%	26%	29%
Donations to Republicans	$10,773,735	$12,421,111	$13,188,803	$14,280,931	$16,216,373	$ 66,880,953
% to Republicans	71%	71%	68%	73%	74%	71%

Source: Center for Responsive Politics (2007).

4. PACs of Firms Operating in the Energy and Natural Resources Sector

As discussed earlier, campaign contributions made to U.S. Senators and House members must be disclosed to the FEC. In addition to the FEC database and its website, the Center for Responsive Politics compiles and makes information on corporate political spending for recent election cycles[1] available on its website (www.opensecrets.org). Thus, I use the data provided by both the FEC and CRP.

In this section, my analysis centers on firms operating in the Energy and Natural Resources economic sector. Such firms are subject to higher regulatory scrutiny because the nature of their business operations inherently exposes them to the public policy arena. The Energy and Natural Resources sector is comprised of high exposure, environmentally sensitive industries such as oil and gas, mining, miscellaneous energy, electric utilities, environmental services/equipment, waste management and fisheries/wildlife (Center for Responsive Politics, 2007). Environmental regulations can significantly influence corporate operations, with the greatest impact on firms in the Energy and Natural Resources sector. Given the strategic importance of such regulations, particularly with the constant pressure applied by pro-environment lobbying groups, it is not surprising that firms from this sector undertake visible and proactive political actions[2] (Hoberg, 1990). For example, Eismeier and Pollock III (1988) note that by 1984, PACs from the Energy and Natural Resources sector already outnumbered those from other industries and consistently ranked among the highest contributors to political causes throughout the mid-1980s. More recent evidence suggests that this level of political involvement persists. For example, the Energy and Natural Resources sector donated over $21 million in PAC contributions during the 2005-2006 election cycle (Center for Responsive Politics, 2007) and was ranked fourth for PAC hard dollar contributions made by industry groupings (Federal Election Commission, 2007). This suggests that firms from the Energy and Natural Resources sector indeed use PAC contributions as a financial incentive tactic to influence legislators and policymakers on matters relevant to them. Table 2 contains information on PAC contribution dollar amounts and the actual number of PACs for all economic sectors defined by the CRP from election cycles 1997-1998 to 2005-2006. These sectors are Agribusiness, Communication/Electronics, Construction, Defense, Energy and Natural Resources, Finance/Insurance/Real Estate, Health, Lawyers and Lobbyists, Transportation, and Miscellaneous Business. The information helps situate the Energy and Natural Resources sector and make comparisons with others. The rankings of the Energy and Natural Resources sector are determined in terms of PAC contribution dollar amounts made to congressional candidates.

Table 3 provides longitudinal descriptive statistics on the total PAC contributions made from the Energy and Natural Resources sector to Senators and House members for every election cycle between 1990 and 2006. Contributions from this sector have steadily increased every election cycle, from $15.2 million in 1990 to $21.9 million in 2006. In addition, the

---

[1] For archival records on earlier election cycles as far back as 1980, the CRP can provide them at a reasonable cost

[2] An estimated 70 percent of the $6.6 billion pollution-related investment for 1975 was made by the utilities, petroleum, refining, chemicals, nonferrous metals, and paper industries. This resulted from entrepreneurial politics, which are generated by proposed policies with perceived benefits that are widely distributed and

data allocate contributions made between Republicans and Democrats, and are depicted in Figure 2 as well. Overall, the giving trend of this sector appears to be heavily directed to candidates from the Republican Party, reflected by an average of 71% versus 29% to their Democrat counterparts. This is consistent with both the pro-business ideology and the incumbency factor since Republicans have taken over the majority of the U.S. Congress since the 1994 election cycle.

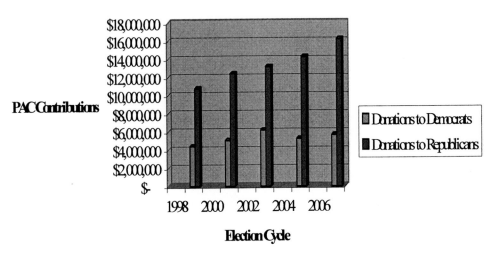

Source: Center for Responsive Politics (2007).

Figure 2. PAC contributions made from the Energy and Natural Resources sector to Senators and House members by political party for election cycles 1997-1998 to 2005-2006.

5. CONCLUSION

These results show that corporations, in general, hold a defined political agenda to achieve specific goals. Figures and tables presented in this chapter reaffirm the prominent political involvement of business in government affairs. Most publicly traded large corporations have a PAC established in a Washington office and this presence represents an integral and essential part of their overall corporate strategy.

Firms operating in the Energy and Natural Resources sector and other heavily regulated industries are more visible in the political arena and media due to the nature of their activities and their large size. However, their objectives often conflict as they attempt to satisfy stakeholders with different interests; that is, enhancing social reputation and obtaining favored legislation at the same time. On one hand, organizations attempt to demonstrate a certain level of corporate social responsibility and utilize vehicles such as charitable contributions, corporate foundations or environmental disclosures in order to legitimize their actions (Patten, 1991, 2002; Roberts, 1992; Cho and Patten, 2006). On the other hand, they must please their shareholders by providing them with reasonable positive returns on investments. To achieve this goal, they need to possess the ability to access and influence

perceived costs that are concentrated in specific segments of industry (Eismeier and Pollock III, 1988). This illustrates that these industries do not remain passive in the political arena.

legislators and public policymakers in their respective line of business. As the evidence of this chapter illustrate, PACs from firms in the Energy and Natural Resources sector are actively participating in government public policymaking to satisfy a biased category of stakeholders, i.e., federal legislators. Other corporate political strategies may include lobbying efforts in Washington and state capitals, grass-roots campaigns, direct visits to legislators and regulators, and issues management departments. Ultimately, these may lead to economic success and increase in profits, which are essentially, as one may presume, the reason why the corporation is created. Despite this variety of options available for political actions, must we, however, abide and accept this economic, rational, self-interest maximizing motivation exhibited by corporate executive management?

REFERENCES

Boies, J. L. (1989). Money, business, and the state: Material interests, Fortune 500 corporations, and the size of political action committees. *American Sociological Review, 54*, 821-833.

Burris, V. (1987). The political partisanship of American business: A study of corporate political action committees. *American Sociological Review, 52*, 732-744.

Center for Responsive Politics. (2007). From http://www.opensecrets.org

Cho, C. H., & Patten, D. M. (2006). The role of environmental disclosures as tools of legitimacy: a research note. *Accounting, Organizations and Society*, doi:10.106/j. aos.2006.09.009.

Clawson, D., & Neustadtl, A. (1989). Interlocks, PACs, and corporate conservatism. *American Journal of Sociology, 94*, 749-773.

Conway, M. (1986). PACs and congressional elections in the 1980's. In A. J. Ciglar, & B. A. Loomis (Eds.), *Interest Group Politics*. Washington, DC: CQ Press.

Dominguez, G. S. (1982). *Government relations : a handbook for developing and conducting the government program*. New York, NY: Wiley.

Eismeier, T. J., & Pollock III, P. H. (1986). Politics and markets: corporate money in American national elections. *British Journal of Political Science, 16*(3), 287-309.

Eismeier, T. J., & Pollock III, P. H. (1988). *Business, money and the rise of corporate PACs in American elections*. New York, NY: Quorum Books.

Federal Election Commission. (2007). From http://www.fec.gov

Green, D., & Krasno, J. (1988). Salvation for the spendthrift incumbent: Reestimating the effects of campaign spending in House elections. *American Journal of Political Science, 32*, 363-372.

Handler, E., & Mulkern, J. R. (1982). *Business in politics : campaign strategies of corporate political action committees*. Lexington, MA: Lexington Books.

Herndon, J. F. (1982). Access, record, and competition as influences on interest group contributions to Congressional campaigns. *Journal of Politics, 44*, 996-1019.

Hoberg, G. (1990). Risk, science and politics: Alachor regulation in Canada and the United States. *Canadian Journal of Political Science, 23*(2), 227-237.

Humphries, C. (1991). Corporations, PACs and the strategic link between contributions and lobbying activities. *The Western Political Quarterly, 44*(2), 353-372.

Jones, W., Jr., & Keiser, K. R. (1987). Issue visibility and the effects of PAC money. *Social Science Quarterly, 68*, 170-176.

Luke, D., & Krauss, M. (2004). Where there's smoke there's money: Tobacco industry campaign contributions and U.S. Congressional voting. *American Journal of Preventive Medicine*, 27(5), 363-372.

Mack, C. S. (1997). *Business, politics, and the practice of government relations*. Westport, CT: Quorum Books.

Mack, C. S. (2001). *Business strategy for an era of political change*. Westport, CT: Quorum Books.

Masters, M. F., & Baysinger, B. D. (1985). The determinants of funds raised by corporate political action committees: An empirical examination. *Academy of Management Journal, 28*, 654-664.

Masters, M. F., & Keim, G. D. (1985). Determinants of PAC participation among large corporations. *Journal of Politics, 47*, 1158-1173.

Mizruchi, M. S. (1992). *The structure of corporate political action*. Cambridge, MA: Harvard University Press.

Patten, D. M. (1991). Exposure, legitimacy, and social disclosure. *Journal of Accounting and Public Policy, 10*(4), 297-308.

Patten, D. M. (2002). The relation between environmental performance and environmental disclosure: a research note. *Accounting, Organizations and Society, 27*(8), 763-773.

Peltzman, S. (1974). Toward a more general theory of regulation. *Journal of Law and Economics, 17*, 211-244.

Roberts, R. W. (1992). Determinants of corporate social responsibility disclosure: An application of stakeholder theory. *Accounting, Organizations and Society, 17*(6), 595-612.

Roberts, R. W., Dwyer, P. D., & Sweeney, J. T. (2003). Political strategies used by the US public accounting profession during auditor liability reform: The case of the Private Securities Litigation Reform Act of 1995. *Journal of Accounting and Public Policy, 22*(5), 433-457.

Ryan, M. H., Swanson, C. L., & Buchholz, R. A. (1987). *Corporate strategy, public policy and the Fortune 500*. New York, NY: Basil Blackwell.

Shipper, F., & Jennings, M. M. (1984). *Business Strategy for the Political Arena*. Westport, CT: Quorum Books.

Smith, M. A. (2000). *American Business and Political Power*. Chicago, IL: The University of Chicago Press.

Stigler, G. J. (1971). The theory of economic regulation. *Bell Journal of Economics and Management Science, 2*(1), 3-21.

Suarez, S. L. (1998). Lessons learned: Explaining the political behavior of business. *Polity, 31*(1), 161-186.

Wright, J. R. (1989). PAC contributions, lobbying, and representation. *Journal of Politics, 51*, 713-729.

In: Contemporary Issues in Business Ethics   ISBN: 978-1-60021-773-9
Editors: M. W. Volcox, Th. O. Mohan, pp. 135-147   © 2007 Nova Science Publishers, Inc.

Chapter 6

CORPORATE RESPONSIBILITY
FOR CIVIL AVIATION SAFETY

Risako Morimoto[*]

CERMAS and Department of Strategy, Toulouse Business School, France

ABSTRACT

This chapter examines how improving daily management practices can increase the level of civil aviation safety. Various internal and external factors have an impact on an airline's flight safety performance. Historically, accident investigations have focused on primary factors related to operational failure and human error. In addition to the training and maintenance programs required by regulatory agencies, airlines have created safety management systems in order to prevent, control, or mitigate primary causes of safety breaches. In recent years accident investigators have begun seeking the latent factors behind primary causes, shedding light on management factors that impact flight safety. Industry efforts are turning to identifying opportunities to proactively address management factors as a way of further improving flight safety.

This research identifies key management factors that are considered to have a significant impact on flight safety, through extensive literature review and in-depth interviews with safety experts. Then, the relative importance of these key management factors are measured by a questionnaire survey with airline employees and civil aviation experts. Thirty-eight individuals from five continents have responded to the questionnaire. The research analysis has indicated that safety culture has the most significant impact on aviation safety improvement. Therefore, management needs to give a priority to enhance organization's safety culture in daily business operations in order to improve safety performance.

[*] T: +33561294712; F: +33561294994; Email: r.morimoto@esc-toulouse.fr

1. INTRODUCTION

Safety remains the highest priority for airlines. The fatal accident rate for scheduled passenger airlines based on International Civil Aviation Organization (ICAO)[1] records have fallen over the past twenty-five years from 2 per million flights to 0.3 per million flights, as efforts have focused on in-house safety management systems for mechanics and flight operations (Learmount 2005). Historically, accident investigations have focused on primary factors related to mechanical failure and human errors. In recent years, the latent factors behind primary causes have started to be investigated, shedding light on management factors that impact flight safety. Industry efforts are turning to identifying opportunities to proactively address management factors as a way of further improving flight safety.

Airlines today are operating in a highly competitive and changing environment. Mergers that cross national boundaries are becoming increasingly common in today's globalised world. This makes organizations more complex in terms of structures as well as the system to deal with mixed cultures. Changing personnel a volatile market, or economic situation are often considered as influences on corporate priority or culture. Commercial pressures on air transport industries today are increasingly high. One of the major components of airlines' operation costs is jet fuel cost, whose price tripled between 2003 and 2005[2]. Various efforts are being made in order to reduce operating costs since airlines are operating in a highly competitive environment. Aircraft often operate up to maximum flying hours and the utilizations of crews reach to the legal limit in order to reduce operating costs. Tough roster hours could well result in increased fatigue of crews. Major airlines' maintenance work is also often outsourced mainly to save operation costs - approximately 51% of maintenance work was outsourced in 2005 compared to 37% in 1996 (Mutzabaugh 2005).

In order to prevent accidents, the cultural factor seems to play an important role, as management needs to react appropriately if the cultural factor is failing. Safety culture is formed if upper management accepts responsibility for safe operations, especially the proactive management of risk. Organizations must have sufficient time, information, expertise, training and contingency plans for special situations and events. Thus, the initiative of improving organizations' corporate responsibility practice being driven and reinforced from upper management seems to be crucial.

The objective of this study is to examine how improved daily management practices can increase the level of civil aviation safety in this fast growing industry. This study critically investigates the role of organizational management in improving aviation safety performance from corporate responsibility aspects. The study identifies key management factors for aviation safety based on the analyses of in-depth interviews and questionnaires conducted with experts in the aviation sector. This chapter is composed of the following four sections. The next section discusses the main issues of aviation safety management addressed in the literature review. Section three describes the methodology used in this study, followed by the presentation of the findings in section four. The last section concludes the study and suggests how aviation safety can be further improved.

---

[1] ICAO is an organization that promotes understanding and security through cooperative aviation regulation
[2] http://www.wbcsd.org

2. LITERATURE REVIEW

Reason (2001) claims that, hazards and errors can occur at all levels of an organization. Safety violations take place due to psychological precursors of unsafe acts, organizational deficiencies including line management decisions, corporate actions including senior management decisions, and inadequate defenses (Reason 2001). Thus, safety management needs the involvement of all the stakeholder groups as well as strong commitments from upper management. Reason (1990) believes that latent failures of the broad management functions of an organization often result in aircraft accidents. Greenfield (1998) claims that accidents can be prevented through good organizational design and management. Flight Safety Foundation, an independent, nonprofit, nonpolitical international organization dedicated entirely to aviation safety, believes that the responsibility for aviation safety belongs to top management[3]. They claim that top management is required to emphasise safety in management's strategic planning, decision making and resource allocation. The vision within an organization, which increasingly fosters an understanding of the importance of safety in the organizations activities, and the responsibility of each individual needs to be developed in order to prevent accidents. Aviation safety audit is a recommended tool of Flight Safety Foundation to maintain a good safety record.

Improving safety is the prime target for airlines and every possible effort ismade to reduce accident rates. However, the question is which part of airline operations needs to be more closely investigated in order to improve safety? Little et al. (1990) suggest that there is the need for further investigation on the impact of corporate instability within the aviation environment driven by commercial pressures and pilots distresses on aviation safety. Boeing (2006) has investigated the primary cause of airline accidents with its worldwide commercial jet fleet from 1996 to 2005. The most significant cause was flight crew error (55%), followed by airplane (17%), weather (13%), others (7%), Air Traffic Control (5%), and maintenance (3%).

Similar results are found in the study conducted by Lu et al. (2006) on the investigation of the causes of accidents based on 189 final accident reports on the National Transportation Safety Board (NTSB) Aviation Accident Database covering FAR (Federal Aviation Regulations) Part 121 scheduled operations between January 1999 and May 2004. The study shows that direct causes of the accidents are led by cock-pit crews (24%), ground crews (23%), turbulence (21%), maintenance personnel (13%), foreign object damage such as birds (8%), flight attendants (4%), air traffic controller (2%), manufacturer (2%), and passenger & FAA's discretional function (e.g., regarding certified approval) for small percentages. Lu et al. (2006) have identified errors caused by pilots as an especially significant primary cause - 38% of major airline crashes and 74% of commuter or air taxi crashes worldwide between the years 1983 and 1996. Another similar study conducted by Bowen and Lu (2004) has assessed the major airline's safety performance in 2001 and 2004. The probability of accidents caused by pilot fatigue was approximately 1.7 cases per one hundred thousand flights. Effective fatigue management requires understanding the relationship between working conditions and fatigue, not merely the simplistic assessment of work-hours scheduled (Harris et al. 2001).

---

[3] http://www.flightsafety.org/corporate_audit.html

The contributing factors to these identified major causes of aviation accidents are poor situational awareness, misjudgment, ineffective communication, operational deficiency, lack of training, non-compliance with standard operational procedure and fatigue (Lu et al. 2006). For example, there was an incident caused by the failure to close a cargo door properly together with the design of the cargo door latch, or other incidents caused by the loss of the vertical stabilizer due to improper maintenance. There were also drunk pilot incident which could well result in serious accidents. Crew awareness and monitoring of navigational systems can prevent CFIT (controlled flight into terrain) accidents. Some pilots believe that advanced electronic navigation systems coupled with Flight Management System computers, or their over-reliance could also be partially responsible for these accidents. Crew Resource Management (CRM) or the Aviation Safety Reporting System is a common method widely used to improve the human factors of aviation safety. Salas et al. (2001) states that Crew Resource Management (CRM) training is generally perceived to produce positive reactions, enhances learning, and promotes desired behavioral changes.

Flight International (2006), the world's leading provider of aerospace news, believes that international aviation safety problems are becoming regionalized and related to ageing technology. According to Flight International (2006), there are two common factors of airlines that are involved in accidents. Those airlines are often based in countries with a struggling economy and have a poor safety record compared with the world average figure. The reasons behind this tendency could be due to the fact that safety oversight in these countries is not their political priority. This may indicate that an airline's culture regarding obeying regulations reflect that of its country's political environment. Safety culture can be reflected in organizational systems in place, attitudes, priorities, and actions, which vary widely across organizations. One of the important elements of a safety culture is a "no-blame" system that allows air and ground crews to report instances of human and mechanical error without fear of retribution. One well-known industry resource for flight safety improvement is Commercial Aviation Safety Team (CAST). CAST is a government-industry cooperative group whose goals include reducing the United States (US) commercial aviation fatal accident rate by 80% between 1997 and 2007, and working with international organizations and regulatory authorities to reduce the worldwide accident rate. CAST encourages worldwide adoption of the program, which includes emphasis on developing a safety culture.

Literature review shows that highly sophisticated safety monitoring systems in terms of engineering, maintenance, operation and crew function already exist. However, the coverage of organizational management issues at all levels is not well covered in great detail. For example, the International Air Transport Association (IATA) has a safety audit system called the IATA Operational Safety Audit (IOSA)[4]. The IOSA is an evaluation system designed to assess mainly the operational management and control systems of an airline. The Canadian Civil Aviation authority has a more comprehensive Safety Management System Assessment Guide, which covers broad general safety issues including roles, responsibilities, and involvement of employees as well as the importance of communications[5]. The Australian Civil Aviation Safety Authority has guidance materials for a safety management system[6].

---

[4] http://www.iata.org/ps/services/iosa/

[5] http://www.tc.gc.ca/CivilAviation/maintenance/Tp14326/Evaluation.htm

[6] http://www.casa.gov.au/

This system briefly includes the importance of the senior management commitment as well as safety officers' responsibilities.

3. RESEARCH METHODOLOGY

This study has two research questions. First, what are the key organizational management factors which are likely to affect aviation safety. Second, what is the relative importance of the key organizational management factors. The study has applied an approach of mixed research method that is both qualitative (interview) and quantitative (questionnaire). Qualitative research produces complete and detailed description of research topics, whereas quantitative research provides statistically reliable and generalisable results. Quantitative research classifies features and counts their occurrences. Findings of the quantitative analysis can be generalised to a larger population, and direct comparisons can be made. However, the picture of the data which emerges from qualitative analysis is much richer than that obtained from quantitative analysis.

This study began with ten in-depth exploratory interviews with carefully selected experts on aviation and safety in order to understand their perceptions about aviation safety and its relationship to organizational management. The interview analysis has collected smaller but focused samples rather than large random samples usually collected for quantitative analyses. Open-ended questions regarding aviation safety and organizational management factors to improve aviation safety have been asked of each interviewee. The sample of interviewees covers flight safety experts, airline managers and pilots in Taiwan, France, United States, Bangladesh, and Colombia. Various nationalities were selected in order to examine any cultural variations. The author has numerous experiences in interviewing with a wide variety of individuals, possessing a proved interview skill. Hence, the study has collected the highest standard of data without any subjective bias. The interviews have identified key organizational management factors for improving aviation safety performance from expert points of view. The interviews were mainly conducted by telephone, due to the diverse location of the respondents' organizations, and lasted for 1 hour on average.

A questionnaire was then designed to validate and rank the key management factors being identified in the interview analysis. The sample size for the questionnaire is much larger than the one for the interview analysis, therefore statistically reliable results can be obtained. The software Opinions Online provided by the Helsinki University of Technology was used to post the questionnaire online[7]. On-line questionnaire has helped to maintain strict confidentiality of the respondents for the sensitive topic, as airlines are cognizant of potential exposure to legal liability or regulatory intervention. Furthermore, the questionnaire was not designed to assess any airline's performance with regard to management factors or flight safety performance.

The questionnaire was translated into the respondents' native language, namely French, Spanish, and Chinese, in order to achieve high response rates. The questionnaire was pre-tested with master students in order to make sure the questions were clear and understood in a consistent manner (Dillman 1978). After the pre-test, some modifications were made in order

---

[7] http://www.opinions.hut.fi/index2.html

to correct ambiguity and misleading parts of the questionnaire, including wording. We have contacted each respondent by email explaining the purpose of the study, together with the address of the web site of our online questionnaire. Several follow-up efforts including email and telephone reminders were made in order to obtain better response rates.

The questionnaire has asked respondents to rank the fifteen organizational management factors according to their impact on flight safety, from 1 (lowest) to 15 (highest). The questionnaire has also invited respondents to suggest additional key management factors. The geographical location of the organization's headquarters that respondents are based in was also asked in order to observe a multicultural variation in the perceived importance of the management factors. The online questionnaire was responded by 38 key representatives in aviation sectors from eight countries. The response rate of the questionnaire was 40%. Fowler (1988) claims that a response rate of less than 20% is unlikely to produce credible statistical results representing a population. The sample size is statistically large enough to draw scientific conclusions. The sectors include airline managers, crew members, other air transport employees, flight safety experts, airport and civil aviation authorities. The questionnaire coverage of the location includes Europe (5%), North America (8%), Latin America (24%), Africa (3%), and Asia (60%). Larger proportions of respondents in Asia and Latin America resulted from our interest in emerging markets. The distribution of the job position that the respondents hold consists of upper management (11%), middle management (55%), crew members (13%) and other employees (21%).

4. FINDINGS

4.1. Key organizational Management Factors

All the interviewees have stated that management factors do influence flight safety outcomes significantly. However, they claim that there are too few studies about airline management factors contributing to aviation safety, or driving primary causes of safety violations. Some of the interviewees have claimed that most of the airline managers on a daily basis (especially in small airlines) are more concerned about everyday business decisions, such as those concerning airline productivity or financial performance than about safety as an ongoing daily and a long-term matter. Some possible reasons for such an attitude could be explained as pressures to present results to airline shareholders, consider flight safety expenditures more as a cost than an investment, a lack of knowledge about the causal dynamics of flight safety, or inadequate communication regarding business decisions and safety goals. There was also a fear among the interviewees that training budgets might be reduced to achieve operational cost savings as training is an expensive activity. The interviewees strongly believe that training is one of the key factors for safety improvement that is directly impacted by organizational management.

Some interviewees suggest that airline flight safety would be better understood as a complete *flight safety management system* rather than a *flight safety program.* This is because flight safety in a system concept is interconnected to all airline activities. Each of the airlines' systems, such as financial, operations, human resource, maintenance, training, ground support, information systems are also involved in flight safety. Furthermore, a system approach to flight safety is a useful way to analyze and understand the contribution of the airline organization to flight safety. System elements would include the operation environment, aircraft, flight crews, operating procedures, and airline organization.

The interviewees all stress that airline managers play an important role in flight safety outcomes. Drivers of the majority of maintenance errors include management, organization, communication, and human performance. The great majority of factors contributing to maintenance errors are internal to an airline organization. These internal factors could be observable, measurable, and controllable by management to at least some degree. Managers implement performance policies and processes, establish organizational structures and communication and reward systems, manage resources, as well as devise and review operating procedures. Managers are also responsible to develop and to maintain a good safety climate within the organizational culture. A good safety climate is characterized by employees sharing similar positive behaviors and attitudes about organization safety. These include management as well as employee commitment to safety, swift and effective management action on safety matters, and the efficient safety communications within the organization. Flight safety is considered a very technical and specialized-area, therefore most airline managers give most or all of the responsibility for flight safety to the Flight Safety Department. This behavior reduces the opportunity to gain vital supports and commitments from all the other areas of the organization, and also discourages an involvement of key management and other employees in flight safety.

According to the interviewees, unions can have a positive or negative effect on safety. Therefore, airline and union management should give a priority to a close and cooperative working relationship in the area of safety. Business changes, such as mergers, are also perceived to disrupt operational processes or organizations themselves with follow-up effects that can impact flight safety. Thus, the implementation of business changes must be carefully planned and executed for minimum disruptions to processes, employees, and operations. Many pilots in a wide variety of airlines being interviewed observed that there is a frequent tendency for managers with inadequate experience on safety or lack of flying experience to fill senior operational positions. Their concern was that these managers might not understand the implications of their decisions.

Based on the analysis of the interviews with experts, the following fifteen management factors listed in Table 1 are considered to have significant impacts on aviation safety. They are safety culture, adequate training, effective safety monitoring system of errors and deviations, flight safety program management, crew coordination, capability (knowledge about safety) and turnover of key management personnel, communication between management and employees, staff workload management, outsourcing of ground services (business changes, especially during busy peak periods), decision-making under workload pressure, management relations with unions, funding for flight safety programs, airline's financial condition, merger & organizational changes, and an organization's budget constraints. Note that no noticeable significant cultural variations in the perception of the interviewees on key management factors for aviation safety were identified.

Table 1. Fifteen key management factors for aviation safety

safety culture	Good corporate culture towards safety can be the key for safety improvement
adequate training	Regular and effective training can enhance organizations' safety
safety monitoring system	Effective monitoring systems of errors and deviations can reduce their occurrences
flight safety program management	Effective flight safety program can enhance safety
crew coordination	Effective crew management can enhance safety
capability (knowledge about safety) and turnover of key management personnel	The level of knowledge and high turnover of key safety management personnel can affect the quality of organization's safety systems
communication from management to employees	Transparency and good flow of information across organizations is important to improve organization's safety performance
staff workload management	Heavy workload can reduce productivity level that is likely to increase errors
outsourcing of ground services	Major business changes (such as outsourcing), especially during busy periods might affect an organization's safety performance
decision-making under pressure	Workload pressure can affect on the quality of decisions
management relations with unions	Union strikes or threats might affect an organization's safety performance
flight safety program funding	Inadequate funding for a flight safety program can reduce the quality of the system
airline's financial condition	Tight financial condition can affect the quality of decisions and practices
merger & organizational change	Organizational changes can lead to corporate cultural clash
budget constraints	Budget constraints can affect the quality of decisions and practices

4.2. The Ranking of Key Organizational Management Factors

Figure 1 shows the ranking of the key organizational management factors being identified based on the analysis of the questionnaire. Note that there were no obvious significant major cultural differences in the perception of the respondents with multi-cultural backgrounds.

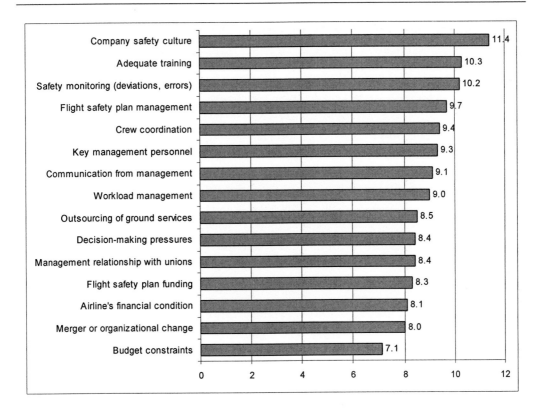

Figure 1. Ranking of key management factors for aviation safety.

The results indicate that safety culture is the most important factor to affect flight safety significantly. To manage safety as an integral part of business would be the key to form a good corporate safety culture. It would also be important to build trust between managers and employees. Clear definitions of each job and responsibility would also make the organizational safety management more effective. Efficient management is well likely to reduce organizations operation costs and create business opportunities, which would also promote effective corporate safety culture. Whole organizations can work towards flight safety from top to the bottom of hierarchy beyond the minimal regulatory requirements is the key concept.

Von Thaden *et al.* (2003) claim that the concept of safety culture in the complex and high-risk aviation industry is often unsystematic, fragmented, and underspecified. According to von Thaden et al., (2003), the following five global components of safety culture could support organizational management to develop, to improve and to incorporate safety culture into their corporate culture. They are organizational commitment, management involvement, a fair evaluation & reward system, employee empowerment, as well as an effective and systematic reporting system. By incorporating these components into the organization's culture, upper management is most likely to identify safety as a core value of the organization and actively promote safety across all levels of the organization. Upper management also needs to express their positive attitude towards safety, even in times of financial difficulty. Moreover, upper and middle management are required to be personally involved in safety activity within the organization, such as seminars, training, active oversight of safety-critical operations, and facilitated communication across the organization. To enhance safety culture, the organization needs a clear and consistent system aligned with its safety priority, promoting safe behavior and correcting unsafe behavior. They also need a reporting system in order to learn from past incidents as well as to identify weaknesses, in the organization before accidents occur. Finally, it is important that individuals, not only senior managers, in organizations show their positive attitude toward safety to initiate and achieve safety improvements.

The questionnaire results show that adequate training was ranked as the second most significant factor for aviation safety improvement. Empirical research suggests that there are substantial differences in the way pilots conduct their work as a function of national culture and that the areas of difference have implications for safety (Helmreich & Merritt 1998). Thus, it is important to raise national, professional and organizational cultural aspects in a training session. For example, collectivists who focus on harmony tend to be better in teamwork and communication, compared to individualists who define situations in costs and benefits for themselves (Helmerich et al 1998). Cultures with high uncertainty avoidance attitude are unlikely to deviate from procedures or regulations. For such a culture, written procedures are needed for all situations and an organization's rule should never be broken. However such a culture may be less creative in coping with novel conditions, which are not covered by procedures. Some cultures have a tendency towards the attitude that juniors should not question the decisions or actions of their superiors and the nature of leadership, which may lead to accidents.

Pilots or crew performance might be affected in abnormal situations, personal problems, high stress, emergency situations. However, professionalism makes pilots or crews do their job efficiently. Strong commitment of senior management or a policy that encourages open communication and avoids denial as a reaction to problems or risks uncovered are also highly likely to improve safety. With strong positive organizational culture, pilots and other groups may accept more readily new concepts such as CRM or its associated training. National culture has positive and negative elements for safety.

According to the questionnaire result, effective monitoring is considered to be the third important management factor for improving flight safety. Good safety monitoring systems enable proactive management of safety risk to discover what conditions should be changed, which is highly likely to reduce deviations and errors. There are various tools for safety improvement being developed that identify and correct predisposing conditions that could lead to incidents or accidents[8].

Finance related management factors were not perceived to be significant in the questionnaire survey. Budget constraint was the lowest in the ranking, which is the 15th. Other finance related factors, namely funding for flight safety programs and airline's financial condition, were also both ranked low. This could suggest that as long as safety culture is properly in place, tight financial conditions might not compromise safety significantly, since safety is always the number one priority. Several additional significant management factors outside the listed factors in Figure 1 suggested by the questionnaire respondents were mostly related to safety culture, safety management programs, and teamwork.

To summarize the research findings, enhancing company safety culture is the key priority for safety management. Upper management is responsible to develop and improve company's safety culture and to incorporate it into the overall corporate culture. The other important

---

[8] For example, some tools developed by NASA are found at http://humanfactors.arc.nasa.gov/ihs/activities/ASMM/

management factors for improving flight safety are effective safety monitoring system, followed by human resource management (including training, management personnel, workload/pressure and union management), external influence management (such as structural changes like outsourcing or mergers) and finance management. Furthermore, good safety culture rooted in organizations at all levels is likely to have a positive influence on all the other factors.

5. CONCLUSION

This chapter has examined how improved safety management can reduce flight accidents. The study presents the key management factors for improving aviation safety performance from corporate responsibility aspects, which were identified in the analysis of the in-depth interview with experts and the questionnaire survey. The interviewees were selected from various countries including the emerging market so that cultural differences were also considered.

All the interviewees have agreed that management factors do influence flight safety outcomes. Some of the interviewees have claimed that most of the airline managers (especially in small airlines) are concerned, on a daily basis, more about everyday business decisions such as those concerning airline productivity or financial performance than about safety as an ongoing daily and long-term matter. The interviewees all stress that airline managers play an important role in flight safety outcomes. Many interviewees have addressed the importance of a system approach to safety, an organizational capacity to deal with any business changes, and the role of managers, training as well as union management for safety improvement. According to the interviewees, unions can have a positive or negative effect on safety. Business changes, such as mergers, are also perceived as being disruptive to operational processes or organizations themselves with follow-up effects that can impact flight safety. Thus, the implementation of business changes must be carefully planned and executed for minimum disruptions to processes, employees, and operations. Many pilots in a wide variety of airlines being interviewed observe that there is a frequent tendency for managers with inadequate experience on safety or lack of flying experience to fill senior operational positions.

The result of the questionnaire has indicated that company safety culture is considered to be the most important factor for aviation safety improvement, followed by adequate training and effective monitoring. Hence, these three key management factors need to be given a great priority in a daily operation. Management must proactively promote safety improvement at all levels of organization with a long-term vision rather than reacting passively after accidents occur. This research has addressed, with empirical data, the importance of management's proactive attitude to enhance organization's safety culture in their management decision making and incorporating it into the organization's culture. Possible initiatives to be implemented are effective training and awareness programs (seminars, workshops or events) on a regular basis that increases the interests and responsibility of each staff across the organizations. These initiatives can raise awareness and help accept and value safety improvement. Strong commitments from upper management are likely to speed up such proactive action.

In the questionnaire, budget constraint was perceived to be the least significant factor in terms of affecting flight safety. Other finance related management factors, namely funding for flight safety programs and airline's financial condition, were also both ranked low. This could suggest that as long as safety culture is properly in place, tight financial conditions might not affect aviation safety significantly. There was no identified major cultural difference in the perceptions of the respondents with multi-cultural background. Several additional management factors suggested from the respondents were mostly related to safety culture, safety management programs, and teamwork.

This study has covered a wide range of respondents both for the interview and the questionnaire, despite the difficulty in obtaining responses due to the busy schedule of the respondents and the sensitivity of the topic. For future research, the geographical locations not covered in this study, such as Australia, can be included in the analysis for further comparison of the perceptions and cultural influences. Moreover, future research could increase the sample size, which would further enhance the credibility of the results. Finally, there is a growing concern about airlines responsibility for tackling climate change issues by reducing greenhouse gas emissions[9]. With projected rising demand of air transport, future research should also conduct a deeper analysis to reduce the environmental impacts of emissions.

ACKNOWLEDGEMENT

Many thanks go to professor Sveinn Gudmundsson at Toulouse Business School France, and John Ash from the University of Cambridge UK for their useful advices. Assistance from Morlene Sschatzer, A. H. M. Shafiul Bari, Hervé Depoilly, LC Chiang, Rommel Zapata-Cano, and, JM Zhang are greatly acknowledged. We thank the ten airline and aviation safety professionals that volunteered to be interviewed, and the many anonymous respondents to the online questionnaire. We also thank Professor Raimo P. Hamalainen and Professor Jyri Mustajoki at the Helsinki University of Technology for the free use of Opinions Online to publish our questionnaire

REFERENCES

Boeing   (2006)   Statistical   Summary   of   commercial   jet   plane   accidents, http://www.boeing.com/news/techissues/pdf/statsum.pdf#search=%22Biman%20Banglad esh%20Airlines%20DC-10%20crash%22.

Bowen, BD & Lu, C-T (2004) 'Proposing a comprehensive policymaking mechanism: the introduction of policy research construct' *International Journal of Applied Aviation Studies*, 4 (1) 31-44.

Dilman, D.A (1978) *Mail and telephone surveys: the total design method,*Santa Barbara, CA, Wiley Interscience.

---

[9] http://www.wbcsd.org

Flight International (2006), *Airline Safety Review 2006*, http://www.flightglobal.com/ SectionHome/SectionDefault.aspx?NavigationID=195&CategoryID=10253&SlotID=6

Fowler, F. J (1988) *Survey research methods*, Sage, Beverly hills, CA

Greenfield, Michael A (1998) *Normal Accident Theory: The changing face of NASA and Aerospace.* A training presentation. 17 Nov. 1998.

Harris, W.C., Sachau, D., Harris, S.C., and Allen, R, (2001), 'Relationship Between Working Conditions and Commercial Pilot Fatigue Development' *Proceedings of the Human Factors and Ergonomics Society* 185-8.

Helmreich R.L (1998), 'Error management as organizational strategy' In proceeding of *the IATA Human Factors Seminar*, Bangkok, April 20-22, pp.1-7.

Helmerich R.L & Meritt, A.C (1998) *Culture at work*, Ashgate, Aldershot, UK.

Learmount, David, (2005), 'Safety First' *Flight International.* 25 Jan. 2005. 4 Jan. 2006. http://www.flightglobal.com/.

Little, L.F., I. C. Gaffney, K. H. Rosen, and M. M. Bender, (1990), 'Corporate Instability is Related to Airline Pilots' Stress Symptoms' *Aviation, Space, and Environmental Medicine* 61: 977-82.

Lu, C-T, wetmore, H, & Przetak, R (2006) 'Another approach to enhance airline safety: using management safety tools', *Journal of Air Transportation*, 11 (1), 113-140.

Mutzabaugh, Ben, (2005) "Today in the Sky: Is Maintenance Outsourcing an Airline Safety Risk?" *USA Today.* 7 March.

Reason, J, T, (1990), *Human error*, Cambridge University Press, UK.

Reason J T, (2001), *Managing the risks of organizational accidents*, Ashgate Publishing, Hampshire.

Salas, E, Burke, C S, Bowers, C A, Wilson, K A, (2001), 'Team training in the skies - Does crew resource management (CRM) training work?', *Human Factors,* 43 (4), pp. 641-674.

von Thaden, T. L., D. A. Wiegman, A. A. Mitchell, G. Sharma, and H. Zhang, 2003, *Safety Culture in a Regional Airline: Results from a Commercial Aviation Safety Survey.* University of Illinois at Urbana-Champaign.

In: Contemporary Issues in Business Ethics
Editors: M. W. Volcox, Th. O. Mohan, pp. 149-161

ISBN: 978-1-60021-773-9
© 2007 Nova Science Publishers, Inc.

Chapter 7

MEASURING CORPORATE RESPONSIBILITY PERFORMANCE

Risako Morimoto[*]

CERMAS & Department of Strategy
Toulouse Business School, France

ABSTRACT

This study addresses the way to develop a new corporate responsibility audit system, which is speedy, simple and easy to conduct. Many organizations today show great interest in assessing their daily operational performance in order to be a good corporate citizen. However, various currently existing corporate responsibility audit systems are often complex and make organizations, especially small & medium size enterprises, hesitate to engage in the corporate responsibility initiative despite their willingness. An audit system without much time, resource or budget constraint is highly likely to encourage more organizations to take part in the corporate responsibility initiative.

This research shows that there is no single broadly accepted definition, despite the widespread debate on corporate responsibility, which makes corporate responsibility audit development truly challenging. This study highlights key issues to be focused on during the development process of corporate responsibility audits, which were identified through extensive literature review and in-depth interviews with key representatives from various sectors in the United Kingdom. The research suggests that the proposed audit system needs to assess the key corporate responsibility performance of organizations comprehensively by their stakeholder groups. The study also discusses what is required for such audit systems to be effectively implemented in order to improve corporate responsibility performance of organizations.

[*] Tel: +33561294712; F: +33561294994; Email: r.morimoto@esc-toulouse.fr

1. INTRODUCTION

Despite the widespread debate on corporate responsibility, a single and broadly accepted definition is still lacking, which makes development of corporate responsibility auditing challenging. This study examines the issues surrounding the development of corporate responsibility auditing based on the analysis of extensive literature review and in-depth interviews conducted with a number of knowledgeable stakeholders from different sectors in the United Kingdom (UK). This research tackles the complex issue of corporate responsibility auditing with a scientific approach, namely the grounded theory.

Many organizations today show great interests in assessing their daily operational performance in order to be a good corporate citizen. Organizations worldwide often have their own corporate responsibility policy. Increasing numbers of organizations also report social, ethical and environmental issues associated with their operations. Initial focus of sustainability reporting was primarily on environmental issues until 1999, though emphasis on economic and social indicators also started to be intensified gradually (White 2005). About 52% of the top 250 companies of the Fortune 500 and 33% of its top 100 companies issued corporate responsibility reports in 2005, which shows approximately 10% increase from 2002 (Jimena 2006). Legislations, legal requirements, or stock exchange policies often make corporate responsibility reporting mandatory. There are also increasingly high pressures for organizations to publish corporate responsibility reports from various stakeholder groups, such as investors, journalists or nongovernmental organizations (NGOs). Investors are becoming highly interested in sustainability issues, and consider environmental, social and governance issues very important for their investment decisions (Odell 2007).

There are various corporate responsibility audit systems that currently exist, though they are often complex and make organizations, especially small & medium size enterprises (SMEs), hesitate to engage in the corporate responsibility initiative despite their willingness. An audit system, which is user-friendly without much financial, resource or time burden, is highly likely to encourage more organizations to take part in the corporate responsibility initiative. This study addresses the way to develop a new corporate responsibility audit system, which is speedy, simple and easy to conduct. Thus, neither huge budgets nor intense workforces are required for corporations, especially SMEs, to improve their daily corporate social responsibility performance.

This study consists of the following four sections. The next section extensively reviews the literature on the current issues surrounding corporate responsibility auditing. Section 3 describes the research methodology applied in this study. Section 4 discusses in detail the research findings. Section 5 provides recommendations for future corporate responsibility audit development based on the research analysis. Section 6 summarizes the chapter and draws some conclusions.

2. LITERATURE REVIEW

The extensive literature review shows that there are vast numbers of studies on corporate responsibility. The definition of corporate responsibility is often a hot topic to debate in those literatures. For example, Durand (2006) claims that there is no universally shared definition of corporate responsibility globally. McClenahen (2005) has tried to define social responsibility. Accountancy Ireland (2006) has conducted a survey to see how chartered accountants' define corporate responsibility, which addresses the wide variety of definitions. Hopkins (2005) has defined corporate responsibility and had set up a framework to measure it. There are three levels, each of which has factors to be assessed in terms of quantitative measurement procedure in the framework. His framework is similar to our proposed auditing framework discussed in this chapter.

There were also many studies on corporate responsibility auditing. Goel and Cragg (2006) have discussed how to improve corporate reporting. Adams (2004) has assessed corporate responsibility reporting reflecting corporate performance as well as the potential of recent standards and guidelines in terms of 'reporting – performance gap'. Doming (2005) has closely examined the concept of ethics auditing and theoretically develops its framework. Waddock (2004) had intended to create corporate accountability using the Global Compact's nine principles. There are frequently large gaps between stated corporate values and daily practices. Thus, Waddock and Smith (2000) have suggested that auditing company's core operating practices by using a corporate responsibility audit is likely to uncover these gaps and proactively improve their management practices. O'Dwyer et al. (2005) have examined current and potential sustainability reporting in terms of their adequacy to meet information needs of NGOs using a questionnaire survey with Irish based social and environmental NGOs. Their findings have proved a wide spread demand among NGOs for mandated externally verified sustainability reporting in an annual report, other corporate reports or on web sites.

Many studies discuss the benefits of practicing corporate responsibility initiatives. The corporate social disclosure practices are considered to be a crucial mechanism for organizations to create transparency and to reveal their social, environmental and ethical performance as well as policies to a variety of stakeholders (Adams 2004; O'Dwyer *et al.* 2005, White 2005). White (2005) emphasizes that managers should engage in social or environmental problems more proactively rather than tackling problems after they had already happened. According to White (2005), organizations adopting sustainability practices are likely to reduce operating costs, improve efficiency, gain a better reputation, be encouraged to develop innovative products and services, and integrate risk management. White (2005) claims that reporting based on Global Reporting Initiative (GRI), a commonly used corporate responsibility reporting guideline, enables external users to monitor progress of an organization towards sustainability, while internal users to identify some actions to take in order to improve their performance (White 2005).

There are also studies pointing out some practical issues attached to corporate responsibility reporting including implementation of the audit findings. Jimena (2006) emphasizes that, organizations with perfect corporate responsibility reports does not necessarily mean that they have the best practice. Furthermore, some managers claim that they presently have overloaded information of organizations' environmental, social and economic issues. However, limited information on organizations' environmental and social impacts is actually reported (Jimena 2006). The implementation issue of corporate responsibility reporting is also another concern. Adams and Frost (2006) claim that there is very little attention on how sustainability information provided in corporate responsibility reporting is actually used by management when making strategic decisions, management planning, performance management or risk management. Furthermore, organizations often fail to provide information how they incorporated the findings of their corporate responsibility reports into their strategic decision making, according to Adams and Frost (2006).

Adams and Frost (2006) have analysed the external corporate responsibility reports of 100 large Australian and 100 large UK companies. The findings highlight that although most large companies disclose their environmental and social issues, their disclosures are usually general and non-specific when reporting their corporate responsibility performance. They have also found that organizations approach to corporate responsibility reporting varies widely, in terms of motivation for reporting, the scope of the data collected, or use of the data in decision making. Each organization has different emphasis in their sustainability improvement and its implementation. Jimena (2005) argue that what should be measured in corporate responsibility reports is organization specific, which depend on organisations' sector, activity, geographical location, legal legislation. Jimena (2006) also points out that some sectors tend to report their sustainability performance compared to others, such as extractive or utility industries.

Unlike financial accounting systems, there are no generally accepted standards of sustainability reporting (White 2005). There are various frameworks for corporate responsibility reporting, such as the commonly used guideline GRI, Social Accountability 8000 (SA8000), or Accountability 1000 (AA1000). The GRI officially launched its third generation of sustainability reporting system (G3) in October 2006. The revision of their system was aimed to increase the robustness of the reporting framework, and to improve the user-friendliness of the guidelines as well as the comparability of sustainability reports[1]. Clarifying the contents and improving the precision as well as consistency the terminology within the guidelines were also the target for the revision.

3. RESEARCH METHODOLOGY

This study applies a qualitative research method in order to investigate a way to develop a user-friendly audit system to measure organization's corporate responsibility performance by providing a fundamental framework upon which an auditing system may be developed, and a theory transformed into practice. The study first reviews existing literature to investigate whether any similar studies had been conducted before, determine the nature of any existing documents, and gain an overview of the main arguments on corporate responsibility audit. Then, the study proposes the preferable measurement of corporate responsibility based on the analysis of qualitative data derived from in-depth interviews conducted with key experts in corporate responsibility.

The research examines the perceptions of key individuals drawn from different sectors in the UK regarding problems in the definition and measurement of corporate responsibility, and proposes a set of indices for corporate responsibility auditing. The data in this study were collected in such a manner as to explore the spectrum of perception in the relevant sectors and to understand the diversity of those perceptions as well as any similarities. This was achieved by means of a tested interview guide. The interview questions used in this study covers definitions of corporate responsibility, advantages and disadvantages that corporate responsibility brings to organizations, connection (if any) between corporate responsibility and sustainable development, problems in the measurement of corporate responsibility, and criteria that could be used to measure corporate responsibility. The interview questions were used in exactly the same manner in all the interviews conducted, including the order of the interview questions in order to maintain the coherency and objectivity.

Total of ten interviewees were drawn from four different sectors in the UK: the government, the private sector, the academic sector, and non-governmental organizations (NGOs), each of which was likely to have a particular perspective on corporate responsibility issues. Two key representatives were selected from each sector, except four representatives from the numerous NGOs in this field. Constraints of time and interviewee availability limited the number of interviews conducted, as with all other qualitative research. Since the data is qualitative and the sample group was carefully selected as a representative of each sector, ten interviews were assumed to be enough to capture the insights of this topic. According to Glaser and Strauss (1967), the basic criterion governing the selection of interview groups for discovering theory is their theoretical relevance for furthering the development of emerging categories, or data themes. In this case, a number of sectors in society are relevant to the understanding of corporate responsibility issues.

Prior to the actual interview, interview questions were tested with five colleagues at the business school in the UK. This process facilitates to find out whether there were any difficulties or ambiguity in understanding the questions (Dillman 1978). Pre-testing was also useful for the interviewer to practice her interviewing skill before the actual interview sessions. Some adjustments were made after incorporating the suggestions and feedback from the test-interview into the original list of the interview questions. The actual interviews for this study were conducted over a period of two months. Each interview lasted one hour on average. Best efforts were made during the interviews in order not to influence our interviewees by not providing interviewer's own views, or mislead them. Thus, objective views without any bias were collected during the interview process. The data recorded during the interview meetings were transcribed, and then verified prior to entry in a computer database. The computer qualitative analytic tool called Nudist has enabled us to categorize statements in the interviews. Each category could then be examined to see its relevance, and possible linkages between the categories or themes could be explored to form and test a theory developed by the established scientific approach, which accounts for the phenomena evident in perceptions and behaviors associated with corporate responsibility.

Data analysis was conducted using an established scientific approach. The methodology used as the basis of this study is the *grounded theory* approach, which is defined as the discovery of theory from data systematically obtained from social research (Glaser and Strauss 1967). In the grounded theory approach, data are collected and a theory subsequently developed to account for the phenomena the data illustrate. The theory is 'grounded' in the data; developed from it by the analysis process and tested in the existing data for verification. This method was selected because of its capacity to generate theoretical explanations from largely qualitative information of the sort captured during the interview programme. This approach is also a robust scientific approach that provides results from diverse and unstructured data.

---

[1] See www.globalreporting.org for further details of G3

4. RESEARCH FINDINGS

According to the interview results, although the concepts in respect to corporate responsibility displayed similarities, the way in which they expressed their views of corporate responsibility varied between and even within different sectors, as shown in Table 1. No exactly identical definitions of corporate responsibility were offered by the interviewees. Several key aspects of corporate responsibility were illustrated by the interview data. These include *voluntary initiatives, responsibility to the community or society, embracing both social and environmental issues in the work of generating profit, responsibility for stakeholder relationships, and sustainability.* Such difference in views indicates that each individual has their own view of corporate responsibility, according to their own interest.

The diversity in the definition of corporate responsibility illustrated by the interview data clearly indicates the complexity of the subject and the difficulty attached to developing a measurement system for corporate responsibility. Any methodology would be exercised to capture the full scope of the difference in individual perceptions. The World Business Council for Business Development (WBCSD), an organization of transnational corporations who advocate for cooperation between business and government to balance economic, social and environmental interests, claims that the variety of definition at the global level is also diverse[2]. After conducting a dialogue with a number of stakeholder groups around the world, the WBCSD has concluded that corporate responsibility means very different things to different people, depending upon a range of local factors including culture, religion, and governmental or legal framework conditions.

There were also several other significant findings in the interview analysis. First, many argue that the market is not attentive to the success of corporate responsibility. Consumer pressure seems to be insufficiently strong. There is a need to create incentives for organizations to change their behavior and integrate corporate responsibility into their policy. In order to do that, the market needs to look at the value of an organisation not only on the basis of financial performance, but also its environmental and social performance. Members of the private sector believe that the effective governance of corporate responsibility would create and protect long-term shareholder values. Hence, regulations would be needed to change the market system if corporate responsibility is to be meaningful.

Many perceive that the government has done a good job so far in respect to corporate responsibility, although it can do even more. NGOs in particular emphasize the requirement for both national and international regulation, despite the fact that the government's preference to date has inclined more towards light touch regulation. This approach has been adopted merely to provide encouragement based upon the idea of corporate responsibility as a voluntary initiative. The importance of good corporate leadership and giving a greater priority to corporate responsibility at board level was also emphasized by many interviewees during the interviews.

There was a claim that one of the advantages of corporate responsibility, having a better reputation, is in fact a minor one. There is a perception that the advantage applies only to large companies, and in specific sectors, such as energy or manufacturing. Corporate responsibility is seen as costly and time consuming, especially for SMEs, which in fact comprise the vast majority of the UK private sector. Therefore incentives will need to be

Table 1. Definition of corporate responsibility in different sectors

Sector	Definition
Academic	* *"Corporate responsibility, which started from environmental issues, environmental impacts, incorporated community programmes and charitable giving, now moving onto people risk, corporate governance, ethical issues as well as shareholder elements as coming from financial services' interest in ethical concerns"* * "Corporate responsibility which embraces both environmental and social issues. Company's responsibility to the community in which it operates or on which it has an impact"
Private sector	* *"Responsible management of a company with respect to its impact on the society"* * "Corporate responsibility, which is important to long-term business success, and is vital to the maintenance of productive long-term relationships with stakeholders"
Government	* *"Voluntary activity which is done above what is legally required by companies or organizations into [sic] how they do business or operate within, with their stakeholders, with their employees, with their customers, purely voluntary initiatives, looking at how perhaps they could be more socially responsible in their business or work dealings"* * "Business contribution to sustainable development"
NGOs	* *"Corporate responsibility which started from the environmental perspective, embraces both environmental and social. The wider responsibilities businesses share in their work of generating profit"* * *"Business contribution to sustainable development"* * *"Sustainability, which implies the social and environmental impacts of companies should be sustainable over a long period of time"* * "Managing and taking responsibility for stakeholder relationships and doing that in consultation with respect for the relevant stakeholder groups"

given to SMEs which have little resources, as corporate responsibility becomes an increasingly important business issue for them in the future, according to the Department of Trade and Industry in the UK. One possibility avenue for applying pressure to SMEs could be through supply chains.

When a successful corporate responsibility auditing system is to be developed, the following issues should be considered. First issue is the disparity of perceptions concerning the definition of corporate responsibility by different sectors, as revealed by the interview data. This indicates a particular difficulty in the process of audit. Second, the widespread criticism of Ticking-Box type assessment systems, a system in which organizations just tick boxes to indicate whether they achieved the indicated assessment criteria, clearly addresses the need to develop an alternative approach to the problem. One another crucial factor for developing a comprehensive corporate responsibility auditing system is to deal with the problem of negative screening. When individuals managing socially responsible funds make their investment decisions, they screen companies to exclude those that produce commodities

---

[2] www.wbcsd.org

and services deemed to environmentally and socially irresponsible, such as weapons, pornography, or tobacco. This is controversial, since it is for debate whether the products or core process of an organization should be the core indicator of its level of responsibility. There was widespread agreement with the idea of emphasizing products. However, some NGOs claim that a change in behavior and organizational commitment to improve their operations is the key issue in assessing corporate responsibility. Involvement of all the stakeholder groups is regarded as the most important issue, as discussed above. Therefore the question concerning whether it is moral to exclude some specific organizations should be asked, and effort should be made to consider the corporate responsibility assessment of any type of organization.

To sum up, this research has highlighted several key items as crucial in developing a corporate responsibility auditing system. The inclusion of all significant stakeholder groups in the auditing process is essential. Careful considerations should be given to the diversity in individual perceptions of corporate responsibility, which makes corporate responsibility audit development challenging. The problem of negative screening should also be addressed. The shortcomings of the 'ticking-box' type approach for corporate responsibility assessment method should also be worth investigated. The measurement of organizations' corporate responsibility performance should be both qualitative and quantitative in nature. The research analysis also concludes that the following six elements were perceived as the key for the achievement of successful corporate responsibility. They are good stakeholder management, good corporate leadership, greater priority for corporate responsibility at board level, integration of corporate responsibility into corporate policy at all levels and in all divisions of business, regulation at the national and international level understood and demonstrated across all areas of business, and active involvement of, and good coordination between, government business, NGOs and civil society.

A theoretical framework was developed in this study to illustrate the factors essential in corporate responsibility as perceived by the different stakeholders (Table 2), including the six key elements listed above. This matrix is an attempt to place the position of each stakeholder group into context with regard to corporate responsibility. The listed outcomes in Table 2 are likely to be expected with the specified combination of the environment and the process for each actor. Understanding the background of corporate responsibility development as viewed by each stakeholder is essential to the development of a meaningful corporate responsibility auditing system.

5. RECOMMENDATIONS

This study proposes a desirable conceptual framework of a corporate responsibility auditing process, incorporating the findings of the extensive literature review and the in-depth interview analysis. The audit method could essentially be in four phases as follows. First stage is the evidence compilation. The client organization collects evidence against each of the audit indices for consideration by the auditor. The second stage is the site visit. The auditor visits the organization and examines the evidence to support each index. Supplementary evidence in the form of documents, interviews, photographs or notes is

Table 2. Theoretical framework illustrating the factors essential in corporate responsibility

Environment	Actor	Process	Six key elements for successful corporate responsibility	Outcome
Competitive market	Private sector	Practice corporate responsibility	i) Good stakeholder management ii) Greater priority for corporate responsibility at board level iii) Integration of corporate responsibility into corporate policy iv) Good corporate leadership	More efficient business, greater share price, long-term business success
CEOs see the commitment increasingly important to creating well-managed company				
Corporate responsibility perceived as a business contribution to sustainable development	NGOs	Putting corporate responsibility in practice by stakeholder dialogue and consultation		Active involvement of and good coordination between government, business, NGOs, and civil society / Meaningful change in corporate behaviour
Corporate responsibility voluntary initiative	Government	Light-touch regulation	More Regulation	Help organizations to tackle sustainability

Table 2. Continued

Environment	Actor	Process	Six key elements for successful corporate responsibility	Outcome
Direct impact on their daily life	Local inhabitants	Positive stakeholder relationship created by corporate responsibility		Less negative impact on local inhabitant and more positive involvement of the community
Society where corporate responsibility is understood better than the past	General public	Transparency created by corporate responsibility		Better quality society
Reputational value insignificant, and no cost & time for corporate responsibility	Supplier	Through supply-chains: pressure from larger corporations	Active involvement of and good coordination between government, business, NGOs, and civil society	SME participation in corporate responsibility
Competitive environment	Employee & contract staff	Positive stakeholder relationship created by corporate responsibility		Motivated, engaged, involved, trained and committed workforce
Corporations are more transparent and people empowered by choice	Clients & customers	Pressure on corporations		Better quality of goods & services
Share prices reflect many factors	Shareholders	Active social responsible investment		Create market for corporate responsibility Greater share prices

collected as required by the auditor. The third stage is the evidence analysis. The auditor scrutinizes all of the evidence against all of the indices and prepares the final report to the client organization. Final stage is the reporting. The client organization is provided with a comprehensive listing of its performance, including the degree of evidential uncertainty for all of the indices.

The proposed corporate responsibility audit framework is designed to be as simple as possible to support prompt completion of the procedure and gain high participation rates of organizations. The proposed audit framework consists of two main sections; a description of the corporate responsibility system architecture, and stakeholder factors. Thus, major aspects of organizations operations and all the stakeholders are included. The main features of the proposed audit are as follows. First, it is designed to accommodate any type of organization without discrimination. Second, it assesses the organization's management system and its relations with all of the stakeholders, which are classified into a set of cohorts. Third, performance against each index is categorised as Essential, Required, or Desirable. Fourth, evidence is identified against a series of indices that characterize the organization's performance in relation to each stakeholder group. Documentary evidence is the most appropriate proof of compliance for any given index, although some verbal evidence, including the results of brief telephone surveys or interviews, is proposed in the case of some indices. The main purpose of conducting the corporate responsibility auditing is to encourage organizations to improve their sustainability performance and to integrate corporate responsibility practice into their organizational culture. Thus, in order to measure how well the auditing system is implemented can be assessed by benchmarking the organizations' performance this year to the previous year performance in order to examine their continuous improvement.

6. CONCLUSION

Organizations often hesitate to engage in a corporate responsibility audit despite their huge interest in assessing their sustainability performance due to resource, time or budget constraints. This research was aimed to facilitate such ever growing organizations' corporate responsibility initiative by investigating how a user-friendly corporate responsibility audit can be developed. The study has examined the definitions of corporate responsibility and key factors necessary to be considered when developing a new user-friendly corporate responsibility auditing system based on the analysis of extensive literature review and in-depth interviews conducted with a number of knowledgeable stakeholders from different sectors in the United Kingdom. The interview analysis has addressed the subjective nature of the topic. Although the concepts of corporate responsibility defined by the interviewees displayed similarities, the way in which they expressed their views of corporate responsibility varied between and even within different sectors. No exactly identical definitions of corporate responsibility were offered by the interviewees, which makes measuring corporate responsibility performance very challenging. Such difference in views indicates that each individual has their own view of corporate responsibility, according to their own interest. Several key aspects of corporate responsibility were illustrated by the interview data. These include *voluntary initiatives, responsibility to the community or society, embracing both social and environmental issues in the work of generating profit, responsibility for stakeholder relationships, and sustainability.*

The research has highlighted several items as crucial in developing a corporate responsibility auditing system as follows. The inclusion of all significant stakeholder groups in the auditing process is essential. There is diversity in individual perceptions of corporate responsibility, which makes corporate responsibility audit development challenging. The problem of negative screening of certain products and services should also be addressed. The shortcomings of the 'ticking-box' type approach for corporate responsibility assessment method should also be worth investigating. The measurement of organizations' corporate responsibility performance should be both qualitative and quantitative in nature.

The research analysis has concluded that the following six elements are perceived as the key for the achievement of successful corporate responsibility operation. They are good stakeholder management, good corporate leadership, greater priority for corporate responsibility at board level, integration of corporate responsibility into corporate policy at all levels and in all divisions of business, regulation at the national and international level understood and demonstrated across all areas of business, and active involvement of, and good coordination between, government business, NGOs and civil society.

This study proposes a desirable conceptual framework of a corporate responsibility auditing process, incorporating the findings of the extensive literature review and the in-depth interview analysis. The proposed corporate responsibility audit system is designed to be as simple as possible to support prompt completion of the procedure. The proposed audit consists of two main sections; a description of the corporate responsibility system architecture, and stakeholder factors. Major aspects of organizations operations and all the stakeholders are included. In order to measure how well the auditing system is implemented can be assessed by benchmarking the organizations' performance this year to the previous year's performance in order to examine their continuous improvement. The concept of corporate responsibility auditing system developed in this research is augmenting and complementary to currently existing systems, such as GRI. The proposed approach differs from the currently existing system in terms of style. The proposed approach challenges the previous system since it is a procedure which is speedy, simple and easy to conduct. It complements in the sense that the most significant factors are extracted to assess whereas the more detailed currently existing approach reconfirms the overall organization's corporate responsibility performance.

ACKNOWLEDGEMENTS

Useful comments and advices from Dr Chris Hope and John Ash from the University of Cambridge UK are greatly acknowledged. Many thanks also go to the interviewees who kindly participated in the interviews for their grate contribution to this research.

REFERENCES

Accountancy Ireland, 2006, volume 38 (3), p.1.

Adams, C.A.: 2004, 'the ethical, social and environmental reporting-performance portrayal gap', accounting, *Auditing & Accountability Journal*, 17 (5), pp. 731-757.

Adams, C & Frost, G (2006) 'CSR reporting' Financial Management, June, pp. 34-36.

Dilman, D.A (1978) *Mail and telephone surveys: the total design method* (Santa Barbara, CA, Wiley Interscience).

Doming, G.: 2005, 'Trust and dialogue: theoretical approaches to ethics auditing', *Journal of Business Ethics*, 57 (3), pp. 209-219.

Durand, A (2006) 'CSR continues to define itself globally' *Caribbean Business*, 11 May, p. 48.

Glaser, B.G. and Strauss, A.L.: 1967, The discovery of Grounded Theory: strategy for Qualitative Research (Weidenfed and Nicolson).

Goel, R & Cragg, W (2006) 'Corporate reporting' *Business and the Environment*, February, p.5-7.

Hopkins, M.: 2005, Measurement of corporate social responsibility, *International journal of Management & Decision Making*, 6(3/4), p.1.

Jimena J (2006) 'Measuring your responsibilities' Canadian Mining Journal June, www.canadianminingjournal.com, p8.

McClenahen, J.S.: 2005, Defining social responsibility, *Manufacturing & Society*, March, pp.64-65.

Odell, A.M (2007) 'Surveyed managers emphasize socially responsible issues', *WBCSD news*, 24 January 2007, www.wbcsd.org

O'Dwyer, B, Unerman, J, & Hession, E (2005) 'User needs in sustainability reporting: perspectives of stakeholders in Ireland' *European Accounting Review*, 14 (4) pp. 759-787.

Waddock, S.: 2004, 'Creating corporate accountability: foundational principles to make corporate citizenship real', *Journal of Business Ethics*, 50 (4), pp. 313-327.

Waddock, S & Smith, N (2000) 'Corporate responsibility audits: doing well by doing good', *Sloan Management Review*, Winter2000, Vol. 41, Issue 2, pp. 75-83

White, G. B (2005) 'How to report a company's sustainability activities' Management Accounting Quarterly, 7 (1), Fall, PP. 36-43.

In: Contemporary Issues in Business Ethics   ISBN: 978-1-60021-773-9
Editors: M. W. Volcox, Th. O. Mohan, pp. 163-176   © 2007 Nova Science Publishers, Inc.

Chapter 8

MISERY AS CORPORATE MISSION: USER IMAGERY AT THE NIGHTCLUB THE SPY BAR

*Niklas Egels-Zandén**

Centre for Business in Society, School of Business, Economics and Law at Göteborg
University, Box 600, SE – 405 30 Göteborg, Sweden

Ulf Ågerup[†]

Marketing Group, School of Business, Economics and Law at Göteborg University
Box 600, SE – 405 30 Göteborg, Sweden

ABSTRACT

Despite extensive corporate responsibility research into both *what* products firm produce and *how* they produce them, research is lacking in one product category in which the *what* and *how* linkage create questionable corporate practice – luxury products. Luxury is in some cases created by companies controlling the so-called user imagery of their customers, i.e., by companies encouraging 'desirable' individuals to consume their products and obstructing 'undesirable' individuals from consumption. This chapter critically analyses the implications of this corporate practice based on a study of Sweden's most luxurious nightclub. The study's results show that the nightclub has organised its activities to allow categorisations of individuals into 'desirable' and 'undesirable' customers. Furthermore, the study shows that a creation of 'misery' for the vast majority of individuals (the 'undesirable') is essential for creating 'enjoyment' for the selected few (the 'desirable'). The chapter concludes by discussing implications for practitioners interesting in altering this situation.

* Niklas.Egels-Zanden@handels.gu.se; +46-31-7862729 (telephone)
† Ulf.Agerup@handels.gu.se; +46-31-93 23 29 (telephone)

INTRODUCTION

When discussing a firm's corporate responsibility, two main issues arise. *What* products does the firm produce, and *how* does it produce these products? Researchers, as well as practitioners, have given much attention to the idea that some products are 'irresponsible' – most notably cigarettes, weapons, alcohol, and gambling products (e.g., Newton, 1993; Kinder and Domini, 1997; Elm, 1998; Havemann, 1998; Maitland, 1998; Brenkert, 2000; Green, 2000). For example, firms producing these products are excluded often from 'ethical' funds (e.g., Kinder and Domini, 1997). Similarly, much attention has been given to *how* products are produced. Lately, this debate has mainly been focused on human and workers' rights in production in developing countries. Hot research topics include: the corporate embracement of codes of conduct (e.g., Frenkel, 2001; van Tulder and Kolk, 2001; Graafland, 2002; Winstanley *et al.*, 2002; Egels-Zandén, 2007), the signing of global collective agreements (e.g., Wills, 2002; Carley, 2005; Fairbrother and Hammer, 2005; Riisgaard, 2005; Anner *et al.*, 2006; Egels-Zandén and Hyllman, 2006, 2007), and corporate operations in controversial markets (e.g., Donaldson 1989, 1996; De George 1990, 1993; Donaldson and Dunfee, 1994; Carroll and Gannon, 1997; Schermerhorn, 1999). Despite the ample research into both *what* products firm produce and *how* they produce them, research is lacking in one product category in which the *what* and *how* linkage create questionable corporate practice – luxury products.

A review of the last years of international publications into corporate responsibility clearly shows that luxury products are a neglected area of research. This lack is likely due to that luxury products generally are not of 'irresponsible' nature (compared to cigarettes, alcohol, weapons, etc.), and that the quality demands and high price range often limit the abuse of human and workers' rights in production (cf. McWilliam and Siegel, 2001). Hence, since previous research has treated the *what* and *how* questions separately, luxury products have escaped its radar. However, this chapter argues that when treated together the *what* in luxury products (i.e., their exclusiveness) leads to problematic aspects in *how* the products are produced and marketed.

The purpose of this chapter is to address this gap in previous research by analysing the intersection between *what* and *how*. More specifically, we focus on the corporate practice of customer base management aimed at influencing the user imagery of the product, and critically analyse the implications of this practice. This is much needed, since previous marketing research into user imagery and luxury products has neglected the corporate responsibility aspects of this practice. Hence, corporate responsibility researchers have neglected the area of luxury products and user imagery, while marketing researchers have studied both luxury products and user imagery but ignored their corporate responsibility aspects. We base our analysis of user imagery on a study of Sweden's most luxurious nightclub – The Spy Bar – and our results show that corporate responsibility as well as marketing researchers be well advised to recognise the corporate responsibility aspects of luxury products and user imagery in future research since the corporate practice entails critical issues for further academic and practitioner discussions.

LUXURY PRODUCTS AND USER IMAGERY

The core idea of 'luxury' is that the product is only attainable for a limited range of consumers (e.g., Berry, 1994; Twitchell, 2002). However, recently there has been a shift in the clientele for luxury products with more affordable, although still expensive, alternatives for 'normal' people being launched (e.g., Twitchell, 2002; Allères, 2005). It is problematic to precisely define 'luxury' (e.g., Dubois *et al.*, 1995; Vigneron and Johnson, 1999), although most people in practice can categorise products into 'luxury' and 'non-luxury' products. In this chapter, luxury is defined as products that are widely desired and more expensive than what their utility motivates (cf. Berry, 1994; Twitchell, 2002). Hence, luxury products are primarily consumed because of their meaning to us rather than because of their utility. Consequently, brand meaning creation is central to the creation of luxury.

Brand meaning is created partly through product design, market communication, but also through the communication between stakeholders in society (Balmer and Gray, 2000) in the form of, for example, public speech and print (Twitchell, 2002), word-of-mouth (Keller, 2003), and user imagery (Aaker, 1996). The idea of *user imagery* is that values are transferred to a brand through the people that are associated with it, i.e., that the brand meaning is dependent on those associated with the brand (cf. McCracken, 1989). This includes both companies' employees and the users of the product (Keller, 2000). Hence, consumers' perceptions of the brand users affect their perception of the meaning of the brand (Aaker, 1996; Schroeder, 2005; Brioschi, 2006). This relationship works in both ways. If 'desirable' individuals consume the brand it instils values of 'luxury' into the brand, and if 'undesirable' individuals consume the brand it has the opposite effect.

This idea of user imagery has led firms to invest in *ideal* users such as sponsored athletes, spokespersons, and people portrayed in advertising to promote the luxury of the brand (Aaker, 1996). The ideal users should not be confused with the target group for the brand, but should rather be seen as a reflection of the image that the firm want to offer the target group (cf. Kapferer, 1994). In contrast to the ideal user who uses a brand because he or she is financially compensated for doing so, the *typical* users are those individuals actually using the brand (Aaker, 1996). In the same way as spokespersons, but arguably even more powerful, these users instil the brand with values by conveying what can be seen as a visual word-of-mouth (cf. Twitchell, 2002; Keller, 2003). The focus in this chapter is on attempts to manage these typical users in order to improve the user imagery.

In essence, user imagery can be used as a tool to create a boundary between 'desirable' and 'undesirable' individuals. Framed in this way, it is clear that user imagery is based on the more general marketing ideal of identifying and targeting certain customer groups. Traditionally, this practice is referred to as positioning which entails segmenting consumers into distinct but homogenous target groups that require similar marketing mixes (e.g., Kapferer, 1994; Aaker, 1996; Keller, 2003). In these positioning strategies, any addition of customers not belonging to the target group is seen as a bonus – a *positive* side effect. However, when applying the user imagery logic additional customers are seen as a *negative* side effect if they are from the 'undesirable' group. Since the consumers are not only perceived as income generators, but also image creators, it is rational for purveyors of luxury to turn away potential consumers if their undesirable characteristics would taint the luxury brand's image. In other words, by employing customer base management to improve brand image, companies sacrifice short term financial gain to create brand meaning. In creating brand meaning, user imagery plays a more central role for luxury products as compared to other product categories, since conventional branding activities are ineffective for luxury products (cf. Baker, 2006). Hence, brand meaning has to be created in alternative ways for luxury products and companies have to rely more on influencing social discourses through tools such as user imagery than traditional activities (cf. Twitchell, 2002).

The boundary creation between 'desirable' and 'undesirable' customers can be expected to affect a person's perception of herself. Several authors have shown that consumption is closely linked to the construction of identities (e.g., Levy, 1959; McCracken, 1986; Belk, 1988), and that this is especially so in consumption of luxury products (Berry, 1994; Vigneron and Johnson, 2004). Hence, by classifying an individual as a 'desirable'/ 'undesirable' consumer, companies influence individuals' identities. As will be shown in the study presented in this chapter, this influence could literally lead to matters of life or death. Despite these corporate responsibility implications, prior research into user imagery has neglected these aspects and solely focused on how firms strategically can employ user imagery to improve the brand personality (e.g., Aaker, 1996). Simultaneously, corporate responsibility research has neglected the research topics of luxury and user imagery, leading to a lack of critical analysis of the implications of this type of corporate practice.

METHOD

To analyse how corporations strive to achieve user imagery through customer base management in luxury products, we make use of a data from a study of Sweden's most luxurious nightclub – The Spy Bar. Data were collected via interviews, observations, and document analysis. The focus in the data collection was on studying the operations of the nightclub in relation to user imagery and customer base management. The Spy Bar is unusual in the sense that individuals from the security firm are the only individuals that the customers interacted with (except for bartenders and DJs). This is true also for the presentation of The Spy Bar on its webpage and in media articles in which the CEO of the security company – rather than the CEO of the nightclub – is the front figure for the nightclub. Hence, the nightclub has outsourced all significant interaction with customers to an independent security company. This has the effect that the head of security at The Spy Bar (also the CEO of the security company) is well known among the general public in Sweden. Given the importance of the security officers, they were the chosen focus in our data collection.

In total, 12 semi-structured interviews (lasting on average one hour) were made with the security officers (including the CEO) working at The Spy Bar. A handful of additional interviews were also made with representatives for The Spy Bar. These interviews were mainly used to provide a background understanding of the directives provided by The Spy Bar management to the security officers. Additionally, 15 semi-structured interviews (lasting on average 30 minutes) were made with customers inside The Spy Bar and potential customers queuing outside the nightclub.

In addition to interviews, observations were conducted during four evenings at the nightclub. During the observation study, the researcher closely followed the security officers' work and interaction with customers. In parts of the observation study, access was granted to the two-way radios used by the security officers. The observation study was focused on two central aspects of the security officers' work – the selection of customers outside the nightclub and the disciplining of customers inside the nightclub.

Finally, written documentations (in the form of web pages and media articles) were used as both input into interviews and as validation of the data received through observations and interviews. There were few inconsistencies between the data obtained in interviews and observations, but some between the data presented in the written documentation and the observations/interviews. In cases of inconsistencies, these were sometimes discussed with the security officers, and we based the below presented descriptions mainly on the data provided in the interviews and observations since these seemed more reliable than the media articles and web pages.

The collected data were used to construct thick descriptions of the activities of the security officers. To validate the descriptions, they were sent to the CEO of the security company who expressed no critique regarding the descriptions of their work. Based on these descriptions of the security officers' activities and the interviews with customers and The Spy Bar management, a 'typical' nightclub evening was constructed (as presented in the empirical section below). Evidently, there are problems in constructing a 'typical' nightclub evening, since nothing is 'typical' in corporate practice. However, this was perceived as the best way to present the empirical data in order to convey an understanding of a nightclub evening at The Spy Bar to the reader.

Night clubs belong to a specific category of luxury products. As shown by Allères (2005), luxury can be divided into different price levels. There is the inaccessible luxury level of yachts and mansions, the intermediate level of cars, watches, and hotels, and finally the accessible level where although the products are more expensive than their substitutes, most people can afford to buy them should they wish to do so. This level covers, for example, champagne, perfume, and the empirical focus of this chapter: nightclub visits. In focusing on nightclub visits, i.e., on attainable luxury products, the purpose of this chapter is not to discuss the problems related to the first two types of offerings and, hence, to question the excluding nature of prices. Rather, the purpose of this chapter is to analyse those products that are attainable for most individuals. In these cases, the limitation has to be achieved in other ways than through prices, and as is shown in this chapter one way to achieve this is influencing user imagery via customer base management.

A 'TYPICAL' EVENING AT THE NIGHTCLUB THE SPY BAR

After midnight a regular Friday evening, a large crowd stands outside a small entrance to a nightclub – The Spy Bar – in the city of Stockholm (the capitol of Sweden). Separating the queuing individuals from the nightclub is a red rope and inside the rope numerous security officers dressed in black suits control the queue; carefully selecting who should be allowed to enter the club. The queue is different from the traditional linear queue. It does not even look like a queue; rather, like an unstructured ocean of people. The head of the security officers (also the CEO of the security company) explains that this queue structure is generally referred to as a 'rainbow' queue and that the purpose of the queue is to allow the security officers to freely select who is allowed to enter the nightclub without having to consider how long each individual has waited outside the club. The CEO mainly controls the selection of individuals himself, making him an influential and well-known figure in Swedish nightlife. He has, for example, been offered to go on tours around Sweden as a celebrity security officer.

While the selection procedure is extremely strict at this hour, it was easier to enter the nightclub earlier in the evening. Then, individuals were allowed to enter that now would not even come close to the 'desirability' status of the selected few that are allowed entrance. The security officers explain this by referring to the need for the nightclub to receive revenues throughout the evening, and that they have fewer individuals to select from early on in the evening. At this hour, the possibility to select individuals is seemingly endless. The management of The Spy Bar has defined the characteristics of those that are to be allowed to enter the nightclub, and the security officers do their best to implement these directives in practice. When asked what they are searching for in a customer, the security officers have difficulties providing a precise answer. Rather, they provide a list of characteristics as to exemplify what they are after. Guests are to be celebrities, over 25 years of age, from the city centre, dressed in Gucci, trendy, financial wealthy, journalists, stock brokers, real estate agents and/or CEOs. While those few with just the 'right' characteristics enter the nightclub quickly, the vast majority of guests wait outside for often over an hour uncertain of if they will be allowed entrance. The length of the wait is also difficult to predict, since the 'rainbow' queue system provides no signals regarding if, and if so when, a person is allowed to enter.

The selection of individuals is a complex and sometimes ruthless process. The security officers establish contact with the visitors through body language and eye contact. Rarely, if ever, is there any verbal communication between the security officers and the visitors other than to inform someone to enter the nightclub or to impolitely answer visitors' attempts to persuade the officers to allow them entrance. Occasionally, the security officers signal (in a hardly noticeable way) to groups of individuals that they are to walk around the block and return without certain members of the group. Hence, the officers force groups to be split into those 'desirable' that will be allowed to enter and those 'undesirable' that will not.

Sporadically, celebrities arrive at the nightclub, walking pass the crowd and straight into the club. This does not seem to surprise anyone. However, sporadically some individuals are allowed to enter the nightclub without fitting the expected characteristics of a Spy Bar customer. The queuing visitors quickly recognise this (they are often highly skilled themselves in judging the likeliness of others entering), and discussions start in the crowd. Some of these unexpected guests wear visible signs indicating that they are part of well-known criminal groups, while other unexpected guests seem to have a close relationship with some of the security officers (most often the CEO). Another surprising event to those in the queue is that some celebrities arrive highly confident of their chances to enter the club, but are denied entrance. This includes famous Swedish actors and Olympic winning sportsmen. Seemingly humiliated these celebrities are forced to leave the queue and continue to another nightclub. Loud discussions start among the other queuing individuals focused on understanding why these celebrities were not allowed to enter. Did the security officers not recognise them? Are the officers incompetent? Are they incapable of making a 'fair' selection?

The answer to why the celebrities were denied access to the nightclub is found inside the club. Here, the security officers are responsible for inducing the 'right' atmosphere to the nightclub. This mainly involves assisting guests and securing that no acts of violence occurs throughout the evening, but it also involves disciplining individuals to behave in a 'correct' way. For instance, visitors standing in certain areas of the nightclub or attempting to climb onto the window-ledges are quickly and harshly reprimanded. If the individuals despite these reprimands do not comply with the 'correct' behaviour, the security officers either make him/her leave the nightclub or restrict the individual's future entrance to the club. Such previous acts of 'incorrectness' (although of more severe nature) were the reasons for denying the above discussed celebrities to enter the nightclub.

In addition to disciplining customers inside the nightclub, the security officers are also responsible for assuring that only 'highly desirable' individuals are allowed entrance into the VIP areas within the club. Hence, The Spy Bar is really two, or even more, nightclubs, sharing little more than the same entrance. In this way, the security officers' sorting of individuals into categories continues inside the nightclub as well.

About forty-five minutes before closing time, the security officers stop allowing individuals to enter the nightclub. However, this is not signalled to those in the queue, leading many to queue until the nightclub closes. The evening ends with the security officers lining up outside the nightclub making sure that everything runs smoothly when the customers leave the club.

THE ROLE OF USER IMAGERY

The conducted study clearly illustrates that the security officers at The Spy Bar use customer base management to influence the user imagery and the nightclub brand in the desired direction. Hence, this study confirms the arguments and results of previous studies that corporations in practice use customer base management to influence user imagery (e.g., Aaker, 1996; Twitchell, 2002). In The Spy Bar case, this practice was explicitly demanded by The Spy Bar management and consciously implemented by the security officers. The security officers even regarded customer base management as one of their most – if not their most – important work task. As the CEO of the security company noted: "Popular nightclubs have strategically organised their activities in order to sort people into an A class and a B class. The entire organisation from the interior to the queue system is designed for this purpose". Furthermore, most security officers did not regard this as problematic or disturbing. Rather, it was seen as the common practice among luxurious nightclubs; a necessary strategy for creating the luxury status of the club.

The Spy Bar's focus on user imagery via customer base management should be seen in the light of that the club had ample opportunities to select customers. Since a nightclub visit is an attainable luxury product (cf. Allères, 2005), most individuals can afford an evening at The Spy Bar and given the perception of the club as the most luxurious club in Sweden numerous individuals attempts to spend an evening at the club. However, the club is limited in size by the building it is occupying, so even if the security officers would have desired to allow all interested individuals to enter the club this would be impossible. Hence, the club is in the rare situation that demand for its product widely exceeds the supply and that the supply capability not easily could be increased.

The security officers used customer base management to influence user imagery in two main ways. First, and most important, when selecting who should be allowed to enter the nightclub. The 'rainbow' queue system at The Spy Bar was an important tool for selecting who is allowed to enter. By creating a crowd of individuals outside the red rope that demarks the division between inside and outside the nightclub, the security officers were able to continuously choose individuals that were perceived as 'desirable'. These 'desirable' individuals included royalties, 'celebrities', wealthy individuals, and 'cool' individuals. Importantly, an individual's spending capability was not the main criterion for the security officers' selections; rather, the officers' attempted to identify an "appearance of luxuriousness". The 'undesirable' individuals, on the other hand, included overweight, poorly dressed, and 'ugly' individuals (especially if these also were immigrants and/or not from the city centre). These individuals were consciously restricted from entering the nightclub, regardless of their spending capability. In addition to the categories 'desirable' and 'undesirable', the security officers also sorted individuals into a 'potentially desirable'/'not undesirable' category. This category filled a central role for the nightclub, since they were to create an as large as possible queue outside the nightclub. Hence, the security officers consciously attempted to maximise the queue outside the club both to create an appearance of popularity, but also to communicate that even the – to an outside observer – seemingly 'cool' and 'desirable' individuals in the queue were not 'desirable' *enough* to enter the nightclub. This practice can be understood as a negative user imagery message: these seemingly desirable individuals are not even qualified to be a 'typical' user of The Spy Bar.

Second, in addition to the queue system, the security officers also used customer base management inside the club. First, in a similar fashion as outside, there were restricted 'VIP' areas within the club only open for especially 'desirable' individuals. Second, the security officers disciplined individuals inside the nightclub that did not act as a 'desirable' individual ought to act. This included evident behaviour such as acts of violence and sexual harassment, but also standing in certain parts of the nightclub and addressing the security officers in the 'wrong' way. Hence, in addition to sorting individuals into 'desirable' and 'undesirable' based on mainly external attributes via different queue systems, individuals were also sorted into 'desirable' and 'undesirable' based on their behaviour inside the nightclub. 'Undesirable' behaviour occasionally led to individuals being forced to leave the club, but more frequently to being restricted in future attempts to enter the club. In this way, the sorting of individuals into 'desirable' and 'undesirable' continued throughout the customers' nightclub visit and effected their future classification. However, since there is not a perfect relation between 'desirable' external attributes and 'desirable' behaviour, some individuals that had 'desirable' external attributes were denied access to the nightclub due to behavioural aspects. For individuals unaware of the behavioural 'problems' of these individuals, this practice sent the message that the security officers were poorly skilled at recognising 'desirability', in turn, potentially threatening the nightclub's user image.

MISERY AS CORPORATE MISSION

There are several implications of the security officers' classification of individuals into 'desirable' and 'undesirable'. First, the 'undesirable' individuals risk spending their weekend queuing outside the nightclub. It is common that individuals spend hours in the queue outside the nightclub, and still are not allowed entrance. Despite this, they return the next weekend to repeat the procedure. Since the 'rainbow' queue system restricts individuals from contact with the security officers, individuals receive no signals of whether they are to be allowed to enter the club or not. Hence, individuals could – and many in fact do – spend much of their weekend queuing outside The Spy Bar.

Second, and even more important, the classification of individuals into 'desirable' and 'undesirable' not only influence individuals' weekend activities, but also their perception of themselves. Numerous authors have shown that consumption is closely linked to individuals' construction of their identities (e.g., Levy, 1959; McCracken, 1986; Belk, 1988), and that this is especially so in consumption of luxury products (Berry, 1994). Hence, to be classified as 'desirable' or 'undesirable', potentially effects individuals' perception of themselves. The vast majority of visitors to The Spy Bar are uncertain of their status when arriving at the nightclub with only a handful being certain of being allowed to enter the club. Hence, most individuals are uncertain of their 'desirability', making them susceptible to security officers' classifications. Our study's results also indicate that the security officers' influence the visitors' perception of themselves – both in a positive and negative way. Those few that are allowed to enter seem to experience improved self-confidence (at least temporarily) perceiving themselves as successful individuals. On the other hand, the majority that are restricted from entering seem to experience worsen self-confidence (at least temporarily) perceiving themselves as less successful than they previously had thought. In an era where individuals are increasingly uncertain of their identity and their value (e.g., Gabriel and Lang, 2006), these 'desirability' signals seemingly have important implications for individuals' identities.

Moving from an individual to an organisational level, the links between the security officers' actions and individuals' identities provide an overall understanding of luxurious nightclubs' operations. As much as nightclubs are providing a service in the form of entertainment, they are also providing a service in ranking of individuals. The results of our study indicate that individuals do not mainly visit the nightclub for the music, drinks etc., but rather for the potential to feel 'desirable', 'successful' and 'exclusive'. However, in order for a selected few to feel 'desirable' and 'exclusive', the majority has to be categorised as the opposite as 'undesirable' and 'unsuccessful'. This is achieved through creating a widespread queue of 'undesirable' individuals outside the club – individuals that the few 'desirable' can feel more successful than. Hence, as much as the mission of nightclubs is to create a feeling of 'successfullness' among the selected few, it is also to create a feeling of 'unsuccessfullness' or 'misery' among the vast majority of individuals interested in visiting the club. The nightclubs (and in the Spy Bar case the security officers) have become judges of our times, classifying individuals into an A and a B group while simultaneously promoting that everyone should want to be in the A group.

This categorisation of individuals as 'undesirable' is not always accepted by the 'unacceptables', making them strike back. In the studied case, this resistance mainly took the form of verbal abuse of the security officers, but sometimes it also led to threats and acts of violence. When reflecting on these forms of resistance, the CEO of the security company said that: "In practice, the 'rainbow' queue system leads to increased frustration and disorder among the guests – the opposite of the task of a security officer". Hence, the CEO of the security company was aware of the connections between their practices aimed at creating an exclusive user imagery and the resistance of the 'undesirable'. In extreme cases, the resistance of the 'undesirable' has led to devastating consequences with frustrated 'undesirables' returning after being denied entrance to the nightclub firing into the queues and at the security officers. This has occurred several times in The Spy Bar nightclub area, although not directly at the nightclub itself. Hence, the practice to categorise individuals into 'desirable' and 'undesirable' customers to improve the user imagery could have severe implications not only for the security officers but also for the individuals queuing outside the nightclub.

CRACKS IN THE FAÇADE

So far, the analysis of the role of user imagery at The Spy Bar has focused on the instances where security officers manage the customer base according to the nightclub's mission. However, there are also instances when this is not the case – when there are cracks in the façade. The most obvious such crack is that the 'desirability' of an individual seems to a related to when the individual attempts to enter the nightclub. A 'desirable' individual at 10-11 p.m. is often an 'undesirable' individual at 1-3 a.m. (not to mention at 4 a.m.). This is due both to that 'desirable' individuals only enter the nightclub scene after midnight, and that it is important for the profitability of the nightclub to receive revenues throughout the evening. This practice can be referred to as a 'geek tax' in the sense that by entering the club early and spending money throughout the evening the otherwise 'undesirable' individuals buy themselves an entrance ticket into the club. However, the consequence of this practice is that 'undesirable' individuals are at the club later in the evening when the 'desirable' individuals arrive. Hence, the 'desirable' individuals are faced with 'undesirable' individuals inside the club, potentially making them doubt the exclusiveness of the club and the 'success factor' of the clientele. Partly, the nightclub solves this by having VIP rooms, protecting highly 'desirable' individuals from mingling with 'undesirable' individuals, but partly the 'problem' remains.

An additional crack in the exclusive user image façade is that the security officers allow some 'undesirable' individuals to enter despite an ample supply of 'desirable' individuals in the queue. This initially puzzling observation is partly explained by some of these 'undesirable' individuals having personal relations with the security officers. The security officers themselves would likely not have been classified as 'desirable' according to their own standards and neither would their friends. However, since decision makers are complex individuals (e.g., Sjöstrand, 1997), as well as bounded rational (e.g., Simon, 1957; Cyert and March, 1963), they make decisions that not necessarily are in-line with the corporate mission. The security officers sometimes prioritised assisting their friends over following the corporate mission, leading to 'undesirable' individuals being allowed to enter the nightclub. In addition to friends, other 'undesirable' individuals that still were allowed entrance belonged to criminal groups and were giving access to the nightclub in order for the security officers and the nightclub to avoid repercussions.

In sum, to enter the nightclub an individual has to either be 'desirable', or 'undesirable' but willing to pay a 'geek tax', or have a personal relationship with the security officers, or belong to a criminal group. Hence, there were several groups of individuals that were, for different reasons, allowed to enter the nightclub and that did not fit the characteristics of a 'desirable' individual. The practice of customer base management to improve user imagery, thus, seems to be somewhat difficult to implement in practice, despite conscious attempts by

The Spy Bar management. These cracks in the façade seemed to negatively affect the user imagery with some individuals noting that the nightclub was not as 'exclusive' and 'successful' as they expected. Consequently, the instances of security officers' selection 'failures' negatively affected the nightclub's user imagery.

CONCLUSION

This chapter has shown that corporate responsibility researchers need to broaden their perspective and analyse the intersection between *what* products that are produced and *how* they are produced in order to capture central corporate responsibility issues. It has also shown that marketing researchers are well advised to include aspects of corporate responsibility into their analyses of user imagery. By addressing these gaps in previous research, this chapter has provided an initial study of the corporate responsibility implications of firms' customer base management strategies aimed at creating an exclusive user imagery. The study's results are distressing, indicating that some companies consciously organise their entire operations in order to sort individuals into 'desirable' and 'undesirable' categories. Furthermore, the employees sorting individuals oftentimes do not perceive this as problematic or unethical, despite being aware of the negative effects of their actions on the 'undesirable' individuals. They are just "doing their job". Based on these results, this chapter has argued that exclusive nightclubs have two sides – one focused on entertaining the selected few and one focused on degenerating the vast majority. This 'enjoyment' and 'misery' of nightclubs are two sides of the same coin with 'enjoyment' being dependent on 'misery' and 'misery' being dependent on 'enjoyment'.

The conducted study has important implications for practitioners interested in altering the situation at exclusive nightclubs. First, the so-called 'rainbow' queue structure could be replaced by a regular queue system. This would shorten the time individuals spend in queues, force the security officers to inform and motivate to each customer why he/she is not welcome, and decrease the frustration induced by the queue system. This fairly simple alteration in the operations of the nightclubs would significantly reduce the problems caused by the strive for an exclusive user image. Second, and more radically, the private security firms could be replaced by police officers, weakening the control of nightclub management on the selection and categorisation of individuals. Such a change would challenge the entire corporate organising for creation of an exclusive user imagery, forcing nightclub management to find alternative (and hopefully less problematic) ways of creating 'exclusiveness'.

ACKNOWLEDGMENT

We gratefully acknowledge the support of Michael Arvidsson, Johan Carlsson, Jacob Jonmyren, and Mattias Magnusson in collecting part of the data for this study.

REFERENCES

Aaker, D. A. (1996). *Building Strong Brands*. New York, NY: The Free Press.

Allères, D. (2005). *Luxe...: Stratégies, Marketing*. Paris: Economica.

Anner, M., Greer, I., Hauptmeier, M., Lillie, N., & Winchester, N. (2006). The Industrial Determinants of Transnational Solidarity: Global Interunion Politics in Three Sectors. *European Journal of Industrial Relations, 12*(1), 7-27.

Baker, R. (2006). *Top 10 Reasons Why Affluent Life Style Marketing is Essential Today*. Dallas: Premium Knowledge Group.

Balmer, J. M. T., & Gray, E. R. (2000). Corporate Identity and Corporate Communications: Creating a Competitive Advantage. *Industrial & Commercial Training, 32*(6), 256-261.

Belk, R. W. (1988). Possessions and the Extended Self. *Journal of Consumer Research, 15*(2), 139-168.

Berry, C. J. (1994). *The Idea of Luxury: A Conceptual and Historical Investigation*. Cambridge: Cambridge University Press.

Brenkert, G. G. (2000). Social Products Liability: The Case of the Firearms Manufacturers. *Business Ethics Quarterly, 10*(1), 21-32.

Brioschi, A. (2006). Selling Dreams: The Role of Advertising in Shaping Luxury Brand Meaning. In J. E. Schroeder, & M. Salzer-Mörling (Eds.), *Brand Culture* (pp. 198-210). New York, NY: Routledge.

Carley, M. (2005). Global Agreements – State of Play. *European Industrial Relations Review, 381*, 14-18.

Carroll, S. J., & Gannon, M. J. (1997). *Ethical Dimensions of International Management*. Thousand Oaks, CA: Sage.

Cyert, R. M., & March, J. G. (1963). *A Behavioral Theory of the Firm*. Englewood Cliffs, NJ: Prentice-Hall.

De George, R. T. (1990). *Business Ethics*. New York, NY: MacMillan Publishers.

De George, R. T. (1993). *Competing with Integrity in International Business*. New York, NY: Oxford University Press.

Donaldson, T. (1989). *The Ethics of International Business*. New York, NY: Oxford University Press.

Donaldson, T. (1996). Values in Tension: Ethics Away from Home. *Harvard Business Review, 74*(5), 48-62.

Donaldson, T., & Dunfee, T. W. (1994). Towards a Unified Conception of Business Ethics: Integrative Social Contracts Theory. *Academy of Management Review, 19*(2), 252-285.

Dubois, B., & Paternault, C. (1995). Observations: Understanding the World of International Luxury Brands: The "Dream Formula". *Journal of Advertising Research, 35*(4), 69-76.

Egels-Zandén, N. (2007). Suppliers' Compliance with MNCs' Codes of Conduct: Behind the Scenes at Chinese Toy Suppliers. *Journal of Business Ethics* (in press).

Egels-Zandén, N., & Hyllman, P. (2006). Exploring the Effects of Union-NGO Relationships on Corporate Responsibility: The Case of the Swedish Clean Clothes Campaign. *Journal of Business Ethics, 64*(3), 303-316.

Egels-Zandén, N., & Hyllman, P. (2007). Evaluating Strategies for Negotiating Workers' Rights in Transnational Corporations: The Effects of Codes of Conduct and Global Agreements on Workplace Democracy. *Journal of Business Ethics* (in press).

Elm, N. (1998). The Business of Unethical Weapons. *Business Ethics: A European Review*, *7*(1), 25-29.

Fairbrother, P., & Hammer, N. (2005). Global Unions – Past Efforts and Future Prospects. *Relations Industrielles/Industrial Relations*, *60*(3), 405-431.

Frenkel, S. (2001). Globalization, Athletic Footwear Commodity Chains and Employment Relations in China. *Organization Studies*, *22*(4), 531-562.

Gabriel, Y., & Lang, T. (2006). *The Unmanageable Consumer*. London: Sage.

Graafland, J. J. (2002). Sourcing Ethics in the Textile Sector: The Case of C&A. *Business Ethics: A European Review*, *11*(3), 282-294.

Green, R. M. (2000). Legally Targeting Gun Makers: Lessons for Business Ethics. *Business Ethics Quarterly*, *10*(1), 203-210.

Havemann, C. (1998). Hawks or Doves? The Ethics of UK Arms Exports. *Business Ethics: A European Review*, *7*(4), 240-244.

Kapferer, J.-N. (1994). *Strategic Brand Management: New Approaches to Creating and Evaluating Brand Equity*. New York, NY: The Free Press.

Keller, K. L. (2000). The Brand Report Card. *Harvard Business Review*, *78*(1), 147-157.

Keller, K. L. (2003). *Strategic Brand Management: Building, Measuring, and Managing Brand Equity*. Upper Saddle River, NJ: Prentice Hall, Pearson Education Ltd.

Kinder, P. D., & Domini, A. L. (1997). Social Screening: Paradigms Old and New. *Journal of Investing*, *6*(4), 12-19.

Levy, S. J. (1959). Symbols for Sale. *Harvard Business Review*, *37*(4), 117-124.

Maitland, G. (1998). The Ethics of the International Arms Trade. *Business Ethics: A European Review*, *7*(4), 200-204.

McCracken, G. (1986). Culture and Consumption: A Theoretical Account of the Structure and Movement of the Cultural Meaning of Consumer Goods. *Journal of Consumer Research*, *13*(1), 71-84.

McCracken, G. (1989). Who is the Celebrity Endorser? Cultural Foundations of the Endorsement Process. *Journal of Consumer Research*, *16*(3), 310-321.

McWilliams, A., & Siegel, D. (2001). Corporate Social Responsibility: A Theory of the Firm Perspective. *Academy of Management Review*, *26*(1), 117-127.

Newton, L. (1993). Gambling: A Preliminary Inquiry. *Business Ethics Quarterly*, *3*(4), 405-418.

Riisgaard, L. (2005). Industrial Framework Agreements: A New Model of Securing Workers Rights?. *Industrial Relations*, *44*(4), 707-737.

Schermerhorn, J. R. Jr. (1999). Terms of Global Business Engagement in Ethically Challenging Environments: Applications to Burma. *Business Ethics Quarterly*, *9*(3), 485-505.

Schroeder, J. E. (2005). The Artist and the Brand. *European Journal of Marketing*, *39*(11/12), 1291-1305.

Simon, H. E. (1957). *Models of Man*. New York, NY: Wiley.

Sjöstrand, S. E. (1997). *The Two Faces of Management: The Janus Factor*. London: Thomson Learning.

Twitchell, J. B. (2002). Living it up: Our Love Affair with Luxury. New York, NY: Columbia University Press.

van Tulder, R., & Kolk, A. (2001). Multinationality and Corporate Ethics: Codes of Conduct in the Sporting Goods Industry. *Journal of International Business Studies, 32*(2), 267-283.

Vigneron, F., & Johnson, L. W. (1999). A Review and a Conceptual Framework of Prestige-Seeking Consumer Behavior. *Academy of Marketing Science Review, 1999*(1).

Vigneron, F., & Johnson, L. W. (2004). Measuring Perceptions of Brand Luxury. *Brand Management, 11*(6), 484-506.

Wills, J. (2002). Bargaining for the Space to Organize in the Global Economy: A Review of the Accor-IUF Trade Union Rights Agreement. *Review of International Political Economy, 9*(4), 675-700.

Winstanley, D., Clark, J., & Leeson, H. (2002). Approaches to Child Labour in the Supply Chain. *Business Ethics: A European Review, 11*(3), 210-223.

In: Contemporary Issues in Business Ethics
Editors: M. W. Volcox, Th. O. Mohan, pp. 177-189

ISBN: 978-1-60021-773-9
© 2007 Nova Science Publishers, Inc.

Chapter 9

Incorporating Ethics and Corporate Social Responsibility through Corporate Governance

María de la Cruz Déniz-Déniz
Universidad de Las Palmas de Gran Canaria, Spain
María Katiuska Cabrera-Suárez
Universidad de Las Palmas de Gran Canaria, Spain

Abstract

The focus of this paper will be to analyse the relationship between corporate social responsibility and corporate governance adopting a stakeholder perspective. Moreover, we also try to go in depth about how internal governance mechanism can contribute both to reinforce company's values and to take into account the stakeholders' interests. So, we explain that the internalisation of stakeholder preferences implies a three- stage process: allocation of ownership rights, board composition, and the influence of important stakeholders. All the above lead us to propose that the future research would aim to clarify the roles and the importance of the diverse participants of the corporate governance systems (owners, directors, managers) in achieving a social responsible behavior of the firm, in order to secure its sustainability and legitimacy.

Introduction

In order to create value, the firm can not ignore the context in which it operates. A network of relationships connects the company to a great number of interrelated individuals and constituencies, called stakeholders (Freeman, 1984; Donaldson and Preston, 1995; Clarkson, 1995). The relationships influence the way a company is governed, and, in turn, are influenced by the company's behaviour (Tencati and Perrini, 2006). Post, Preston, and Sachs

(2002) states that the capacity of a firm to generate sustainable wealth over time, and hence its long term value, is determined by its relationships with critical stakeholders.

According to Freeman and Velamuri (2006), once of the most basic level of stakeholder awareness has been achieved, the entrepreneur or manager must understand that the continued survival and profitability of the company depend on effectively sustaining the cooperation with the stakeholders over the time. The competitive, macroeconomic, regulatory and political environments are so dynamic that they make it necessary for the initial stakeholder arrangements to be revised on a constant basis. Management according to the stakeholder approach is the effective balancing over time of multiple stakeholder interests.

If the entire set of stakeholder relationships becomes strategic for the long-term success and survival of a company, shareholder value can not be considered a sufficient objective and a sufficient measure in order to assess the quality of business management (Tencati and Perrini, 2006). According to the authors, the concept of extended enterprise focused on stakeholder linkages calls for rethinking the nature, purposes and behaviour of companies. Therefore, the stakeholder view of the firm is at the basis of a new governance model which informs a company's activities and its relations. In this enlarged view of the governance model, stakeholders become an essential part of the extended organisation and their role is crucial for a successful management. Therefore, it seems necessary to study which governance structures are more suitable to accomplish those multiple responsibilities of the firm.

Based on those ideas, the focus of this paper will be to analyse and discuss the relationships between corporate social responsibility and corporate governance adopting a stakeholder perspective. Moreover, we also try to go in depth about how internal governance mechanism can contribute both to reinforce company's values and to take into account the stakeholders' interests.

CORPORATE SOCIAL RESPONSIBILITY AND CORPORATE GOVERNANCE: A STAKEHOLDER PERSPECTIVE

The stakeholders' theory represents a major contribution of business ethics (Freeman, 1984; Alkhafaji, 1989). It encompasses the view that a corporation consists of, and, arguably, is responsible to, a number of stakeholders –parties that affect or are affected by the corporation (Freeman, 1997). It rejects the view that a corporation is responsible only to stockholders, and argues that other stakeholders' concerns are also relevant and merit consideration (Radin, 2002). So, stakeholder theories seek to identify those individuals or entities (e.g. the firm, managers, employees, customers, suppliers, community) and explore the relationships between them. Stakeholder analysis is a particularly good way to build mediation between power and responsibility, because "power cannot be viewed in isolation from responsibility, and it is this power-responsibility relationship that is the foundation for calls for corporate social responsibility" (Carroll, 1989:17). According to Carroll (1979) this CSR can be defined as the economic, legal, ethical and discretionary expectations of society about the organization. So, companies must respond to numerous social demands, as well as to their technical, economic and legal obligations.

Radin (2002) indicates that stakeholder theorists share some insights when they try to dispel a few common misunderstandings. The first common misunderstanding that the stakeholder theory attacks is that stockholders are the only legitimate claimholders, or stakeholders (Friedman, 1970; Davies and Kay, 1997). This fallacy encompasses the traditional assumption that a financial investment (e.g. through stock ownership) is necessary to ground a claim on the firm. This is clearly not true. There is abundant evidence that individuals and entities other than stockholders have legitimate claims on the firm (Schwarcz, 1996). The second misunderstanding is that stockholders and their interests are primary. It is true that managers can not legally behave in a fiscally irresponsible manner so as to wrongfully interfere with firm profitability and stockholder returns, but this is not to say that those are the manager's only concerns. Managers have overriding responsibilities to other stakeholders, many of which are codified in law. For example, consumer protection law, labour and safety laws, and environmental protection law underscore the prevalence of multiple stakeholder concerns.

The assumption of stakeholder theorists has been that shareholders already have the power to ensure that their interests are taken into account by the firm and its managers. Then, they try to demonstrate that shareholders' rights should be limited or circumscribed by the rights or interests of other stakeholder groups (Heath and Norman, 2004). So, stakeholder theorists call for a change in the basic definition of modern corporations from a stockholder perspective to a stakeholder perspective (Lozano, 2000). That stakeholder perspective can fit what Quazi and O'Brien (2000) define as a broad vision of CSR that seeks to build sustainable relationships with society. That strong commitment to CSR includes extensive responsibilities to various stakeholder groups (Heath and Norman, 2004). However, according to the shareholding vision, the companies' function is to provide goods and services that lead to the maximization of short-term profits. That narrow vision of CSR (Quazi and O'Brien, 2000) recognizes no social responsibility beyond the obligation to maximize shareholder value (Heath and Norman, 2004).

Building on the above ideas, it has been stated that corporate governance must be concerned with the processes by which organizations are directed, controlled and held accountable in order to secure the economic viability as well as the legitimacy of the corporation (Neubauer and Lank, 1998; Cadbury, 1999). This way, corporate governance can be understood as a process by which corporations are made responsive to the rights and wishes of multiple stakeholders (Freeman, 1984, Hilb, 2005). According to Bonn and Fisher (2005), corporate governance deals with the rights and responsibilities of an organization's board, its management, shareholders and other stakeholders.

Therefore, a stakeholders' definition of corporate governance can be adopted that contrasts with the shareholding definition (Pieper, 2003; Letza et al., 2004), which regards the corporation only as a legal instrument for shareholders to maximize their own interests. The shareholding perspective is considered to be too limited a view to build a relevant theory of corporate governance (Charreaux and Desbrières, 2001). This is so because the corporation has a collective rather than an individual identity and executives are the representatives and guardians of all corporate stakeholders' interests (Hall, 1989). According to Driver and Thompson (2002), we can establish that a stakeholders' approach to corporate governance might be a more logical or rational system, a fairer or more democratic system, and one that provides better performative outcomes. Arjoon (2005) establishes that giving an effective response to different stakeholders implies that corporate governance can be achieved by adopting a set of principles and best practices. A great deal depends upon the fairness, honesty, integrity in which companies conduct their affairs.

It is precisely the concerns about the activities of organizations and the recent corporate scandals that have resulted in an increase in the attention being paid to corporate governance. Bodies such as the OECD and stock exchanges have developed corporate governance principles that include references to business ethics; that is, it is argued that an organization's approach to ethics must be addressed in its corporate governance framework (Bonn and Fisher, 2005; Jesover and Kirkpatrick, 2005).

Anyway, discussion and good intentions will have no effect on actual corporate social responsibility if they do not have solid foundations in ownership, board or stakeholder structure (Thomsen, 2006). According to this author, stakeholders can influence a company through market transactions and contracts but transaction costs and information problems set a limit to use contractual mechanisms. So, non-market mechanisms must be used instead (Zingales, 2001) in a way that the internalisation of stakeholder preferences implies a three-stage process: allocation of ownership rights, board composition, and the influence of important stakeholders.

Thomsen (2006) establishes that the sequential emphasis on first ownership, then board structure and then stakeholder structure is not accidental. Formally, corporate values are determined by the owners at the annual general meeting or the decision to set values is delegated indirectly to the board. So, ownership is prior to other factors which influence corporate values. The decision of whether or not acquire ownership of the firm implies that residual control rights are allocated to certain owners and not to others. Owners may then delegate responsibility to the management board. They or their management agents may then decide to include relevant stakeholder representatives on the board, or they may decide not to. And finally, the board may decide to form and honour implicit contracts with stakeholders, or it may decide not to. The outcome will depend on the preferences of the relevant decision makers as well as their decision mandate.

THE INTERNALISATION OF STAKEHOLDERS PREFERENCES: OWNERSHIP, THE BOARD AND CONTRACT WITH STAKEHOLDERS

Ownership

Although one solution to contracting problems between a firm and a stakeholder is to internalise the stakeholder-firm relationship through ownership, ownership shares are not generally distributed across the various stakeholder groups in accordance with their stakes in the company (Thomsen, 2006). That is so because of different reasons. Firstly, not all stakeholders have sufficient capital or risk willingness to invest in ownership. This is a standard impediment to employee ownership. Secondly, not all of them have the information to be efficient owners. This is an obstacle to government ownership and for financial investors. Thirdly, the cost of collective decision making for owners with highly diverse resource endowments, preferences and information could be prohibitive. Then, companies with homogeneous owners will be more efficient, for example if they belong to the same family or the same community (relatives, members of a cooperative).

Therefore, ownership is a matching problem in which owners with specific characteristics (access to information, capital and knowledge) are matched with firms which have their own specific characteristics (size, activities, technology) (Thomsen, 2006). Himmelberg et al. (1999) and Zhara et al. (2000) argue that directors and managers with low ownership levels are more likely to take opportunistic actions by supporting projects that advance their own interests instead of creating value for the firm's stakeholders.

The above is a particular case of the principal- agent problem described by the agency theory (Jensen and Meckling, 1976; Fama and Jensen, 1983). This model has had a profound influence on corporate governance theory (Jensen, 1993). A central premise of this theory is that management decisions are strongly influenced by the ownership status of each decision maker who serves on a corporation's board of directors (Schulze, Lubatkin and Dino, 2003). The basic assumptions are that principals/owners wish to maximize profits (or value for the shareholder), while agents/managers have other interests (high compensation, low effort, preferences of expenditure, empire-building etc.). Although this supposition may be sufficient for many purposes, strictly speaking, it is only an approximation of the more general idea that owners (as well as managers) wish to maximize their utility, which may depend on other factors such as their specific cultural and value systems.

On the other hand, there are works that have found not only the presence of majority shareholders in large companies (*e.g.*, Holderness and Sheehan, 1988; Gedajlovic, 1993; La Porta, *et al.*, 1999; Thomsen and Pedersen, 2000), but also that they are active on the corporate governance, as opposed to the idea of Berle and Means that managers are not responsible to anybody due to the stock dispersion (La Porta et al., 1999). According to these last authors, those larger companies often tend to have majority shareholders who, in most cases, are an individual or family, normally the company founder or his descendants. The degree and nature of ownership required to establish effective control will depend upon the institutional context in which a firm is located and also, the strategic control of a firm can also be attained with low ownership levels through the establishment of pyramids and cross-holdings, or the existence of covenants that allow the family to appoint the CEO or board members, or even bypass the board for certain decisions (Carney, 2005). In terms of the agency theory, those controlling shareholders are ideally placed to supervise the management, and in fact the top management is normally part of the controlling family, but at the same time, they have the power, and possibly the interest to expropriate the small shareholders (Jesover and Kirkpatrick, 2005; Yeh, 2005). Therefore, the fact that the cash flow is in the hands of the majority shareholder reduces but does not eliminate the incentive to expropriate value from the firm at the expenses of small shareholders and, we could say, the rest of the stakeholders of the firm.

Also, this concentration of ownership in the hands of the largest shareholder may lead to a greater incentive for him/her to run the firm properly because it would directly increase his/her own wealth (Yeh, 2005). Moreover, high managerial equity holdings could influence the managers' attention to stakeholder interests. In this sense, owner-managers probably have a much bigger stake in the firm than other stakeholders (Jansson, 2005). Thus, they could have incentives to maintain product quality, to promote innovations and respond more effectively to changing environments, to avoid negative reputations stemming from bad environmental policies, to improve their behaviour toward communities and to maintain good employee relations (Johnson and Greening, 1999). However, the possibility that the principals/owners may have objectives other than maximizing value is rarely considered in the literature (Thomsen and Pedersen, 2000). In this sense, the identity of the owners may be an important factor to consider.

Thomsen and Pedersen (2000) conclude that, given the high levels of concentration of ownership in Europe, the identity of the owners is crucial in understanding corporate management on the continent. So, although all owners generally benefit from a high share price, they will differ in the priority they give to value compared with other objectives. Galve and Salas (1995) argued that the nature of the majority shareholders may influence the results, not only because of their different objectives, but also the agency costs incurred in contracts that seek to maintain the cohesion of the group, or those that regulate the conflict with other minorities.

Concretely, the ownership being in the hands of one family may cause serious power struggles because company conflicts and family conflicts become intertwined, and, above all, it may create problems regarding the size of the company due to the limitations that self-financing means. Also, the family's involvement in the company's management may result in unqualified people holding managerial posts, in other words family entrenchment, although one of the gravest mistakes, is still frequent (Thomsen and Pedersen, 2000).

The Board

The board composition decision allocates board seats over the set of potential board members, which include the stakeholder representatives as well as professional managers and board members (Thomsen, 2006). Boards are normally elected by the owners, who delegate many decision rights concerning corporate values to the board. In companies that separate ownership and control this implies that managers play a pivotal role in creating or changing corporate value systems and the composition of the board is a key determinant of this process.

The literature has discussed the question of how boards should be composed in order to best fulfil their functions: service, resource dependence and control (Johnson, Daily and Ellstrand, 1996). The notion of the board's composition, in reality, includes the difference between a board formed of directors functioning independently of the firm and its management team (specifically the CEO), and a board mainly made up of members of the management team (Dalton et al., 1998). However, truly independence requires that members of the board have no personal and/or professional affiliation with the company, its management team, its parent, or any firm with which the company does business (Klein, Shapiro and Young, 2005). However, as recent corporate failures have shown, leaving up to the "formal" standards is not enough. More attention should be paid to correct governance attitude and behaviour of directors and management. In fact, corporate governance is about "doing the right things" and "doing the things right" (Van de Berghe and Levrau, 2004).

Relationships with critical stakeholders may be internalised by having them represented on the board as non-executive members (Evan and Freeman, 1993; Louma and Goodstein, 1999). This way, stakeholder representation could promote procedural fairness by providing means of ensuring that stakeholder considerations are more directly represented in corporate decision making. Thus if corporate social concerns about the stakeholder is view as important and legitimate it is likely to be institutionalised within social structures -in particular within board of directors. Ibrahim et al. (2003) found that the presence of non-executive directors (NEDs) in the boardroom was likely to lead to a company engaging in socially responsible activities, on the basis that NEDs hold wider organisational roles that their executives counterparts (Johnson and Greening, 1999). Although NEDs are governed by the same legal responsibility as other board members, it is argued that the nature of their role leads them to adopt a more counter-balancing view than other executive members (Kakabadse et al., 2001; Kakabadse, Kakabadse, and Barrat, 2006). According to McNulty and Pettigrew (1999), NEDs play an influencing role in the setting of strategy, thus contradicting the belief that they act merely as a rubber stamp to the desires of the executives (Kakabadse, Kakabadse, and Barrat, 2006). The authors state that the role of NEDs has become more professional, with many boards now using specialist recruitment agencies to source prospective NEDs with specific knowledge and skills.

Johnson and Greening (1999) establish that NEDs hold both profit goals, in line with agency theory, and wider non-profit goals, displaying a strong stakeholder orientation, recognising that the organisation has responsibilities to groups other than shareholders. These authors believe that the value of NEDs is in considering and addressing external constituencies, thus improving the organisations' relationship with its environment. They stimulate a desire on the part of insiders to "keep the house in order", particularly through good governance (Dutton and Jackson, 1987; Fombrun and Shanley, 1990). According to Barrat (2005), individuals capable of understanding and anticipating the complex demands that may be made on the organization, and, as a result, instituting appropriate governance procedures, are being recognised as an invaluable resource.

The standard assumption is that the board should aim to maximise shareholder value, but actual owner interest may not be homogeneous (Thomsen, 2006). First, large investors may be concerned with ethical and political concerns as well as stock returns (Woidtke, 2002) and so my small shareholders. Secondly, large owners like founding families or other corporations may be concerned about their non-ownership business relationships with the firm (Thomsen and Pedersen, 2000). Third, founders and their families my have their own idiosyncratic ideas about the company's mission (Morck, et al, 1988). So, the board will need to take non-owner stakeholder consideration into account, even if shareholders value remains the overall goal. In fact, successful boards should strive to deliver both shareholder value and value for the rest of the stakeholders and both legality and legitimacy (Hilb, 2005). Again, one way to do this is to include representatives from the relevant constituencies.

According to Hermalin and Weisbach (2000), the gains from improved stakeholder relations have to be weighed against potentially increasing costs of collective decision making related to managing conflicts of interest and larger board size. An alternative solution is to invite decision experts who are believed to understand the needs of the critical stakeholders to sit on the board, but it is not clear to what extent such representation will work as a safeguard for stakeholders interests (Thomsen, 2006). In fact, it may be that outside directors with less knowledge of the firm and with less of a financial stake may lower company efficiency by distracting managers and by causing them to focus on short-run goals (Klein et al., 2005).

Another important question on relation to the board is it leadership. The firm's leadership structure defined by whether the CEO is also the board's chair is one structural mechanism about which there is controversy. According to Howton, Howton, and McWilliams (2005), combining the CEO and board chair positions leads to a single individual having a concentrated power base that will allow the CEO to make decisions in his or her own self-interest, which ultimately are at the expense of the firm's stakeholders. However, others (e.g. Coles et al., 2001; Boyd, 1995) suggest that with such combination the direction of the firm is more unambiguous than it would be with two individual occupying these top level positions. Additionally, the CEO-board chair has more complete knowledge of the firm than an outsider (that is, an independent board chair) has. Furthermore, as an insider for the firm, the CEO has greater commitment to the firm than an outside board chair. The inconclusive evidence and opinions on this respect lead Howton, Howton, and McWilliams (2005) to suggest that the firm's leadership configuration may be closely associated with other control mechanisms, in particular the composition of the board of directors, that allow a corporate governance from a stakeholders point of view.

Contracts with Stakeholders

According to Thomsen (2006), a third way for companies to internalise stakeholders concerns is to increase their creditability and trustworthiness through implicit contracts based on reputation, corporate culture or socialisation. Intuitively, the emphasis placed on different stakeholder values should reflect their relative bargaining power (Berheim and Whinston, 1986; Mitchell, et al., 1997; Scott and Lane, 2000) which should again reflect their impact on the overall value creation in the firm. For example, in labour intensive industries more emphasis might be placed on employee satisfaction.

Fombrun (1996) states that reputation may be built by consistent behaviour over a long period of time and facilitated by communication. Following Kreps (1990), a reputation for honesty is a valuable asset which will be lost if the company is not truthful. Commitments to employee satisfaction, customer value, and creditor protection may also be valuable, self-sustainable assets. For example, the literature contains references to family companies associated with values like product quality, respect for, and protection of the employees, involvement with the community, family sacrifice to support the company financially, continuity and integrity in the management policies, corporate approach, etc. (Donnelly, 1964, Ward, 1987; Leach, 1993; Poza, 1995; Neubauer an Lank, 1998; Miller and Le Breton-Miller, 2003). Those ideas form part of the "legend" that has been built around family business about features such as concern for reputation, long-term orientation, respect for tradition and family values, etc. Therefore, it is argued that family companies are unlikely to uproot their employees; they usually maintain their installations in the original places; the owner families generally sit on the boards of hospitals, churches, schools, and charities that contribute to the welfare of the local community (Ward, 1987; Lansberg, 1999; Gnan and Montemerlo, 2002).

Thomsen (2006) considers that socialisation is another way in which stakeholders concerns may conceivably be internalised, not only in corporate values, but also even in the minds and identity of the managers. Managers' identities are affected by representing the organisation in its relationships with stakeholders (Scott and Lane, 2000). In this sense, stewardship theory (Davis, Schoorman and Donaldson, 1997) states that managers whose needs are based on growth, achievement and self-realisation, and who are intrinsically motivated can make better use of organisational objectives than personal ones. Similarly, managers who identify with their organisations and are strongly committed to organisational values are more likely to serve organisational ends. This way, managers will identify with organisational values and prefer cooperative behaviour, which could facilitate implicit contracting with external stakeholders. In fact, commitment to the community, the workers and other stakeholders is congruent with the idea of collective benefit that constitutes one of the basic principles of this theory. Along those lines, Davis *et al.*(1997) argue that, in heterogeneous organizations whose stakeholders' interests compete with one another, the stewards are motivated to take decisions that they perceive as the best for the group's interests, in line with the principles of Rawlsian ethics. As a result, it can be said that these leaders are motivated by power in a social rather than a personal sense (Peay and Dyer, 1989). A person motivated by social power wishes to build an organization more for the benefit of society than for personal glory. From an ethical point of view, it can be said that a legitimate use is made of power (Gallo and Melé, 1998). From this point of view, the role of the board could be one of providing service and advice rather than monitoring and control, and therefore board structures could rely on insiders or affiliated outsiders (Klein et al., 2005: Van den Berghe and Levrau, 2004).

CONCLUSION

At this point, we can state that the corporate social responsibility orientation will ultimately depends on the nature of firms owners. The social orientation of the firm will depend on the values of those owners and of their representatives both on the board and the management teams.

The idea of shareholders primacy is undergoing an internal transformation. That way, a notion of corporate responsibility in which shareholding activism becomes the means by which society holds corporate management to account is gaining importance. In the course of the past decade a shift in the content of shareholder value has occurred, which reflects the stakeholder critique of that period: this reflects the idea that shareholders should exercise their power not as representatives of the market but as agents of society as a whole. Shareholder have the right to call managers to account not because of an a priori ownership claim, but essentially because it is in society's interests that they should perform this task (Deakin, 2005).

The future research would aim to clarify the roles and the importance of the diverse participants of the corporate governance systems (owners, directors, managers) in achieving a social responsible behavior of he firm, in order to secure its sustainability and legitimacy.

REFERENCES

Alkhafaji, A.F. (1989) *A Stakeholder Approach to Corporate Governance: Managing in a Dynamic Environment*. New York: Quorum Books.

Arjoon, S. (2005) Corporate Governance: An Ethical Perspective, *Journal of Business Ethics*, 61, 343-352.

Barrat, R. (2005) The role and contribution of the non executive director: implications for corporate social responsibility in the boardroom, *Unpublished PhD. Thesis, Cranfield University, School of Management.*

Bernheim, D.B. and Whinston, M.D. (1986) Common Agency, *Econometrica*, 54 (4), 923-42.

Bonn, I. and Fisher, J. (2005) Corporate Governance and Business Ethics: Insights from the Strategic Planning Experience, *Corporate Governance*, 13, 730-738.

Boyd, B.K. (1995) CEO duality and firm performance: a contingency model, *Strategic Management Journal*, 16 (4): 301-312.

Cadbury, Sir A. (1999) What Are the Trends in Corporate Governance? How will They Impact your Company? *Long Range Planning*, 32, 12-19.

Carney, M. (2005) Corporate Governance and Competitive Advantage in Family-Controlled Firms, *Entrepreneurship Theory and Practice*, May, 249-265.

Carroll, A. B. (1979) A Three-Dimensional Conceptual Model of Corporate Social Performance, *Academy of Management Review*, 4, 497-505.

Carroll, A. B. (1989) *Business and Society. Ethics and Stakeholder Management*. United States: South-Western Publishing Co.

Clarkson, M.B.E. (1995) A stakeholder framework for analysing and evaluating corporate social performance, *Academy of Management Review*, 20: 92-117.

Coles, J.W.; McWilliams, V.B. and Sen, N. (2001) An examination of the relationship of governance mechanisms to performance, *Journal of Management*, 27 (1): 23-50.

Charreaux, G. and Desbrières, P. (2001) Corporate Governance: Stakeholder versus Shareholder Value, *Journal of Management and Governance*, 5, 107-128.

Dalton, D.R., Daily, C.M., Ellstrand, A.E. and Johnson, J.L (1998) Meta-analytic Reviews of Board Composition, Leadership Structure, and Financial Performance, *Strategic Management Journal*, 19, 269-290.

Davies, E. and Kay, J. (1997) Shareholders aren't Everything, *Fortune,* febrero 17

Davis, J.H., Schoorman, F.D. and Donaldson, L. (1997), "Toward a stewardship theory of management", *Academy of Management Review*, Vol. 22, pp. 20-47.

Deakin, S. (2005). The coming transformation of shareholder value. *Corporate Governance*, 13, 11-18.

Donaldson, T. and Preston, L.E. (1995) The stakeholder theory of the corporation: concepts, evidence, and implications, *Academy of Management Review*, 20 (1), 65-91.

Donelly, R.G. (1964). "The family business". *Harvard Business Review*, 1:427-445.

Driver, C. and Thompson, G. (2002) Corporate Governance and Democracy: The Stakeholder Debate Revisited, *Journal of Management and Governance*, 6, 111-130.

Dutton, J.E. and Jackson, S.E. (1987) Categorizing strategic issues: links to organizational action, *Academy of Management Review,* 12 (1), 76-90.

Evan, W. and Freeman, R.E. (1993) A stakeholder theory of the modern corporation: Kantian Capitalism. In Beauchamps and Bowie N (Eds), *Ethical theory and business*, 75-93. Englewood Cliffs, NJ: Prentice Hall.

Fama, E.F. and Jensen, M.C. (1983), "Agency problems and residual claims", *Journal of Law and Economics,* Vol. 2, pp. 327-349.

Fombrum, C.J. (1996) *Reputation: Realizing value from the corporate image*, Boston: Harvard Business School Press.

Fombrum, C.J. and Shanley, M. (1990) What's in a name? Reputation building and corporate strategy, *Academy of Management Journal*, 33 (2), 233-258.

Freeman, R. E. (1984) *Strategic Management. A stakeholder Approach*. Boston: Pitman/Ballinger (Harper Collins).

Freeman, R.E. (1997) Stakeholder Theory. In P.H. Werhane and R.E. Freeman (ed.) *Encyclopedic Dictionary of Business Ethics*. Malden, MA: Blackwell Publishers Ltd.

Freeman, R.E. and Velamuri, S. R. (2006) A new approach to CSR: Company stakeholder responsibility. In Kakabadse, A. and Morsing, M. Corporate social responsibility Reconciling aspiration with application, 9-23. Palgrave Mcmillan. UK.

Friedman, M. (1970) The Social Responsibility of Business is to Increase its Profits, *New York Times Magazine*, 13, September, 122-126.

Gallo, M.A. and Melé, D. (1998). *Ética en la empresa familiar*. Editorial Praxis. Barcelona. Spain.

Galve Gorriz, C & Salas Fumás, V. (1995). Propiedad y eficiencia de la empresa: teoría y evidencias empíricas. *Información Comercial Española*, 740,119-129.

Gedajlovic, E. (1993). Ownership, strategy and performance: Is the dichotomy sufficient? *Organization Studies*, 14, 5, 731-752.

Gnan, L. and Montemerlo, D. (2002) The Multiple Facets of Family Firms' Social Role: Empirical Evidence from Italian Smes'. Research Forum Proceedings of the Family Business Network 13th Annual Conference. Helsinki, Finland.

Hall, K.L. (1989) *The Magic Mirror: Law in American History*. New York: Oxford University Press.

Heath, J. and Norman, W. (2004) Stakeholder Theory, Corporate Governance and Public Management: What Can the History of State-Run Enterprises Teach us in the Post-Enron era? *Journal of Business Ethics*, 53, 247-265.

Hermalin, B. and Weisbach, M.E. (2000) Boards of directors as an endogenously determined institution. A survey of the economic literature. *Social Science Research Network*

Hilb, M. (2005) New corporate governance: from good guidelines to great practice. *Corporate Governance*, 13, 569-581.

Himmelberg, C.P.; Hubbard, R.G. and Palia, D. (1999) Understanding the determinants of managerial ownership and the link between ownership and performance. *Journal of Financial Economics*, 53 (3): 353-384.

Holderness, C.G. and Sheehan, D.P. (1988). The role of majority shareholders in publicy held corporations. An exploratory analysis. *Journal of Financial Economics*, vol 20, 317-346.

Howton, S.D.; Howton, S. W.; and McWilliams V.B. (2005). Management, governance and corporate responsibility. In Doh, J.P and Stump, S.A. *Handbook on responsible leadership and governance in global business*, 243-258. Edwarg Elgar. UK.

Ibrahim, N.A.; Howar, D.P. and Angelis, J.P. (2003) Board members in service industry: an empirical examination of the relationship between corporate social responsibility orientation and directorial type, *Journal of Business Ethics*, 47 (4), 393-401.

Jansson, E. (2005) The Stakeholder Model: The Influence of the Ownership and Governance Structures, *Journal of Business Ethics*, 56: 1-13

Jensen, M.C. and Meckling, W.H. (1976), "Theory of the firm: Managerial behavior, agency costs and ownership structure", *Journal of Financial Economics*, Vol. 3, pp. 305-360.

Jensen, M.C. (1993). The modern industrial revolution, exit, and the failure of internal control systems. *The Journal of Finance*, Vol. XLVIII, n°3, 831-880.

Jesover, F. and Kirkpatrick, G. (2005) The Revised OECD Principles of Corporate Governance and Their Relevance to Non-OECD Countries, *Corporate Governance*, 13, 127-136.

Johnson, R.A. and Greening, D. W. (1999) The Effects of Corporate Governance and Institutional Ownership Types on Corporate Social Performance, *Academy of Management Journal*, 42, 564-576.

Johnson, J.L., Daily, C.M. and Ellstrand, A.E. (1996) Boards of Directors: A Review and Research Agenda, *Journal of Management*, 22, 409-438.

Kakabadse, A.P.; Korac-Kakabadse, N.; Ward, K. y Bowman, C. (2001): Role and contribution of non executive directors, *International Journal of Corporate Governance*, 1, 4-7.

Kakabadse, A.P.; Kakabadse, N.K. and Barrat R. (2006) CSR in the boardroom: contribution of non executive director (NED). In Kakabadse, A. and Morsing, M. Corporate social responsibility Reconciling aspiration with application, 284-299. Palgrave Mcmillan. UK.

Klein, P., Shapiro, D. and Young, J. (2005) Corporate Governance, Family Ownership and Firm Value: The Canadian Evidence, *Corporate Governance*, 13, 769-784.

Kreps, D.M. (1990) Corporate culture and economic theory, In Alt, J.E. and Shepsle, K. (Eds), *Perspectives on positive political economy*, Cambridge: Cambridge University Press.

Lansberg, I.S. (1999) *Succeeding Generations*. Boston, MA: Harvard Business School Press.

La Porta, R; López de Silanes, F. & Shleifer, A. (1999). Corporate ownership around the world. *The Journal of Finance*, LIV, 2, 471-517.

Leach, P. (1993). *La empresa familiar*. Ediciones Granica. Barcelona, Spain

Letza, S., Sun, X. and Kirkbride, J. (2004) Shareholding versus Stakeholding: A Critical Review of Corporate Governance, *Corporate Governance*, 12, 242-262.

Louma, P. and Goodstein, J. (1999) Stakeholders and corporate boards: institutional influences on board composition and structure, *Academy of Management Journal*, 42 (5), 553-563.

Lozano, J.M. (2000) *Ethics and Organizations: Understanding Business Ethics as a Learning Process*. Netherlands: Kluwer Academic Publishers.

McNulty, T. and Pettigrew, A. (1999) Strategists on the board, *Organisational Studies*, 20, 47.

Miller, D. and Le Breton-Miller, I. (2003) Challenge versus Advantage in Family Business. *Strategic Organization*, 1, 127-134.

Mitchell, R.K.; Agle, B.R. and Wood, D.J. (1997) Toward a theory of stakeholder identification and salience, *Academy of Management Review*, 22 (4), 853-886.

Morck, R.; Shleifer, A.y Vishny, R. (1988) Management Ownership and market valuation: an empirical analysis, *Journal of Financial Economics*, 20 (1): 293-315

Neubauer, F. and Lank, A.G. (1998) The Family Business: Its Governance for Sustainability. London, GB: McMillan Press LTD.

Peay, T. and Dyer, W. (1989). "Power orientation of entrepreneurs and succession planning". *Journal of Small Business Management*. January:47-52.

Pieper, T. (2003) Corporate Governance in Family Firms- A literature Review. In M. Huse, H. Landström, and G. Corbetta (ed.) *Governance in SMEs-Contributions from the 2nd International Doctoral Course on Governance in SMEs*. Sandvika: Norwegian School of Management.

Post, J.E.; Preston, L.E. and Sachs, S. (2002) Managing the extended enterprise: the new stakeholder view, *California Management Review*, 45 (1), 6-28.

Poza, M.E. (1995) *A la Sombra del Roble: La Empresa Privada Familiar y su Continuidad.* Ohio, United Status: Editorial Universitaria para la Empresa Familiar.

Quazi, A. M. and O'Brien D. (2000) An Empirical Test of a Cross-National Model of Corporate Social Responsibility, *Journal of Business Ethics,* 25, 33-51.

Radin, T.J. (2002) From Imagination to Realization: a Legal Foundation for Stakeholder Theory. In M.L. Pava and P. Primeaux (ed.) *Re-Imagining Business Ethics: Meaningful Solutions for a Global Economy.* Netherlands: Elsevier Science Ltd

Schulze, W., Lubatkin, M. and Dino, R. (2003). Toward a theory of agency and altruism in family firms. 19th EGOS Colloquium, Copenhagen, Dinamarca.

Schwarcz, S.L. (1996) Rethinking a Corporation's Obligations to Creditors, *Cardozo Law Review,* 17, 647-690.

Scott, S. G. and Lane, V. R. (2000) A stakeholder approach to organizational identity, *Academy of Management Review,* 25 (1): 43-62.

Tencati, A. and Perrini, F. (2006) The sustainability perspective: a new governance model. In Kakabadse, A. and Morsing, M. Corporate social responsibility Reconciling aspiration with application, 94-111. Palgrave Mcmillan. UK.

Thomsen, S. (2006) Corporate governance and corporate social responsibility, In Kakabadse, A. and Morsing, M. Corporate social responsibility Reconciling aspiration with application, 40-54. Palgrave Mcmillan. Gran Bretaña

Thomsen, S. and Pedersen, T. (2000). Ownership structure and economic performance in the largest european companies. *Strategic Management Journal,* 21, 689-705.

Van den Berghe, L.A.A. and Levrau, A. (2004). Evaluating boards of directors: What constitutes a good corporate board? *Corporate Governance,* 12, 461-478.

Ward, J. L. (1987), *Keeping the family business healthy,* Jossey-Bass, San Francisco, CA, USA.

Woidtke, T. (2002) Agents watching agents? Evidence from pension fund ownership and firm value, *Journal of Financial Economics,* 63 (2), 99-131.

Yeh, Y. (2005) Do Controlling Shareholders Enhance Corporate Value? *Corporate Governance,* 13, 313-325.

Zhara, S.A.; Neubaum, D.O. and Huse, M. (2000) Entrepreneurship in medium size companies: explaining the effects of ownership and governance systems, *Journal of Management,* 26 (5): 947-976.

Zingales, L. (2001) Corporate Governance. Working Paper presented at the National Bureau of Economic Research and published in the *New Palgrave Dictionary of Economics and the Law.*

INDEX

D

E

H

I

J

Q

R

S

T